STANDARD BIBLE COMMENTARY

ACTS

Edited by ORRIN ROOT
and John W. Wade

STANDARD PUBLISHING
Cincinnati, Ohio
3175

© MCMLXVI
The STANDARD PUBLISHING Company
Cincinnati, Ohio
Printed in U.S.A.

Foreword

The book of Acts holds a unique place, not only in Scripture, but in all literature. Countless volumes of church history have been written, but here in the pages of God's Word is the one and only dependable record of the church in its beginning and during the first thirty years of its existence. Those were formative years: the church of the living God was taking shape for an endless life. Those were vigorous years: the church was weak in worldly power and wealth, but it was pulsing and pushing with the power of God's Spirit. Those were years of greatness: the church was small in numbers, but tremendous in the greatness of its God.

There were prophets in the church in those days. The apostles and others spoke as the Holy Spirit gave them utterance. Consequently we can perceive in the record a norm, a standard, for the preaching of the gospel and for the life of the church.

This does not mean the church was perfect or that its pristine purity was totally unsullied. There was Simon the sorcerer of Samaria as well as Simon Peter, the stone. There was Ananias the liar as well as Ananias the devoted disciple of Damascus. There were false teachers who would have fastened the church forever in the fetters of Judaism. There were problems, but there were solutions. There were controversies, but there were decisions. By inspiration of God the lines were clearly drawn. Truth and falsehood were known as what they were; right and wrong were called by their true names. Therefore the norm perceived in the record is God's norm, and therein lies much of the value of this book.

This commentary is presented in the hope that it will help many to grasp the wealth of Acts, not to lock it unused in vault or treasure chest, but to spend it freely in right living and proper direction of God's church. The comments herein are not designed for profound scholars and theologians; they are working thoughts for working people who in their busy lives still find time to work for the Lord and His church.

Most of the material in this volume is not appearing for the first time. It has been gathered from past issues of *Bible Teacher and Leader,* a Sunday-school quarterly that has been growing in popularity since 1944 and for several years has been published also as an annual in more substantial binding for the student's library. From all the studies of Acts since 1944, those parts presenting a verse-by-verse exegesis of the Scripture have now been assembled with some additions to form a brief but comprehensive commentary on the whole of this matchless book from God's Word.

—Orrin Root

CONTENTS

MAPS AND CHARTS

Introduction to
The Acts of the Apostles

by LEWIS A. FOSTER

The book of Acts occupies an important position in the New Testament. It serves as a bridge between Christ and the church, between the gospel and how it was spread. Commonly, though not always in the early manuscripts, it stands between the Gospel narratives and the epistles. Without the book of Acts one would have no record of the happenings immediately following the life of Christ and of the beginnings of the church. Without the background found in Acts one would have no key to the travels of Paul and to the setting of his epistles.

The book of Acts is a bridge in other ways. Geographically it provides a span between the early stages of the church in Jerusalem and the spread of the gospel across Asia Minor and Greece to Rome. The book of Acts supplies examples of the preaching of the apostles that can be compared with the message of their epistles. It shows the rise of problems and persecutions confronting the church in its earliest days. It provides the only extant history of the church during the first century. Since it is a God-inspired history, its significant choice of detail and the accuracy of its records are assured. Through the study of this book one can understand better the will of God, the work of the Spirit, and the nature of the church. One must study this book to gain an understanding of the divine pattern of what the church ought to be and to do.

AUTHORSHIP

The Acts of the Apostles is the second part of a two-volume work in which the Gospel of Luke is the first volume. Both volumes were dedicated, as was common among historical works of that period, to a certain patron, Theophilus (Luke 1:3; Acts 1:1). It was also customary for the second volume of a historical work to summarize the first volume as the second was begun. The author of Acts does just this: "The former treatise have I made, O Theophilus, of all that Jesus began both to do and teach . . ." (Acts 1:1).

Internal Testimony

Although the first volume bears the name of Luke, the author does not specify his name in the records of either Luke or Acts.

"We" Passages. One notes, however, in the course of the second volume, certain passages make use of the pronoun "we," thus including the author as a companion of Paul in his travels (Acts 16:10-17; 20:5-16; 21:1-18; 27:1-7; 28:7-16). It is incredible that an historian as careful with details as this author proves to be would have no significant purpose in the employment of these "we" passages in contrast with the use of the third person pronoun elsewhere. From this, therefore, one concludes that the author was present with Paul in the particular events described in the "we" passages in the book of Acts.

Luke by Elimination. These "we" passages include the period in Paul's life when he spent two years in prison at Rome (Acts 28). From this Roman imprisonment Paul wrote, among other epistles, Philemon and Colossians. In these epistles he sends greetings from his companions: Epaphras, Mark, Aristarchus, Demas, Luke (Philemon 23, 24), Jesus Justus (Colossians 4:11). The author of the book of Acts should be among these companions, for he was present according to the "we" passages and his works reflect a man of such caliber that he would be one of those named in the group. But it could not be Aristarchus, because he is given by name in Acts 27:2, and would be designated in the third person, not "we." Epaphras did not arrive in Rome in the company of Paul, but is counted as one of the Colossians (Colossians 1:7; 4:12). Tychicus, Aristarchus, Timothy, and Mark are all mentioned by name in the book of Acts and are thus eliminated as the possible author. Demas is a doubtful candidate because of later desertion (2 Timothy 4:10). Jesus Justus is designated as one of the circumcision, but Acts reflects an author of Gentile background in its pages (e.g., Acts 1:19). The field of those eligible for the authorship of Acts can be narrowed to give at least some indication in favor of Luke; and his name is not specified in Acts, thus making possible the simple "we" references to himself. Titus is another name familiar among the companions of Paul but missing from the pages of Acts; but he is not found among those named in Rome with Paul.

Luke the Physician. Colossians 4:14 states, "Luke, the beloved physician, and Demas, greet you." A physician would be an educated man having in all probability a formal training such as is exemplified in the Greek employed in these two volumes, Luke and Acts.

External Testimony

The earliest of the external testimonies to the authorship of the Acts of the Apostles appears in the Canon of Muratori (A.D. 170), where the explicit statement is made both concerning "The Third Book of the Gospel" and concerning "The Acts of All of the Apostles" that Luke was the author. Irenaeus also gives an extended account concerning the work of Luke, who "was inseparable from Paul and was his fellow-worker in the gospel" (*Against Heresies* 3.14.1). Clement of Alexandria (*Stromata* 5.12) and Tertullian (*Against Marcion* 4.2) give equally explicit testimony concerning the authorship. Origen (Apud Eusebius, *Church History* 6.25), Eusebius, and Jerome (*Commentary on Isaiah* 3.6; *De Viris Illustribus* 7) give their uniform testimony as well. Eusebius adds the note, "Luke being by birth one of the people of Antioch, by profession a physician, having been with Paul a good deal, and having associated intimately with the rest of the apostles, has left us examples of the art of curing souls that he obtained from them in two divinely inspired books . . ." (*Church History* 3.4). Thus the tradition supporting Lukan authorship of Acts is undisputed in its uniformity and fits well the internal notices. Some have attempted to maintain that the later evidence from external sources may have been derived from deductions made by the ancients based upon the same internal notices extant today, but not upon any additional information. Such a position merely emphasizes the uniformity of the testimony both external and internal, and for want of any real evidence against the Lukan authorship the identification of the author remains well established.

DATE

Strong arguments can be given in favor of a date of the composition of Acts immediately after the last event which it records.

Early Date (A.D. 63)

Relation to Later Events. Within the pages of the book of Acts one finds no allusion to events that happened after the close of the two years of Paul's imprisonment in Rome. This silence might not be so striking but for the importance of certain events that happened soon afterward: the martyrdom of James in Jerusalem; the persecution of the Christians in Rome (A.D. 64); the martyrdom of Peter and Paul (possibly A.D. 67); the destruction of Jerusalem (A.D. 70).

The Outcome for Paul. If Luke knew concerning the outcome of the Roman trial or the end of Paul's life, why did he not mention it at the close of the book of Acts? It has been suggested that if Paul's death had been recorded at the close of Acts it would have drawn a parallel in the minds of people between the Gospel narrative and the death of Christ, and the book of Acts and the death of Paul. This parallel, so it is argued, was to be avoided, for the death of Paul did not have the significance that Christ's death and subsequent resurrection held. If, however, the book of Acts would have concluded with the freeing of Paul from prison, why was this not recorded? What better defense of Christianity could one produce than that the case was won? Whatever the outcome of these events, the simplest explanation for the reason they do not appear at the close of the book is that they had not yet happened, and the author stops when he has caught up with the course of action.

The Ending of Acts. Even so, the ending of Acts seems to be abrupt as a close to a two-volume work. It ends simply with these words: "And Paul dwelt two whole years in his own hired house, and received all that came in unto him, preaching the kingdom of God, and teaching those things which concern the Lord Jesus Christ, with all confidence, no man forbidding him" (Acts 28:30, 31).

Numerous explanations have been given for this sudden close to Acts. Some have suggested that the author anticipated a third volume. There is slight indication of this in that the book of Acts refers to the previous volume with the Greek word *proton* which means "first" technically, and not "former" as it is ordinarily translated (Acts 1:1). The superlative degree, *proton*, is sometimes used, however, where the comparative would be expected (John 1:30). But grammatically the author might have been planning a third volume rather than comparing the second volume only with one other. If a third volume was anticipated, reasons for its absence have been conjectured: (1) the author died before fulfilling his plans; (2) further information was suppressed because of Paul's martyrdom (without foundation and contrary to other evidence); (3) another possibility might be added: the third volume of Luke's work is actually, viz., the extant collection of Paul's epistles. Although it has not been commonly noted, it is possible that Luke made the earliest collection of Paul's epistles and published them as a third volume with the two others, Luke and Acts. Another enigma noted by many is the absence of any mention of the Pauline epistles within the book of Acts. If we had only Paul's epistles, Paul would seem to be preeminently a writer. If we had only the book of Acts, we would know nothing of Paul's writing activity, but would consider his journeys for Christ as paramount. An explanation of this silence in Acts about the epistles may be that Luke knew he was going to publish Paul's epistles, and he refrained from making any reference to them, since this was to be his third volume. This same careful division of material is noted concerning the life of Christ in the book of Acts. Little is said in the book of Acts on this subject because it had been presented in the first volume. It is true that in the book of Acts one finds allusions to the life of Christ, but these are in the speeches of those occupying a place in the narrative of Acts or at the very beginning of Acts as the second volume is linked to the first.

Even if Paul's epistles are an actual third volume of Luke's work, this still leaves a needed explanation for the abrupt closing of Acts. Interesting detail is gleaned from Philo's *In Flaccum* where a certain Lampon was held in custody for two years while waiting trial; and this period is described as the "longest time." From this example we would conjecture that the Roman law stipulated two whole years would be the extent of time a man could be held awaiting the appearance of his accusers. If his accusers did not come within this period, it would seem logical that an automatic release would be in order. This fits extremely well the predicament of Paul. Since his Jewish accusers had been unable to gain a decision in their own homeland, they would have been reluctant to travel to Rome and risk drawing the ire of the Roman authorities for failing to gain a conviction. This type of default-release also fits the notes in Philemon (22) and Philippians (2:24) where Paul expressed his expectation to come to see the recipients of the letters shortly, although he was at present in prison. Finally, this gives added meaning to the careful choice of words that Luke made when he wrote "two *whole* years" (Acts 28:30). The significance then of this phrase would be that Paul had served his time and was expecting automatic release at the end of this period of two full years. (See Henry J. Cadbury, "Roman Law and the Trial of Paul," in *The Beginnings of Christianity*, F. J. Foakes Jackson and K. Lake, eds., Vol. 5 [1933], pp. 330-333.)

No More Information. Finally, the conclusion that best gives explanation why Luke does not include more information to round out the close of his volume is that there was nothing more to tell, for nothing else had as yet happened. This dovetails with all of the other notes and details both from silence and from the positive notices.

Middle Date (A.D. 80)

Those who maintain this middle theory of dating claim it is necessary because the Gospel of Luke would not have been written until after the destruction of Jerusalem in A.D. 70 (cf. Luke 21:20; Mark 13:14; Matthew 24:15). This position, however, is advocated by those who deny the validity of predictive prophecy and cannot see how a real foretelling of the destruction of Jerusalem could be possible. Therefore they maintain that Luke, and thus Acts, must have been written after the destruction had actually taken place. Following this line of reasoning, it is also claimed that the author of the book of Acts made use of the Gospel of Mark in his first volume. Since it is claimed that Mark was not written until after A.D. 65, the writing of Luke's Gospel would necessarily come some time after this, and the second volume of Luke's work would be still later. Thus the date of about A.D. 80 rests entirely upon interpretations and theories in other areas and especially those theories that are based upon erroneous presuppositions. It is dangerous to base a dating entirely upon related interpretations in any case; but when such a dating is built upon positions that not only lack substantiation but deny the dependability of the Scriptures, it must be rejected.

Late Date (A.D. 100)

E. J. Goodspeed suggests a date of about A.D. 80-90 for Luke-Acts, based upon his interpretation of literary characteristics, subject interests, church organization, etc. He accepts the Lukan authorship; but the reasons he gives for dating Acts in the 90's can readily be used to date it no later than the early 60's. (See Donald Guthrie. *The Gospels and Acts: New Testament Introduction* [1965], p. 313.) Another reason that some use to argue that Acts must come at the close of the first century or the beginning of the next century is an alleged relationship to Josephus. The details recorded about Theudas (Acts 5:36 ff.) do not match the man and deeds recorded of a Theudas in Josephus' work, *Antiquities* 20, 2, 1 ff., dating from A.D. 94. There are two ready explanations for this lack of agreement. Either one of these reports is in error, or else Luke and Josephus describe two different men who bear the same name. It certainly falls far short of demonstration that Luke has made use of Josephus. In fact, the differences between the accounts of Luke and Josephus have drawn the most attention. These differences indicate that Luke did not know Josephus rather than that he borrowed from Josephus.

The weight of contemporary scholarship seems to be moving toward the traditional early date. That such a liberal scholar as Adolf Harnack even a generation or more ago should revise his dating of Acts several times in his studies and each time move his dating earlier is significant. This shows the weight of testimony that forced his final conclusion to the earliest date, when Paul's trial in Rome had not yet come to its conclusion.

PURPOSE AND OCCASION

The Title of Acts

The title commonly ascribed to Luke's second volume falls short of conveying the full purpose of this writing. Probably the title was not given to the second volume by the author himself, but came to be used to distinguish the second volume of this work from the first. The Sinaiticus manuscript simply bears the title, "Acts," whereas Vaticanus and Beza and also Sinaiticus in the subscription entitle it "The Acts of the Apostles." Obviously we do not have all of the acts of all the apostles recorded here. In fact, very few of the apostles are represented in any individual manner. Only Peter and Paul stand out as the leading figures in the apostolic line. The appellation, "Acts," is a common word to be used as designating a history of some great individual. For example, Callisthenes, a nephew of Aristotle, composed a work, *Acts of Alexander,* and Sosylus, a comrade and instructor of Hannibal, wrote the *Acts of Hannibal.*

The Theme

The theme of the work seems to be best summarized in the eighth verse of the first chapter. It is the ordinary procedure of an ancient historian to begin his second volume by summarizing the first volume and then then also indicating the direction of his second volume. Luke has summarized his first volume in his opening phrases, "All that Jesus began both to do and to teach" (Acts 1:1). Then the direction of the second volume seems to have been reported in the words of Jesus: "Ye shall be witnesses unto me both in Jerusalem, and in all Judaea, and in Samaria, and unto the uttermost part of the earth" (Acts 1:8). Thus the book of Acts tells of the spread of the gospel from Jerusalem to the uttermost part of the earth, even Rome.

History

The significance of the book of Acts as an historical account of Christian origins cannot be overemphasized. Here is a book that tells of the founding of the church, of the spread of the gospel, of the beginnings of the actual existence of congregations and evangelistic efforts in the apostolic pattern. One of the unique aspects of the Christian religion is its firm historical foundation. The life and teaching of Jesus Christ are established in the four Gospel narratives, but without the book of Acts we would have no coordinated account of the beginnings of the church.

Apology

As one reads the events of the book of Acts, he is struck by the relationship of the Christian in the world, both to the Jews and to the Gentiles. In this respect the book, by recording the passage of events in the early years of the church, presents a defense of Christianity against various forms of Jewish attack for the purpose of Jewish conversion. It also presents an encouraging account of the confrontation of Christianity with pagan thought and the Roman government and society (see Acts 25:8).

Trial Brief

One specific aspect of the apologetic value of the book might be seen from the occasion of its writing. If the book of Acts comes from the end of Paul's imprisonment in Rome while he was waiting trial, the period of writing would be the very interval of time when

Paul could have been preparing for his defense. The preceding two years of imprisonment in Caesarea would have provided an admirable time for Luke to examine eyewitnesses in Judea and to gather his material concerning Jesus, His life and teaching, and to be writing these down during the Caesarean imprisonment of Paul. Then the Roman imprisonment that followed would have provided opportunity for writing the second volume. But if this work of Acts comes from this particular period, it is quite possible that the author bore in mind an immediate use to which this second volume, and the first volume as well, might be put. If Paul's case came to trial in Rome, it would have been a distinct advantage if a document such as the book of Acts could have been placed in the hands of the Roman authorities as a type of court brief. Acts would have given the Roman authorities some information about the origins, activities, and goals of the Christian movement. Also, it would have helped these officials understand how others had treated Christians.

As far as Roman courts are concerned, it is significant that throughout the book of Acts there is no record of a conviction of a Christian in a Roman court. Either the case was dismissed or the accused Christian was declared innocent. Although this document may not have been used in such a way, it would have provided the strongest type of testimony. If Acts was used as a trial brief, this use does not exhaust its meaning and the ultimate purpose. But this immediate need may have been served by this timeless testimony inspired of God.

Missionary Record

Another suggestion has been made for the ultimate purpose of the book of Acts as an account of conversions and nonconversions (J. W. McGarvey, *New Commentary on Acts of Apostles* [1873], p. xviii.) Although this does not account for all the incidents recorded in Acts, this certainly is an emphasis found in the book and one that gives this account a timely place in the study of man and the way of salvation. The record tells of the missionary zeal of the whole church, for as the Christians were scattered abroad they went everywhere preaching the word (Acts 8:4). All roads led to Rome in this period of history, and it is to be expected that the spread of the gospel took the course from Jerusalem, across Judea, from Samaria to Antioch, and from Syria to Asia, Macedonia, and Achaia, and finally to Rome.

The Acts of the Holy Spirit

This evangelistic effort of the early church was carried on under the guidance and in the work of the Holy Spirit. Many have noted this emphasis as the outstanding characteristic of the book of Acts.

Some have even suggested that a more appropriate title of the work would be "The Acts of the Holy Spirit." Plumptre in the last century suggested the title, "The Gospel of the Holy Spirit." The Gospel narratives emphasized the work of Jesus which He began; His continuing work is carried on through the person of the Holy Spirit in the record of the second volume.

The Tubingen Theory

F. C. Baur is named the father of the nineteenth-century Tubingen school of interpretation that tried to rationalize the Christian religion to such an extent that naturalistic causes were claimed for all of the events associated with the development of the church. This school of skepticism maintained that in the book of Acts one finds a deliberate attempt to harmonize two divergent streams appearing in the beginnings of the Christian movement. Peter was used along with James to represent a Judaizing school, and Paul was used to represent the antithesis in a gospel for the Gentiles. After a period of time these two antithetical schools were synthesized in the Roman Catholic Church, said these skeptics. The book of Acts is interpreted as a late document of the church that was produced with the deliberate plan of presenting both Peter and Paul in such a way that they were brought together in a harmony they did not enjoy in actual life (so the Tubingen school alleged). Thus the document is called an attempt to inject a note of harmony into the history of the early church.

It is true that the book of Acts emphasizes the lives of Peter and Paul. It is also true that in a surprising way one can find parallel accounts for incidents that happened first in the life of Peter and then in the life of Paul. It is also true that in the early church friction did develop between those of a Jewish background and those of Hellenistic origins. But all of this gives no justification for maintaing a necessary antagonism for the duration of Peter's and Paul's lives.

The choice of Peter and Paul as the leading figures in the book of Acts is not because of their friction, but because they are worthy representatives of the very work that Luke desires to portray. The parallelism between their two lives does not need to discredit the trustworthiness of the account. If Luke is a careful and orderly historian who enjoys presenting a certain symmetry in his work, this does not mean that what he recounts is false and simply fabricated. In fact, one might expect to find a certain similarity in the lives of Peter and Paul, since they preached the same gospel, they received the same power of the Lord, and they had the same dedication of life to His work and service. Although at the conference in Jerusalem the problem of Judaizers was presented, it ended with a decision upon which both Peter and Paul were agreed (Acts 15:1 ff.;

Galatians 2:1 ff.). In Galatians an occasion of disagreement in Antíoch is noted, but there is no indication that this resulted in a lasting rift (Galatians 2:11-14). The bitterness and envy that Baur and the Tubingen school claimed existed between Peter and Paul simply does not square with the facts. This false assumption has led to mistaken interpretation, not only of the book of Acts, but also of the Gospels and epistles of the New Testament.

LIBERAL ATTACKS

A concerted effort has been made by some to undermine the credibility of the book of Acts. In this attempt two main lines of attack have been used. One concerns the historicity of the account in conjunction with the author's evident claim to be a companion of Paul upon some of his journeys, and the other concerns the recording of the speeches in Acts.

The Conference in Jerusalem

The illustration most used to attack the trustworthiness of the book of Acts is the conference in Jerusalem about whether Gentile converts should be forced to keep the law of Moses (Acts 15). In the second chapter of Galatians Paul describes a meeting in Jerusalem that has many similarities to the conference described in the fifteenth chapter of Acts (same subject matter, same people, same places, same agitators, and same general results). But beyond these similarities are certain alleged differences. The book of Acts reflects less tension in the scene, and the speeches and conversations are different. It has been suggested, however, that the Galatians account tells of a preliminary meeting of Paul and Barnabas with the apostles, whereas Luke describes the later public sessions and decrees of the whole church. Differences in the purposes of the narrators and the passage of time after the event must also be taken into account.

Visits to Jerusalem

Objection is also made that the conference is numbered as Paul's third visit to Jerusalem by the book of Acts, but as the second in the Epistle to the Galatians: (1) Acts 9:26 ff.; Galatians 1:18; (2) Acts 11:30, 12:25; (3) Acts 15:1 ff.; Galatians 2:1 ff. The answer to this difference in numbering lies in the purpose of his recording these visits in Galatians. Paul is not actually listing his visits to Jerusalem, but he is describing his contact with the apostles. Since on the second visit recorded in Acts there seems to have been no contact with the apostles, he simply omits it from the listing in Galatians. Lightfoot points out that when the offering was delivered as described in Acts 11:30, it was brought to the elders and not to the apostles. Lightfoot conjectures that the apostles were out of the city at that time because of the persecution that descended upon the church in that particular period.

The Portrait of Paul

Haenchen is an example of a recent critic who strives to point out the discrepancy between the portrait of Paul in Acts and that of the epistles (*Die Apostelgeschichte* [1961], pp. 100 ff.; cf. D. Guthrie, *New Testament Introduction*, Volume I [1965], p. 325). Haenchen claims that Paul is described as a wonder worker in Acts, but is not thus reflected in his epistles. Also, Paul is a convincing speaker in Acts, but is not so presented in his epistles. One has only to read 2 Corinthians 12:12 to see the presence of miraculous gifts not only in the church but in the work of Paul, although he does not emphasize this aspect in the writing of his epistles. Reading 2 Corinthians 10:10 concerning unimpressive speech, one must not take as final criterion what the enemies of Paul are saying about him, or what Paul himself in his own modesty says elsewhere of his abilities, but one has only to read his epistles to know of his gift to express himself. The book of Acts corroborates this gift of expression in Paul.

Historical Notes

Some critics raise doubts about the accuracy of Acts by questioning whether a companion of Paul would have written the accounts of Paul's conversion as they are written. For example, three accounts of Paul's conversion are given in the book of Acts: 9:1-9; 22:6-16; and 26:12-18. The position is taken that these accounts leave out the important point that Paul had seen the Lord. But one finds in 9:17 and in 9:27 such a record. Thus the emphasis that Paul gives in the epistles is corroborated in the book of Acts. Another alleged contradiction in the conversion accounts, between Acts 9:7 and 22:9, is readily resolved when one realizes that the Greek *akouo* (used in 9:7) can mean either "hear" or "understand" and the word phone (used in 22:9) means either "sound" or "intelligible voice." Thus the former passage assures us that Paul's companions heard the sound, and the latter passage informs us they did not understand what was spoken.

Another ground of criticism is the silence in the Acts account about the considerable collection that Paul took pains to make for the saints in Jerusalem (e.g., Romans 15:25, 26, 30-32). But one does find indirect reference to this in Acts 24:17. Also in Acts 20:4 one finds a list of men who accompanied Paul, and this admirably corresponds to the group one would expect to accompany the offering. Although the book of Acts does not duplicate the material found in the epistles, its harmony of witness adds to the credibility rather than detracts from its trustworthiness.

Speeches

The speeches recorded in Acts have been questioned on several counts. Here the problem is posed as to whether the speeches reported in the book reflect the true words and thoughts of the speakers or whether they are the inventions of the author himself.

Conventional Practice of Ancient Historians. In considering this question, the customary practices in antiquity must be considered. It is true that ancient historians were accustomed to attempt ingenuity in interjecting speeches at appropriate intervals to describe the situation at hand, and at the same time to dramatize the action. Thucydides is the classic example; he even gives specific information on the subject of speech-making and its role in the recording of history (*History of the Peloponnesian War* 1.22.1). It is generally accepted that the writing of these speeches gave the historian an opportunity to show his real ability in giving a speech that was appropriate to the situation, in a wording that was appropriate to the speaker. But the historian also felt a strong obligation to report speeches accurately, for Thucydides adds, "Of course adhearing as closely as possible to the general sense of what was actually said."

Regardless, however, of the historian's practice of rephrasing speeches, it is improper to discount at the outset the speeches of the book of Acts. One indeed finds the speeches are carefully distributed throughout the book and the words would certainly not be the full extent of what was spoken on each occasion. For example, Peter's speech on the Day of Pentecost must have lasted more than the three minutes it takes to read the account; and Luke so specifies: "With many other words did he testify and exhort" (Acts 2:40). But even though these recorded speeches are condensations, this does not mean they are unfaithful to the meaning and the main thrust of the original speeches.

Speakers in Acts and Their Epistles. When we compare the speeches of individuals in Acts who have also written New Testament epistles, we find remarkable resemblances between their recorded speeches and their writings.

Indications From the Gospel of Luke. Another interesting comparison is made when one examines the Gospel of Luke and notes the speeches of Jesus there. In laying the Gospel accounts alongside one another, one finds more of a uniformity in preserving the words of Jesus' speeches than in the narrative portion of the accounts. This may indicate two things. One is that the Gospel writers were more particular to preserve the original wording of Jesus' speeches; the other is that the Gospel writers wrote independently in dealing with transitions and settings.

Verisimilitude. Another way of assessing the speeches in Acts is to note the teachings, the theology, and patterns of sermonizing that are employed. In these matters, one finds that the speeches are faithful to the earliest times and to the beliefs and emphases of the early church insofar as we know them.

HISTORICAL TRUSTWORTHINESS

In the face of numerous attacks upon the dependability of the author of Acts, one would expect to find little to commend a careful, detailed work in his writings. On the contrary, every page of Acts abounds with sharp, precise points to delight the historian. It is only false presuppositions and insufficient knowledge of the facts that lead some investigators to false interpretation and alleged discrepancies. Ramsay wrote, "Certainly he [Luke] flatly contradicts the assertions of the modern critics; but, as we shall see, he is right and they are wrong" (*The Bearing of Recent Discovery on the Trustworthiness of the New Testament* [1911], page 225). No scholar of this century has done more to point up the historical accuracy of Acts than Sir William Ramsay. Among his many books pertaining to this subject, his work, *St. Paul the Traveller and the Roman Citizen* is the classic. Henry J. Cadbury, although a liberal and disclaiming any purpose of establishing the accuracy of Acts in his volume, *The Book of Acts in History*, nevertheless readily admits, "Except scholars who specialize in the ancient cultures few readers of the Book of Acts recognize how well it fits its contemporary setting" (1955, preface).

The account of the book of Acts covers a period of about thirty years, and reaches the territory from Jerusalem to Rome. Luke's descriptions of these times and places are filled with all manner of population and civilization, variety of administration, Jewish cities, court scenes in Caesarea, dramatic scenes in the capitals of Antioch, Ephesus, Athens, Corinth, and Rome. Various Greek cities and barbarian country districts and Jewish centers are covered. Yet in all this the terminology chosen is at all times the proper nomenclature for each time and place. In Acts 13:7 and 18:12 one reads of "proconsuls" (A.S.V.) in Cyprus and Achaia. One reads in 13:50 "chief men" or "first men" at Antioch in Pisidia, in 14:13 the "priest" of Jupiter (Zeus in Greek) at Lystra, and in 16:35 the "magistrates," "serjeants," "keeper," or in the Latin, "praetors" and "lictors." Especially in Acts 17:6 one has a good example of the accuracy of Luke. The word employed here for the "rulers" in Thessalonica is "politarchs." Nowhere else in all of Greek literature is this word found. Some scholars for a time believed this word was simply coined by the author of the book of Acts. In more recent years, however, a stone bearing an inscription with the word politarch was unearthed; and the site of this discovery was Thessalonica, the very place where Luke had reported "politarchs." Some fourteen instances of the use of this term have to date turned up in inscriptions, all of them in Macedonia or environs, and five of these in Thessalonica itself.

In like manner the "townclerk" of Ephesus (19:35) has been verified by coins and inscriptions as the executive officer of that democratic city. The "Asiarchs" with the people's assembly and the trades also fit the local scene at Ephesus. The "first man" ("chief man") of Melita (28:7) and the "captain of the guard" at Rome in 28:16, supply two more examples of precisely the right teminology. We should note also such details as the Italic and Augustan cohorts at Caesarea in 10:1 and 27:1.

Careful Observation

Not only does one have historical accuracy in the book of Acts, but also exact and minute observation. Some have maintained it could be proved from his vocabulary that Luke was a physician (W. K. Hobart, *The Medical Language of St. Luke* [1882]). However, H. J. Cadbury has somewhat reduced the effectiveness of this argument. He has shown that the physician of the first century did not have a peculiar vocabulary of his own, but that other authors who were not physicians shared the same vocabulary (Henry J. Cadbury, *The Style and Literary Method of Luke* [1919]). But this does not prove that Luke was not a physician.

Others have been impressed with the preciseness of Luke's wording in other areas. James Smith wrote a book in 1848 entitled *Voyage and Shipwreck of St. Paul* in which he showed how free Luke's account was from ordinary errors of a landsman. In fact, he became so impressed with the preciseness of the terminology that he felt Luke must have been a sailor. Although it is not proper to press these details that far, it is evident that Luke expressed himself in carefully chosen words.

Faithful Record

All of this helps to indicate the fact that Luke, so careful in his minute details, is trustworthy on all counts. Furthermore, his honesty and fidelity to the truth are portrayed in recording the shortcomings in the church as well as the successes. One finds that discontent is recorded between the Grecian and the Hebrew widows (6:1). One finds that division and differences are recognized (15:2; 21:20 ff.), and that sin calls forth its consequences (5:1 ff.). The unhappy contention between Paul and Barnabas is not suppressed but simply recorded (15:39).

SOURCES

One might enquire whether Luke relied upon any sources of information other than his own observations and the guidance of the Spirit.

Travel Log

The "we" passages of the book of Acts (16:11-17; 20:5-21; 27, 28) indicate that Luke actually accompanied Paul's party in some of the travels recorded in the book of Acts. That this is a diary source which has simply been copied in by a later author is not feasible. The careful work of this author could not allow the changes of the pronoun "they" to "we" simply upon the whim of turning from one written source to another written source. Furthermore, the linguistic characteristics found in the "we" sections are shared by other sections as well. It is quite possible that Luke may have kept personal records along the way and that these particular portions of the book of Acts are dependent upon his own personal notes of the happenings.

Personal Knowledge

Since Luke was traveling with Paul's band, it was possible for him to investigate the eyewitnesses during these travels—those who were concerned in the very incidents he was recounting. Thus he had access to firsthand accounts of any events that he had not personally witnessed.

Other Possible Written Sources

In Donald Guthrie's *Introduction to the New Testament,* Volume I (1965), pp. 330-344, there is an extensive treatment of different theories concerning the sources of Luke's account. Some say that Luke had access to written sources for the earlier portion of the book of Acts, in which are recorded incidents that occurred in Palestine. The basis for this position is that Aramaisms are present in that portion of Acts that do not recur in the later portions. Another explanation to this phenomenon, however, is that Luke deliberately alters his style when he leaves the land of the Jews. This is in keeping with the practice of ancient historians. Aristotle enunciates the rules of appropriate speech to the actor on the stage, and this is likewise true of the historian in his description of the action in his narrative. His language should be in keeping with the setting of the action. This provides ready explanation of the definite alteration in language that occurs between chapters 1-12 and chapters 13-28. This is another indication of Luke's keen determination to keep all details appropriate and accurate throughout the account.

THE TEXT

The textual problems associated with the book of Acts deserve some attention. There are two distinct traditions among the texts in the record of the book of Acts. The oldest majuscules (B, Aleph, A, C), the Alexandrian writers, along with the early manuscript P45, attest to the Alexandrian or Neutral text. The variant form is traced back to the second century through such manuscripts as Codex D, the Old Latin version, the Latin Fathers, the Old Syriac version, and P38 and P48. These sources contain what is called the Western text. In this problem of the book of Acts the Alexandrian text is more often the shorter account and more polished in style, whereas the Western text has additions and frequent variations.

Many suggestions have been made to attempt a solution to this problem of variants in the text of Acts. In 1894 Fredrick Blass propounded the theory that both textual forms actually stemmed from the work of Luke. He conjectured that Luke first drafted the copy which has been preserved through the Western text, but this was only a rough draft from which he made his final edition, and this is preserved in the Alexandrian text. This theory has been modified once and again through the years. Theodore Zahn in 1916 supported it in his study of the text. Later, A. C. Clarke proposed that the Alexandrian text is actually an abbreviation of the original Western text. The theory has been enlarged to include several texts, some of which may have circulated and formed the basis for the Western text before the authoritative form of the text became the basis of the Alexandrian testimony.

The more probable view holds that the Western text forms a deviation from the Alexandrian text, which was the original. Ropes in his comprehensive work (*The Beginnings of Christianity*, Part I, *The Acts of the Apostles*, Volume III [1926]) suggests that the Western text may derive from the recension of the original and was made about A.D. 150, when there was a rewriting to clarify the texts, and expansions were added from oral tradition. Martin Dibelius makes the suggestion that the use of the book of Acts in liturgy did not begin until the last third of the second century and may have been responsible for some of the variants that came about that time. C. C. Torrey has suggested that these problems can be resolved by positing an Aramaic document earlier than the original Greek and that the Western text may be explained as insertions to make the text more acceptable to Jewish readers.

The most likely explanation still stands that the Western text is a later departure from the original text. Why it should be so much more pronounced in its variant readings than other New Testament books is a question that lies unsolved.

CHRONOLOGY

The chronology of the book of Acts is important to the dating of the epistles of Paul. Unfortunately, all of the crucial points that might fix a positive dating of the events in the book of Acts have a possible leeway of a year or two in one direction or another. There are, however, enough fixed historical points that can be gleaned from secular history to lay alongside the Biblical narrative to make it worthwhile to attempt a fixing of dates.

Paul's Conversion

A study of the city of Damascus shows that Roman coins were struck in the reigns of Augustus and Tiberius, but none have come from the time of Caligula and Claudius; but then in Nero's reign Roman coins again appear. It is maintained that following the death of Tiberius in March, A.D. 37, Aretas was given power that he had not possessed because of an enmity with Augustus and Tiberius. In the time of Caligula, with this new authority given to Aretas, his people could strike their own coins. This would explain the passage in 2 Corinthians 11:32 which specifies that Aretas had control in Damascus. Since he died in A.D. 40, it must have been sometime between 37-40 that Paul was threatened in Damascus. This would leave 34 as the earliest date for Paul's conversion (Galatians 1:17; cf. Acts 10:23 ff.).

Conference in Jerusalem

The Galatian letter states that Paul went up to Jerusalem three years after his conversion (i.e., A.D. 37), and also indicates that fourteen years after his first visit to Jerusalem as a Christian, Paul went up again to Jerusalem, this time with Barnabas and Titus. If this fourteen years is to be added to the year 37, the year 51 would result for the conference in Jerusalem.

The Missionary Journeys

The first missionary journey preceded the conference in Jerusalem, but followed the death of Herod Agrippa (A.D. 44, see Acts 12: 20 ff.; cf. Josephus, *Ant.* 19.8.2). The second missionary journey followed the conference in Jerusalem and can be checked by another major historical landmark in the books of Acts, the proconsulship of Gallio. A fragmentary inscription from Delphi contains a letter from the Emperor Claudius in which mention is made of Gallio. The number twenty-six is used in enumerating the times Claudius had been declared imperator. In August, A.D. 52, he was declared imperator for the twenty-seventh time, so this inscription must have preceded that date. Thus Gallio must have been proconsul in Corinth in the spring or summer, 51-52 or 52-53. In exceptional cases a man might be proconsul for more than one year, and this allows the slight possibility of a date ranging all the way 50-52 or 52-54. Thus we have justification for dating Paul's arrival in Corinth in A.D. 52. This is the precise year that Paul would have been in Corinth if the Jerusalem conference had been held in the year 50 or 51. This leads us to conclude that the second missionary journey, which includes an eighteen-month stay in Corinth, probably began in 51 and may have ended in early 53. Paul's third missionary journey, which included a three-year stay at Ephesus (54-57), ended with his arrest in Jerusalem.

The Years of Imprisonment

Another important landmark in the historical records is the governorship of Felix and the arrival of his successor, Festus. Paul was brought to Caesarea to stand trial under Felix, the brother of Claudius' favorite freedman, Pallas. Felix, however, was recalled by Nero, probably in A.D. 59 (see W. M. Ramsay, *Pauline Studies* [1906], p. 348; H. J. Cadbury, *The Book of Acts in History* [1955], p. 9 ff.) and this was after two years of Paul's imprisonment in Caesarea. Following his appeal to Caesar under Festus, Paul was shipwrecked in the next year on his way to Rome. The final two years (61-63) of the Acts account are spent in Rome as Paul awaits trial. This provides a workable chronology for fitting together the events of the book of Acts and the writing of Paul's epistles. Numerous uncertainties and problems, however, complicate the exact dating.

CONTENT

The contents of the book of Acts can be divided in many different patterns according to the emphasis one wishes to place.

In Orderly Fashion

Luke is so careful in his details, and so aware of balance and orderly presentation of material, that one is fascinated as he goes deeper into the way events are unfolded. For example, Luke lays down a principle and then is accustomed to giving an illustration pointing up the principle: e.g., "Neither was there any among them that lacked: for as many as were possessors of lands or houses sold them, and brought the prices of the things that were sold, and laid them down at the apostles' feet: and distribution was made unto every man according as he had need" (Acts 4:34, 35). Then Luke gives a good example and a bad example of this. Joses, who by the apostles was surnamed Barnabas, was the good example (4:36-37), and Aananias and Sapphira were the bad examples (Acts 5:1 ff.). This introduces an instance of another procedure of Luke. He makes a practice of giving the reader a little snapshot of the individual figures who are to occupy a more central position later on. Thus he has already introduced Barnabas to the reader as the good example of giving before Barnabas becomes the important companion of Paul in the first missionary journey (Acts 13:1). Paul, too, was earlier introduced in a snapshot when he allowed the placing of the garments at his feet at the stoning of Stephen (Acts 7:58).

Chronological Panels

If one chooses to trace the course chronologically and geographically, the book of Acts might be divided up into the following panels (See C. H. Turner, "Chronology of the New Testament," *Hast-*

ings Dictionary of the Bible I, p. 421 ff.). The first period runs from 1:1–6:7 where one finds a summation verse: "And the word of God increased; and the number of the disciples multiplied in Jerusalem greatly." This section tells of the founding of the church in Jerusalem and the preaching of Peter.

With 6:8 a new period of the spread of the gospel throughout Judea is begun with the presentation of Stephen and his work and his death. In 9:31 another summation verse is given: "Then had the churches rest throughout all Judaea and Galilee and Samaria, and were edified; and walking in the fear of the Lord, and in the comfort of the Holy Ghost, were multiplied." Now the church has extended throughout the regions just named.

In the third section, beginning with 9:32, the extension of the church to the area of Antioch, including the conversion of the Gentile Cornelius, is recounted. This extends to 12:24 where we find another summation verse: "But the word of God grew and multiplied."

Then in the fourth period, extending from 12:25 through 16:5, the church spreads through Asia Minor. "And so were the churches established in the faith, and increased in number daily. "

The fifth period, including the section 16:6 through 19:20, is a record of the taking of the gospel to Europe and the strengthening of the church in Asia Minor. Corinth and Ephesus are the particular provincial capitals that are important in this section. The period closes with the verse, "So mightily grew the word of God and prevailed."

The sixth period extends from 19:21, as Paul's plans to go to Rome are enunciated, to the end of the book, where Paul is found preaching the word of God daily to those who are brought to him while awaiting his coming trial in the capital of the empire. This is the extension of the church to Rome and ends with Paul's ministry in captivity.

BIBLIOGRAPHY

Bruce, F. F. *The Book of Acts.* (*The New International Commentary on the New Testament.*) Grand Rapids, Michigan: Wm. B. Eerdmans Publishing Company, 1955.

Guthrie, Donald. *Pauline Epistles.* (*New Testament Introduction*, Vol. I.). Chicago: Inter-varsity Press, 1961.

Harrison, Everett F. *Introduction to the New Testament.* Grand Rapids, Michigan: Wm. B. Eerdmans Publishing Company, 1964.

McGarvey, J. W. *Commentary on Acts*. Lexington: Transylvania Printing and Publishing Company, 1873.

Rackham, R. B. *The Acts of the Apostles*. In *Westminster Commentaries*. London: Methuen and Company, 1906.

Ramsay, W. M. *Saint Paul the Traveller and the Roman Citizen*. Grand Rapids, Michigan: Baker Book House, 1949.

Thiessen, Henry Clarence. *Introduction to the New Testament*. Grand Rapids, Michigan: Wm. B. Eerdmans Publishing Company, 1950.

CHRONOLOGICAL OUTLINE OF ACTS

EARLY DAYS OF THE CHURCH
About A.D. 30-45

ABOUT A.D.

Prelude   **30**
Ascension of Jesus (1:1-11)
Choice of Matthias (1:12-26)

Beginning of evangelism (2:1-47)   **30**

The church in Jerusalem   **30-35**
Beginning of persecution (3:1—4:31)
Christian sharing (4:32—5:16)
Continuing persecution (5:17-42)
Choice of the seven (6:1-6)
Martyrdom of Stephen (6:7—7:60)

Conversion of Saul (9:1-22)   **35**

In Judea and Samaria   **35-40**
Christianity in Samaria (8:1-25)
Winning of an Ethiopian (8:26-40)
Return of Saul (9:23-31)
Peter in Judea (9:32-43)

The Gospel to the Gentiles   **40-43**
Conversion of Cornelius (10:1—11:18)
The church at Antioch (11:19-30)

Herod's Persecution (12:1-25)   **44**

PAUL'S FIRST MISSIONARY JOURNEY
About A.D. 45-49

Choice of Missionaries (13:1-3)
Cyprus
Conversion of deputy (13:4-12)
Saul called Paul (13:9)

Perga
Desertion of Mark (13:13)

Antioch of Pisidia
Successful preaching (13:14-43)
Expulsion from Antioch (13:44-52)

Iconium
Successful preaching (14:1-3)
Flight from Iconium (14:4-7)

Lystra
Mistaken for gods (14:8-18)
Paul stoned (14:19, 20)

Derbe
Preaching and teaching (14:20, 21)

Return to starting point (14:21-28)

Jerusalem conference (15:1-35)

PAUL'S SECOND MISSIONARY JOURNEY
About A.D. 50-53

Barnabas replaced by Silas (15:36-40)

Syria and Cilicia
Joined by Timothy (15:41—16:5)

Continuing westward
Asia and Bithynia bypassed (16:6-8)
Troas
Macedonian call (16:9)
Luke joins the party (16:10, 11)

Philippi
Conversion of Lydia (16:12-15)
Paul's arrest (16:16-24)
Conversion of the jailer (16:25-40)

Thessalonica
Successful preaching (17:1-4)
Flight to Berea (17:5-10)

Berea
Nobility of the Bereans (17:10-12)
Opposition of the Jews (17:13-15)

Athens
In synagogue and market (17:16, 17)
On Mars' Hill (17:18-34)

Corinth
Eighteen months' stay (18:11)
Aquila and Priscilla (18:1-4)
Opposition of the Jews (18:5, 6)
Successful preaching (18:7-11)
First and Second Thessalonians written
Trial before Gallio (18:12-18)

CHAPTER 1

1. The former treatise have I made, O Theophilus, of all that Jesus began both to do and teach.

The former treatise. The reference is to the Gospel according to Luke, written by the same author and addressed to the same person. *O Theophilus.* The name is Greek, meaning "lover of God." *Of all that Jesus began both to do and teach.* In the Gospel, Luke had written essential items of Jesus' total ministry on earth. But that constituted only the beginning of Jesus' whole mission, which is to continue through His church.

2. Until the day in which he was taken up, after that he through the Holy Ghost had given commandments unto the apostles whom he had chosen.

Until the day in which he was taken up. Luke's Gospel brought the story of Christ up to the day of His ascension. *After that he . . . had given commandments.* Several times and in various places the Lord gave the climactic charges which we call the great commission. See Matthew 28:16-20; Mark 16:14-18; Luke 24:36-49; John 20:19-23; 21:1-17. All of these commands to preach the gospel, baptize believers, and to supply spiritual leadership to the saints were given before the final charge on the day of His ascension. *Through the Holy Ghost.* "God anointed Jesus of Nazareth with the Holy Ghost and with power" (Acts 10:38). At least from the time of His baptism, Jesus lived and spoke with a full commitment to the Spirit of God. *The apostles whom he had chosen.* These were the carefully appointed witnesses. After the resurrection Christ appeared "Not to all the people, but unto witnesses chosen before of God" (Acts 10:41).

3. To whom also he shewed himself alive after his passion by many infallible proofs, being seen of them forty days, and speaking of the things pertaining to the kingdom of God.

The Lord took the initiative in every appearance to the apostles, coming into their presence, speaking to them by name, displaying the wounds of the cross, and even eating with them to convince them of the reality of the resurrection. *After his passion.* The suffering and death of Christ are thus indicated. *Being seen of them forty days.* This is the only place where we are told how long it was from the resurrection to the ascension. *Speaking of the things pertaining to the kingdom of God.* Jesus used the occasion of His appearances to the apostles, first to convince them that it was He and that He was truly risen, and second, to explain the things which they had not formerly understood (Luke 24:44-48).

4. And, being assembled together with them, commanded them that they should not depart from Jerusalem, but wait for the promise of the Father, which, saith he, ye have heard of me.

Being assembled together with them. The marginal reading in the American Standard Version says, "eating with them." *They should not depart from Jerusalem.* This does not contradict the previous commands to preach to the whole world; it simply directs the time and manner for beginning that preaching. See also Luke 24:49. *But wait for the promise of the Father.* The promise of

2

ACTS 1:5-7ACTS 1:5-7

the "great and terrible day of the Lord" had been given in Joel 2:28, 31 and Zechariah 2:10. The outpouring of the Spirit on the Day of Pentecost fulfilled these prophecies. *Which, saith he, ye have heard of me.* On the night before His betrayal, Jesus had given full and specific promises concerning the coming of the Comforter, the Holy Spirit (John 14–16).

There was good reason for selecting the holy city for the birthplace of the church, also for choosing the date of one of the great Jewish festivals for the time. On such occasions myriads of Jews flocked there as they made their holy pilgrimages to worship God. The gospel could then be declared to a waiting multitude of the faithful, who in turn would carry the glad tidings back to their respective homelands, in the various nations of the Mediterranean world. Jerusalem was evidently the best place to begin.

5. For John truly baptized with water; but ye shall be baptized with the Holy Ghost not many days hence.

John had said to the multitudes on the banks of the Jordan, "I indeed baptize you with water unto repentance: but he that cometh after me is mightier than I . . . he shall baptize you with the Holy Ghost, and with fire" (Matthew 3:11). Baptism denotes an overwhelming. Even as in John's baptism in water, so in the Holy Spirit there was a complete overwhelming of the human spirit in the Spirit of the living God. Perhaps the apostles appreciated only in small degree the power this divine gift would bestow. They could only wait in patience. The period of waiting, however, was not very long.

"Not many days" was limited to ten, and then the promise was fulfilled in a manner of which the apostles had never dreamed.

6. When they therefore were come together, they asked of him, saying, Lord, wilt thou at this time restore again the kingdom to Israel?

When they therefore were come together. This meeting is not the same as the one mentioned in verse 4, although they could not have been far apart. This was Jesus' last meeting with the eleven apostles before His ascension. Luke gives us some of the details in his "former treatise." See Luke 24: 50, 51. *They asked of him, saying, Lord, wilt thou at this time restore again the kingdom to Israel?* This question from the apostles comes to us as a shock, and no doubt it was a disappointment to Jesus. Not yet had they given up the idea that the Lord would establish a material kingdom, drive out the hated Roman conquerors, and make Israel the leading nation of the world. They did not ask Him if He would "restore the kingdom." That they assumed. Their question was, would He do it at this time, that is, during the "not many days hence." Not until He departed from them, and sent His Spirit to direct them, did the apostles finally abandon their hope for the earthly kingdom.

7. And he said unto them, It is not for you to know the times or the seasons, which the Father hath put in his own power.

Jesus did not bother to correct their mistaken idea about the nature of His kingdom. The Holy Spirit did that on the Day of Pentecost, and the apostles never again made any such mistake. Jesus did rebuke their curiosity. "The Apostles were to be not so much prophets of the future, as witnesses of the past."—Dummelow.

8. But ye shall receive power, after that the Holy Ghost is come upon you: and ye shall be witnesses unto me both in Jerusalem, and in all Judaea, and in Samaria, and unto the uttermost part of the earth.

The apostles expected Jesus to restore an ancient kingdom; He empowered them to establish a new one. They wanted to be under-officers in a Jewish empire; He made them heralds of a world-wide reign. *Ye shall receive power.* This promise is not general to all Christians. It is given for a specific time and for a divine purpose to a selected and limited group—the apostles. *After that the Holy Ghost is come upon you.* This was the visitation and the power which the Lord had promised on the night before His crucifixion. The Spirit would bring Jesus' commands to their memory (John 14:26); through them He would testify of Christ (John 15:26); He would reprove the world of sin, of righteousness, and of judgment (John 16:8); He would glorify Christ and guide the apostles into all truth (John 16: 13, 14). He also empowered them to speak in foreign languages and to accomplish miracles which convinced their hearers of the authority by which they spoke. *Ye shall be witnesses unto me.* A witness is one who speaks of the things he has seen and heard. *The uttermost part of the earth.* The message is for people, wherever people live. The apostles are still the witnesses of Christ, conveying their written testimony, the New Testament, to all nations.

9. And when he had spoken these things, while they beheld, he was taken up; and a cloud received him out of their sight.

When he had spoken. Luke 24:51 says that he was received up "while he blessed them." *While they beheld.* The Scriptures emphasize the visible, bodily resurrection, ascension, and return of Christ. It destroys beforehand any theories that these are merely figures of speech designed to describe the survival of the human spirit beyond death. *A cloud received him out of their sight.* Our curiosity cries out for more details, but the record is given, not to satisfy curiosity, but to preserve essential or important facts.

10. And while they looked stedfastly toward heaven as he went up, behold, two men stood by them in white apparel.

The two men were obviously angels in human form. John 20:12; Mark 16:5; and Acts 10:30 describe angels in similar terms.

11. Which also said, Ye men of Galilee, why stand ye gazing up into heaven? this same Jesus, which is taken up from you into heaven, shall so come in like manner as ye have seen him go into heaven.

Why stand ye gazing? Their lingering gaze was most natural under the circumstances. The angel called them from musing to active service. *This same Jesus . . . shall so come in like manner, as ye have seen him go.* Nothing could be more plain. The person, the visible presence, and the manner of appearance are all to be the same. Of these things, as well as of the resurrection, the apostles are eyewitnesses.

12. Then returned they unto Jerusalem from the mount called Olivet, which is from Jerusalem a sabbath day's journey.

Far from being sorrowful over the departure of their Lord, Luke tells us at the close of his former treatise that they "returned to Jerusalem with great joy" (Luke 24: 52). When the Lord told His disciples that He would leave them, their hearts were filled with sorrow (John 16: 6). Now that He was gone with the promise that He would soon return in the Spirit and abide with them forever, their attitude of defeatism was changed to that of victory. They had such confidence in the outcome that they felt they had really won the battle before it was fought. They had seen Jesus, triumphant over the grave, crowned with the halo of eternal glory, rise above the clouds as He ascended to the right hand of God. The disciples retraced their happy steps to Jerusalem, there to await the next startling event, the coming of Christ's Spirit to endow them with the power needed to carry out the plans that would change the world.

13. And when they were come in, they went up into an upper room, where abode both Peter, and James, and John, and Andrew, Philip, and Thomas, Bartholomew, and Matthew, James the son of Alphaeus, and Simon Zelotes, and Judas the brother of James.

It may be that this was the same upper room in which Jesus kept the Passover with His disciples and instituted the Lord's Supper (Mark 14: 15). This upper room seems to have been a meeting place where the early disciples met frequently for worship. The names of eleven apostles are given here. The account tells us that Judas, after his defection and betrayal of his Lord, went out and hanged himself. The other apostles were all present. When Jesus was led away from Gethsemane, we are told that His disciples, meaning the twelve "forsook him, and fled" (Mark 14: 50). It was hardly to be expected that they would ever assemble again. Save for the crowning event in Jesus' life that followed, it is probable that not one of them would ever have made one move to continue the work Jesus had trained them so well to do. Peter, frequently the spokesman of the group, thrice denied that he had ever known Jesus. Thomas refused to believe the report of the resurrection. James and John had been rebuked by Jesus in their disappointing effort to secure the best positions in the new kingdom. And Judas Iscariot had left a blot of disgrace upon the band by his deed of infamy. Nevertheless, in all the others, except Judas, a new spirit had entered. They were changed men. The cowardly fickle group had become so courageous and militant that they were now ready to follow their leader in life and, if need be, in death.

14. These all continued with one accord in prayer and supplication, with the women, and Mary the mother of Jesus, and with his brethren.

Prayer was the natural and proper exercise during the days of waiting for the promised coming of the Holy Spirit. Luke 24:53 indicates that the place of prayer was the temple, rather than the upstairs dwelling place of the apostles.

Apparently the entire group of one hundred and twenty were included

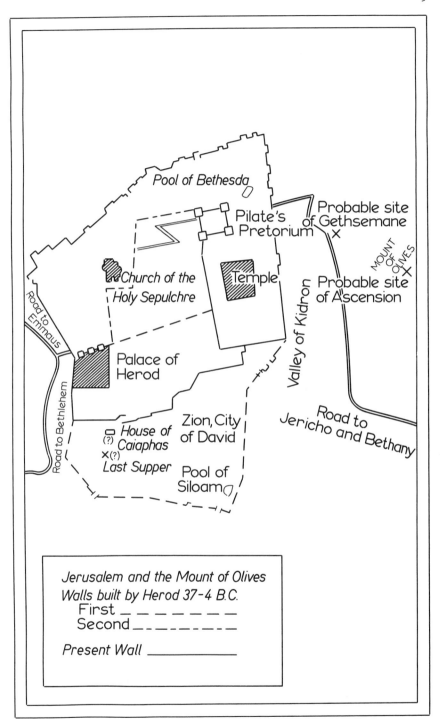

Pool of Bethesda

Pilate's
Pretorium

Probable site
of Gethsemane
×

Church of the
Holy Sepulchre

Temple

MOUNT OF OLIVES
×

Probable site
of Ascension

Road to
Emmaus

Valley of Kidron

Palace of
Herod

Road to Bethlehem

House of
Caiaphas
×(?)

Zion, City
of David

Road to
Jericho and Bethany

Last Supper

Pool of
Siloam

Jerusalem and the Mount of Olives
Walls built by Herod 37-4 B.C.
    First _ _ _ _ _ _ _ _
    Second _ _ _ _ _ _ _ _

Present Wall _____

in the season of worship. Special mention is made here of the women. A band of women were active during the days of Jesus' ministry in Galilee, helping to provide the necessary funds required for the various gospel efforts of Jesus and His disciples. See Luke 24: 10. It probably was those same women who joined the apostles in worship. Mary the mother of Jesus is mentioned, as are His brethren. This is significant. Before the resurrection Jesus' brethren did not believe in Him, and had no sympathy with His missionary work. Such is the personnel of the group that held the great prayer meeting. *Prayer and supplication.* No one knew better than they their total helplessness and inability, unaided, to carry out the world-wide plans of their Lord. It was an utterly impossible task. They were, no doubt, praying for guidance and strength to execute the great commission given into their hands. They prayed with one accord. They had been well-taught concerning the importance of unanimous agreement concerning the things for which they prayed.

15. And in those days Peter stood up in the midst of the disciples, and said, (the number of names together were about an hundred and twenty.)

An hundred and twenty is a small number in comparison with the thousands who had flocked about Jesus during His ministry, and even in comparison with the more than five hundred who saw Jesus after His resurrection (1 Corinthians 15:6). But it is a large number to leave their daily work and continue for ten days in prayer together. *Peter* was a natural leader among the disciples. He now *stood up* to introduce a matter of business.

16. Men and brethren, this scripture must needs have been fulfilled, which the Holy Ghost by the mouth of David spake before concerning Judas, which was guide to them that took Jesus.

As a reason for the suggestion he was about to make, Peter called attention to a *scripture* from the Old Testament, a passage written by *David* under the inspiration of the *Holy Ghost* or Holy Spirit. This, Peter said, was a prophecy *concerning Judas, which was guide to them that took Jesus.* This betrayal by Judas is recorded in Luke 22:47, 48. See also Luke 22:3-6; Matthew 26: 14-16, 47-50.

17. For he was numbered with us, and had obtained part of this ministry.

Judas not only was a disciple of Jesus, but was also one of the twelve apostles, appointed to share the same service that the others were to undertake.

18. Now this man purchased a field with the reward of iniquity; and falling headlong, he burst asunder in the midst, and all his bowels gushed out.

This verse and the following one are not the words of Peter, but a note inserted by Luke to explain why it was necessary to replace Judas. Peter did not need to make such an explanation, because the people with him already knew these facts. Luke's statement is strikingly different from that in Matthew 27:3-8, but not contradictory. Judas got *a field* by flinging down the money in the presence of the priests, who took it and made the purchase as Matthew records. Judas hanged himself as Matthew records; but he hanged himself on something that broke, or else his body began to decay and come apart, so that he fell and *burst asunder.* By coincidence or otherwise, this may have been done in the very field that was purchased with his "blood money."

19. And it was known unto all the dwellers at Jerusalem; insomuch as that field is called in their proper tongue, Aceldama, that is to say, The field of blood.

There were two reasons for this gruesome name: Matthew mentions one (27:6-8), and Luke records the other.

20. For it is written in the book of Psalms, Let his habitation be desolate, and let no man dwell therein: and his bishoprick let another take.

Here Luke takes up again the speech of Peter, which he interrupted after verse 17 to insert the note about Judas. Peter quoted from Psalm 69:25 and Psalm 109:8. The word translated *habitation* properly means a tenting place, a place for a brief stop—a fitting designation for the place where Judas met his end. As a burial place for penniless strangers, it became *desolate,* shunned by the living. The apostleship of Judas is here called a *bishoprick,* which literally means the position of an overseer or superintendent. Probably it is to be taken in a more general sense as simply his office, his position, or his work. A modern colloquial translation might be "his job."

21. Wherefore of these men which have companied with us all the time that the Lord Jesus went in and out among us.

Since David had said in the psalm, "His bishoprick let another take,"

Peter said someone else should be chosen to take the place of Judas. This must be a man who had been with the apostles and the Master through all of Jesus' ministry.

22. Beginning from the baptism of John, unto that same day that he was taken up from us, must one be ordained to be a witness with us of his resurrection.

Peter here emphasized and defined the time mentioned in the last part of verse 21. It extended from the time when John the Baptist was baptizing to the time when Jesus ascended into heaven. One who had been with the apostles throughout that time would know Jesus very well and so would be qualified to be *a witness,* along with the other apostles, *of his resurrection.* He would also be thoroughly acquainted with Jesus' teaching and able to repeat it to others (Matthew 28:20).

23. And they appointed two, Joseph called Barsabas, who was surnamed Justus, and Matthias.

From among the hundred and twenty these two were nominated as possible successors to Judas. Perhaps they had been with Jesus throughout His ministry more continuously than anyone else in the group. Possibly their known ability also was considered.

24. And they prayed, and said, Thou, Lord, which knowest the hearts of all men, shew whether of these two thou hast chosen.

After finding two men who seemed qualified to be apostles, the group did not proceed to elect one. Instead they asked the Lord himself to make the choice. This was appropriate, since He personally had chosen the other apostles (Luke 6:13-16).

25. That he may take part of this ministry and apostleship, from which Judas by transgression fell, that he might go to his own place.

The one chosen was to be a minister, which means a servant, and an apostle, which means one who is sent. He would share the duties of the other eleven apostles, assuming the part that fell to one, the part that Judas forsook when He joined the enemy and betrayed the Lord. Whether *his own place* here means Aceldama or hell, the traitor no longer had any place among the apostles.

26. And they gave forth their lots; and the lot fell upon Matthias; and he was numbered with the eleven apostles.

The method of giving or casting *lots* is not described here or elsewhere in the Bible. One method used in ancient times was to put names on pebbles or other small objects. These were placed in a jar or vase and one was drawn out at random, or the vase was shaken until one fell out. In this case the disciples asked and expected that the Lord would direct the result, and the Bible gives us no reason to doubt that He did.

CHAPTER 2

1. And when the day of Pentecost was fully come, they were all with one accord in one place.

Pentecost was one of the most important feasts of the Jews. See Deuteronomy 16: 16 and Exodus 23: 16. Pentecost occurred on Sunday, just fifty days after Jesus rose from the dead on the "first day of the week." When that memorable day came, our text says the disciples were all with one accord in one place. There is a question about the place. Some say the upper room of Acts 1: 13. Others believe it was a room in the temple. There is a question also about who composed the group. The nearest antecedent to "they" is "apostles" of the previous verse. But, it has been noted that the English rule counts for nothing in the Greek language. There is a possibility that all the one hundred and twenty disciples were there praying and waiting for the coming of the Spirit.

2. And suddenly there came a sound from heaven as of a rushing mighty wind, and it filled all the house where they were sitting.

There was the sound of a windstorm, but no wind. The sound came from the heavens to the apartment where the apostles were. There it remained, filling the place. No wonder the hearing multitudes in the city marveled and were drawn to the spot (v. 6).

3. And there appeared unto them cloven tongues like as of fire, and it sat upon each of them.

The American Standard Version marginal reading speaks of "tongues like as of fire distributing themselves among them." Here was the appearance of fire without the heat of it. The firelike tongues stirred the tongues of the apostles to speak with miraculous power. The distribution of the tongues brought to each separate apostle the power and the language to speak to some person before him in the native language of that person.

4. And they were all filled with the Holy Ghost, and began to speak with other tongues, as the Spirit gave them utterance.

They were all. The apostles, as indicated in the closing verse of the first chapter. *Filled.* This was the baptism, or engulfing, of the Holy Spirit, so complete that in this moment He, rather than their own minds, controlled their words. *Holy Ghost.* In later translations He is called the Holy Spirit. *Began to speak with other tongues.* The Living Oracles translation says, "in other languages." Men from fifteen named nations heard and understood the one gospel in their native tongues (v. 11). *As the Spirit gave them utterance.* Jesus had promised that when the apostles were brought before the synagogues in persecution for preaching the gospel, an adequate answer would be given them (Matthew 10: 20). This was not a time of persecution, but the promise was nevertheless most dramatically fulfilled in this moment.

5. And there were dwelling at Jerusalem Jews, devout men, out of every nation under heaven.

And there were dwelling at Jerusalem Jews, devout men. There were three classes of Jews in the city at that time: natives who were born there; those of the dispersion who had spent most of their lives abroad, but who had returned to the holy city to spend their last days in worship at the temple; and the third class consisted of the countless pilgrims who came from the various nations, where they were making their homes, to worship at the feast of Pentecost. *Every nation under heaven.* Philo is reported to have said there was no nation in which some Jews did not dwell.

6. Now when this was noised abroad, the multitude came together, and were confounded, because that every man heard them speak in his own language.

The external gift of the tongues like as of fire was a sign, not for the sake of the apostles; they did not need it. It was for the sake of the assembling multitudes. Well might these assembling Jews be confounded, confused, both by seeing the strange phenomenon of the cloven tongues and by hearing those unlettered apostles speak in tongues that they had never learned. The miracle succeeded well in its purpose. Not only did it bring together on short notice a vast assembly to hear the gospel message; it also opened their hearts to give earnest heed to the things that were spoken.

7. And they were all amazed and marvelled, saying one to another, Behold, are not all these which speak Galilaeans?

Jerusalem was the one center of all Jewish culture. Galilee was a rather remote province, where there were no great centers of intellectual or religious culture. The standards of education were subnormal. They spoke a corrupt dialect of Aramaic, the native language of the nation, which was so marked that a native could be detected by his speech. It was generally thought that Galilee could produce nothing good. See John 1: 46; 7: 52.

8. And how hear we every man in our own tongue, wherein we were born?

Practically all of those assembled

Jews were bilingual: they understood both Greek and Aramaic. But each of them also understood a third language, that of the country in which they were born and reared. It is not necessary to assume that each visitor heard the sermon of Peter in his own tongue, but, in the beginning of the morning's meeting, the various languages were spoken by the apostles. The miracle of tongues had done its work. Its purpose of confirming the truths spoken by Peter a few moments later was wholly effective. "They were all amazed." They knew that something extraordinary had occurred when mere Galileans were speaking in languages they had never learned.

9. Parthians, and Medes, and Elamites, and the dwellers in Mesopotamia, and in Judaea, and Cappadocia, in Pontus, and Asia.

Parthia was a great nation, extending from India to the river Tigris. It was the one nation that Rome was unable to conquer. Elam is the early Bible name for Persia. Mesopotamia is the territory between the two rivers Euphrates and Tigris. It included Babylonia. Josephus says that in one city alone, Nisibis, there were "many ten thousand men [Jews]" and that at the time all Babylonians were subject to the Parthians (*Antiquities* 18: 9: 1). Judea is mentioned. Many of those present were permanent residents of the homeland. Cappadocia was west of the Euphrates. Pontus, in northern Asia Minor, bordered on the Black Sea. Asia, a small province in the western part of Asia Minor. The land was filled with Jewish people.

10. Phrygia, and Pamphylia, in Egypt, and in the parts of Libya about Cyrene, and strangers of Rome, Jews and proselytes.

Phrygia was in Central Asia Minor. Pamphylia was south on the seacoast of Asia Minor. Paul and Barnabas landed there when they began their missionary tour in Pisidia. In the city of Alexandria, Egypt, next to Rome in population, almost one half of the people were Jews. According to Philo, the Jewish philosopher, they had their own ruler. In Cyrene "There were four classes of men . . . the fourth of Jews. Now these Jews are already gotten into all cities; and it is hard to find a place in the habitable earth that hath not admitted this tribe of men, and is not possessed by them" (Josephus—*Antiquities* 14: 7: 2). Many thousands of Jews lived in Rome. When the embassy from Jerusalem seeing the deposition of Herod Archelaus called upon the Roman senate they were joined by eight thousand resident Jews. A few years before the date of this passage the emperor Tiberius had ordered all Jews to leave Rome. Many, no doubt, returned to Jerusalem, and were there for the feast of Pentecost. The proselytes were pagans converted to Judaism.

11. Cretes and Arabians, we do hear them speak in our tongues the wonderful works of God.

The island of Crete was in the eastern part of the Mediterranean Sea. The Jews were numerous enough there to cause serious political upheavals. Arabians were largely Ishmaelites, dominating the large peninsula of that name. Many were proselytes, and a large Jewish element dwelt among them. All these people gave evidence that the gift of tongues miraculously conferred upon the apostles by the Holy Spirit of God was real.

12. And they were all amazed, and were in doubt, saying one to another, What meaneth this?

All who understood the preaching in any language knew that the apostles were telling the wonderful works of God (v. 11), probably the works God did through Jesus (v. 22). The amazing and puzzling thing was that they were hearing these works described in their many languages by uneducated Galileans. A Median, for example, probably never before had heard public teaching in the Median language in Jerusalem. His astonishment grew as he learned that a dozen other local dialects also were being spoken fluently by men of Galilee.

13. Others mocking said, These men are full of new wine.

It is easier to scoff than to consider, and there are always some who take this easy way. A man of Cyrene, hearing the speech of Media, might thoughtlessly leap to the conclusion that it was mere drunken gibberish. If he cared to investigate, he might find that the message was perfectly clear to a Median beside him; and if he turned his attention to another apostle he might hear the message in his own Cyrenian language. Some careless people, of course, regarded the feast day as a holiday rather than a holy day; they were not inclined to give serious attention to anything.

14. But Peter, standing up with the eleven, lifted up his voice, and said unto them, Ye men of Judaea, and all ye that dwell at Jerusalem, be this known unto you, and hearken to my words.

The record is so brief that we cannot picture the scene accurately in detail. Apparently all the apostles had been talking in various languages at the same time. Possibly they continued to do so while Peter spoke as here recorded; possibly the rest now fell silent and allowed Peter to speak for all of them. No doubt all of them gave approximately the same message, but a part or a summary of Peter's sermon is recorded for us. He *lifted up his voice* to be heard above the murmur of the amazed crowd. *Men of Judaea* were those who lived in Jerusalem and the towns near it. *Dwell* usually suggests a permanent home, but in this case *ye that dwell at Jerusalem* seems to mean those whose homes were elsewhere but who now were staying in Jerusalem for a short time to celebrate the feast of Pentecost. Verse 5 makes this meaning clear.

15. For these are not drunken, as ye suppose, seeing it is but the third hour of the day.

The hours were numbered from sunrise; *the third hour* was midmorning. Of course it was possible to be drunk at that time, but it was not probable. Peter merely called attention to the improbability in passing, knowing that the rest of his speech would show that he was not drunk.

16. But this is that which was spoken by the prophet Joel.

The following verses quote a passage from Joel 2:28-32. The fulfillment of part of this was what amazed Peter's hearers.

17. And it shall come to pass in the last days, saith God, I will pour out of my Spirit upon all flesh: and your sons and your daughters shall prophesy, and your young men

shall see visions, and your old men shall dream dreams.

The last days obviously were already present, since what God promised for those days was now being seen. Probably the phrase here is to be taken as meaning all the days of the new covenant, all the days of the Christian age. *I will pour out of my Spirit upon all flesh.* This was not completely fulfilled on that Day of Pentecost, but it began to be fulfilled. The Spirit of God was poured out on a dozen men of Galilee. Before the day was over the gift of the Holy Ghost (v. 38) was given to three thousand (v. 41). In years that followed, the like gift was given, not to every person in the world, but to some persons of every nation. *Your sons and your daughters shall prophesy.* To prophesy is to speak or write a message received from God directly, not through a book or through another teacher. The apostles were prophesying as they spoke under the direction of the Holy Spirit. In the days that followed, the gift of prophecy was given to others in the church (1 Corinthians 12:28; Ephesians 4:11). Both men and women were so gifted (Acts 11:27, 28; 21:8, 9). *Visions* and *dreams* sometimes were God's methods of guiding His people (Acts 9:12; 10: 9-16; 16:9).

18. And on my servants and on my handmaidens I will pour out in those days of my Spirit; and they shall prophesy.

This repeats the thought of verse 17.

19. And I will shew wonders in heaven above, and signs in the earth beneath; blood, and fire, and vapour of smoke.

Signs or miracles evident on that Day of Pentecost were the sound like that of wind, the tongues like fire, and the speaking in languages unknown (vv. 2-4). Innumerable other signs had been seen in the ministry of Jesus (v. 22). These signs were *in the earth;* the *wonders in heaven above* waited for another time during "the last days," the days of the Christian age. *Blood, and fire, and vapour of smoke.* Some take this fire to refer to the "tongues like as of fire" mentioned in verse 3; but since *blood* and *vapour of smoke* are not mentioned at this time, it may be better to expect all three of these signs or wonders at a later time.

20. The sun shall be turned into darkness, and the moon into blood, before that great and notable day of the Lord come.

These "wonders in heaven above" seem to be among those Jesus foretold in connection with His return (Matthew 24:29, 30). Perhaps *that great and notable day of the Lord* is the day of His coming. If so, the prophecy of Joel spans the Christian age from the day of Peter speaking to the day of Jesus' return.

21. And it shall come to pass, that whosoever shall call on the name of the Lord shall be saved.

Throughout the age foretold by Joel the way is open for men and women to turn to God and find salvation. Peter went on to lead his hearers to do this.

22. Ye men of Israel, hear these words; Jesus of Nazareth, a man approved of God among you by miracles and wonders and signs, which God did by him in the midst of you, as ye yourselves also know.

Men of Israel. Most of Peter's hearers were in Jerusalem because they were loyal Jews, observing the feast according to the law. *Jesus of Nazareth, a man.* Peter began with his hearers where they were. They knew Jesus as a man. Peter proceeded to convince them that He was the Messiah. *Approved of God among you by miracles and wonders and signs.* The Living Oracles translation says, "Recommended to you by God." The threefold mention of "miracles, wonders, and signs" is simply for the sake of emphasis. The whole ministry of Jesus was replete with evidences of power. *Which God did by him.* Jesus himself had insisted that His words and works were not His own, but were given Him from above. *As ye yourselves also know.* The audience included many permanent residents of Jerusalem, who had observed much of the ministry of Jesus. Some who had come to the city for the Passover had witnessed the closing scenes of His life and had remained the fifty days to Pentecost. Still others had heard the reports of Him, whose name was on the lips of all.

23. Him, being delivered by the determinate counsel and foreknowledge of God, ye have taken, and by wicked hands have crucified and slain.

The Living Oracles translation speaks of the "declared counsel . . . of God." The sacrifice of Christ was according to the age-long purpose of God for man's redemption. See Revelation 13:8. He himself knew and predicted His death, declaring that He had power to lay down His life and power to take it again (John 10:18). This did not remove the responsibility of those who sought to destroy Him. "Truly the Son of man goeth, as it was determined: but woe unto that man by whom he is betrayed!" (Luke 22:22). *Ye have taken, and by wicked hands have crucified and slain.* It was the Jewish people who had demanded Jesus' death and prevented Pilate's releasing Him. The Jewish leaders used, as their tools, the Roman courts and soldiers, men who were both "without the law"—that is, outside the Mosaic covenant—and acting in many respects contrary to their own law.

24. Whom God hath raised up, having loosed the pains of death: because it was not possible that he should be holden of it.

God hath raised up. Both the fact of the resurrection and its cause were evident. Men slew Him; God raised Him up. *Having loosed the pains of death.* The "pains of death" are generally considered to be the birthpangs by which death brought forth life in the resurrection. Dummelow's commentary suggests, however, that the line should read, "Loosed the snares [or cords] of death." *It was not possible that he should be holden of it.* The central fact of the Gospels. How could death contain Him who was life? How could the destructive power of Satan triumph permanently over the Son of God?

25. For David speaketh concerning him, I foresaw the Lord always before my face, for he is on my right hand, that I should not be moved.

The quotation is from Psalm 16:8-11. David spoke in the first person, apparently referring to himself, and no doubt he was sincerely expressing his joy over his own close personal relation with God and his own hope of redemption. But he was a prophet, and the Spirit of God guided his words to express at the same time a prophecy of Jesus. Peter said David spoke of Christ (v. 31), but he did not say he spoke of Christ only. Much that is prophetic in the Old Testament has a double interpretation, in which the closer event is in some way typical of another event far in the future. *David's* inspired song had some reference to himself, but Peter pointed out that it referred even more fittingly to the Christ (vv. 29-31). Paul gave the same interpretation to this psalm (Acts 13:35-37).

26. Therefore did my heart rejoice, and my tongue was glad; moreover also my flesh shall rest in hope.

The first part of this verse follows the verse before it. Because of the presence and help of God, the psalmist rejoiced and gave thanks—and so did the Christ of whom he prophesied. The latter part introduces the following verse. The psalmist's hope was not for the spirit only, but also for the *flesh,* the body.

27. Because thou wilt not leave my soul in hell, neither wilt thou suffer thine Holy One to see corruption.

Hell here represents the Hebrew *sheol* and the Greek *hades.* It means not the place of eternal torment, but the place of the dead, good or bad. The point of the verse is that death is not permanent; its application is given a few verses later.

28. Thou hast made known to me the ways of life; thou shalt make me full of joy with thy countenance.

God has revealed both the way to live on earth and the way to life everlasting. Both David and Jesus anticipated eternal joy in the presence of the Father—and so may all of us. This verse ends the quotation from David; the next verse begins Peter's application of it.

29. Men and brethren, let me freely speak unto you of the patriarch David, that he is both dead and buried, and his sepulchre is with us unto this day.

The death of David was a matter of record. His tomb was still known. No one had ever claimed that his body and returned to life. It did "see corruption": it lay in the tomb and decayed (Acts 13:36). Therefore the "Holy One" of verse 27 is not David, even though David's hope for his own body lay in the imperishable life of that "Holy One."

30. Therefore being a prophet, and knowing that God had sworn with an oath to him, that of the fruit of his loins, according to the flesh, he would raise up Christ to sit on his throne.

All Peter's hearers would agree that David was a prophet inspired of God. Any evidence cited from David's writings would carry great weight with them. They also well knew God had promised that David's descendants would be enthroned forever (2 Samuel 7:11-16; Psalm 89:3, 4). They agreed that the Christ they expected would be a descendant of David.

31. He seeing this before spake of the resurrection of Christ, that his soul was not left in hell, neither his flesh did see corruption.

Having been shown that the "Holy One" of verse 27 was not David, the hearers would readily agree that He was the Christ. All of David's descendants who had ruled as kings in Jerusalem were dead and buried, as was David himself.

32. This Jesus hath God raised up, whereof we all are witnesses.

The ancient Scriptures promised that the Christ would not be left in death and His body would not decay. The twelve apostles standing there could testify, of their own personal knowledge, that Jesus had been raised on the third day after His death. He and only He fulfilled the prophecy. He was the Christ!

33. Therefore being by the right hand of God exalted, and having received of the Father the promise of the Holy Ghost, he hath shed forth this, which ye now see and hear.

By the right hand of God exalted. The Living Oracles translation has "to the right hand of God." Christ's exaltation was not only by the power of God (see Philippians 2:9-11), but it elevated Him to the place of peculiar authority in the administration of the universe—at God's right hand. *Having received of the Father the promise.* Jesus spoke of the coming of the Holy Spirit as "The promise of the Father, which, saith he, ye have heard of me" (Acts 1:4). *He hath shed forth this.* The American Standard Version says, "He hath poured forth this." The outpouring of the Spirit was "the first official act of Jesus as ruler of heaven and earth." *Which ye now see and hear.* The facts just declared were things which Peter could have known only by revelation, but the proof that Peter spoke by revelation was before their eyes.

34. For David is not ascended into the heavens: but he saith himself, The Lord said unto my Lord, Sit thou on my right hand.

David is not ascended. The things which David wrote in Psalm 110:1 could not apply to himself, for he was "both dead and buried, and his sepulchre is with us unto this day" (Acts 2:29). *The Lord said unto my Lord.* The whole of Psalm 110 is Messianic. It is an address of God to Jesus, whom David calls Lord, in spite of the fact that Jesus was a descendant of David according to the flesh. This psalm is so quoted and applied by Jesus himself (Matthew 22:44; Mark 12:36), by Paul in 1 Corinthians 15:23-28, and by the writer to the Hebrews (Hebrews 1:13). *Sit thou on my right hand.* The place of honor and authority, where Christ is said to be, where He, "maketh intercession for us" (Romans 8:34).

35. Until I make thy foes thy footstool.

The American Standard Version translates, "the footstool of thy feet." God will see to it that the enemies of Christ are brought low in subjection to Him, to be trodden upon if He will. Compare Philippians 2:9-11.

36. Therefore let all the house of Israel know assuredly, that God hath made that same Jesus, whom ye have crucified, both Lord and Christ.

This is the planned climax of the sermon—the declaration to which all the rest has pointed. *That same Jesus, whom ye have crucified.* There was to be no uncertainty in the Lord's identity. It was Jesus, the prophet of Nazareth, the man whose death they had brought about by their opposition, false testimony, and insistence that He be crucified. *God hath made . . . both Lord and Christ.* Men despised and destroyed Jesus; God raised Him and glorified Him. The term "Lord" signifies complete authority. Compare Luke 6:46.

"Christ" is equivalent to "Messiah," the one chosen and anointed to be the complete prophet, priest, and king over God's people.

37. Now when they heard this, they were pricked in their heart, and said unto Peter and to the rest of the apostles, Men and brethren, what shall we do?

The words of Peter, leading up to and including especially the declaration in the preceding verse, had accomplished in their minds what the ministry of Jesus and the Pentecostal miracles had only approached. "Faith cometh by hearing, and hearing by the word of God" (Romans 10:17). *They were pricked in their heart.* The Living Oracles translation has, "pierced to the heart." Convinced that what Peter said was true, they experienced fear and regret to an extreme degree. *What shall we do?* This question comes naturally to the lips of anyone suddenly convinced that he is in a perilous situation and desiring a way of escape.

38. Then Peter said unto them, Repent, and be baptized every one of you in the name of Jesus Christ for the remission of sins, and ye shall receive the gift of the Holy Ghost.

Jesus had promised to give to Peter the keys of the kingdom of heaven, "binding and loosing" that which would be bound and loosed in heaven. This verse shows the fulfillment of that promise. The kingdom was opened with these words. *Repent.* The Living Oracles translation has, "reform." The inquirers had already believed and evidenced godly sorrow for their wrong. Compare 2 Corinthians 7:10. They needed now to bring their minds and their deeds into submission to Christ.

A literal translation of the word rendered "repent" is "rethink," or "change your mind." *Be baptized every one of you in the name of Jesus Christ for the remission of sins.* Jesus had said "Repentance and remission of sins should be preached in his name among all nations, beginning at Jerusalem" (Luke 24:47), and "He that believeth and is baptized shall be saved" (Mark 16:16). The American Standard Version renders the line, "be baptized . . . unto the remission of your sins," and the Living Oracles translation is even more explicit: "be . . . immersed . . . in order to the remission of sins." These are true to the Greek as Luke wrote it, indicating that baptism into Christ is for the purpose of remission of sins. *Ye shall receive the gift of the Holy Ghost.* On the conditions stated, the believer receives the Holy Spirit as a gift. He becomes to each one a strengthening presence and fruit-producing power. See Galatians 5:22, 23. This is not the same as the miracle-producing baptism of the Spirit.

39. For the promise is unto you, and to your children, and to all that are afar off, even as many as the Lord our God shall call.

The promise. Peter had just promised "the gift of the Holy Ghost" to those who would "repent and be baptized" (v. 38), but *the promise* probably meant more than this to his hearers. They were familiar with the Old Testament promise of endless blessings through the Messiah, and now Peter had proved that the Messiah was Jesus (v. 36). Even though they had killed Him, the ancient promise was still theirs if they would repent and give themselves fully to

Him. *Unto you, and to your children.* God's mercy was offered to the people of that generation and to their descendants. The Messiah's kingdom was to be an everlasting kingdom. *And to all that are afar off.* The promise was not only to Jews who worshiped God, but also to Gentiles who were far from Him and His people. They too could be redeemed if they would accept the Messiah, repent, and be baptized. The kingdom was to be universal as well as eternal. Such was the message the Holy Spirit gave through Peter, though Peter himself did not understand it until later (Acts 10). *Even as many as the Lord our God shall call.* In sending the gospel to "every creature" (Mark 16:15) God extended His call and offered His promise to everyone in the world. The blessings of Messiah's kingdom are actually received, of course, only by those who respond to His call.

40. And with many other words did he testify and exhort, saying, Save yourselves from this untoward generation.

Luke recorded only a part of what Peter said, perhaps only enough to give us the trend of the message. Peter may have showed at length how Jesus fulfilled the prophecies of the Messiah. Jesus himself had done this after His resurrection (Luke 24:27, 44-47). Peter probably urged his hearers again and again to respond to God's call with sincere repentance and obedience. It is Jesus who saves, surely, but *save yourselves* indicates that the people who would be saved must do something for their own salvation. They must give themselves to the Saviour; He does not take them against their will. They must turn away from the *untoward generation,* the perverse people among whom they live. They must abandon their selfish sins and misunderstanding of the Messiah. They must follow the truth as Jesus revealed it.

41. Then they that gladly received his word were baptized: and the same day there were added unto them about three thousand souls.

Those who believed Peter were "pricked in their heart" (v. 37), conscience-stricken, frightened when they realized they had killed God's Christ. When Peter assured them that they could be forgiven and receive God's blessing instead of His wrath, they *gladly received his word* and in obedience to it *were baptized.* Thus the number of disciples was increased by *three thousand souls*—a tremendous response, surely, but only a small fraction of what it might have been. The number of people at Jerusalem for a great feast has been variously estimated to be from one to three million. Even with three thousand converts we see the word of Jesus verified: "Strait is the gate, and narrow is the way, which leadeth unto life, and few there be that find it."

42. And they continued stedfastly in the apostles' doctrine and fellowship, and in breaking of bread, and in prayers.

The church was now a reality, a vigorous band of people, drawn and held together by no other force than their belief in the risen Christ. *They continued stedfastly.* Their continuing steadfastly implies regular meetings in the interest of each individual Christian, and of the collective group. *Apostles' doctrine.* The apostles' doctrine was important. As yet there was not a single book of the New Testament written. But the church inherited the Old Testament from the Jews, and that was taught by the apostles—not as a law to be followed, but as fulfilled by the Christ. The apostles had been thoroughly taught by Jesus in His private school. They knew His teaching and His life, climaxed by the crucifixion, resurrection, and ascension. Guided in addition by the Holy Spirit, which they had received in full measure, how competent they were to teach the three thousand who had just been placed under their guidance and care. *Fellowship.* The early church continued steadfast in the fellowship. Paul writes about "the fellowship in the gospel" (Philippians 1:5). He also tells us about the Christians of Macedonia, who contributed so liberally to relieve the suffering of the poor saints, and who urged him to take upon himself "the fellowship of the ministering" unto them (2 Corinthians 8:1-4). Christian fellowship, then, includes more than meeting together for worship, where song and praise to God are prominent features. Whatever the church does in common is regarded as fellowship. *Breaking of bread.* The breaking of bread was prominent in early worship. This does not mean daily meals. They are referred to elsewhere in a different connection (v. 46). This points to the regular observance of the Lord's Supper. *Prayers.* Prayers were an essential part of the worship program. This was no new feature for those early Christians. They were all Jews, brought up in the synagogues, where, in the Old Testament worship, prayer was prominent.

43. And fear came upon every soul:

and many wonders and signs were done by the apostles.

And fear came upon every soul. This was not the terror caused by oppressors and persecutors. Rather it was reverence, awe, such as that felt by Peter, James, and John on the mount of transfiguration (2 Peter 1:17, 18). The hush caused by the eternal presence filled their souls with an attitude of humble worship that changed their whole concept of life. *And many wonders and signs were done by the apostles.* The wonders and signs performed by the apostles showed the immediate presence of God and placed His stamp of approval on the work of His human agents.

44. And all that believed were together, and had all things common.

The church in Jerusalem grew with amazing rapidity. Twenty-eight years later there were tens of thousands ("myriads," footnote, American Standard Version) of believers in the city. The word "together" here means the fraternal spirit that prevailed among all the disciples; they were one in interest, in effort, and in the eternal hope. "All things common" is limited by subsequent Scripture. It seems the church had a common treasury to which the members voluntarily contributed. From it funds were drawn to meet the necessary expenses of the Christian work, especially in the charities of the church.

45. And sold their possessions and goods, and parted them to all men, as every man had need.

The early Christian plan was purely voluntary, each one deciding how much of his wealth he would give to the church. When Ananias and Sapphira contributed the price of a piece of property they had sold, and misrepresented the amount, Peter reminded them that there had been no compulsion in the matter. They had been free to do as they pleased with their money (Acts 5:4). A number of men of wealth, including the missionary Barnabas, did sell part of their possessions, and laid the price at the apostles' feet. It was the time for a generous expression of liberality, when the rich helped the poor.

46. And they, continuing daily with one accord in the temple, and breaking bread from house to house, did eat their meat with gladness and singleness of heart.

In the temple. The early church, for a number of years, was composed of Jewish Christians. They were freed from the law of Moses, and it no longer had dominion over them. Yet they continued to worship in the temple, and worshiped on the Sabbath Day in the synagogues with the Jews. Yet on the Lord's Day they met in a new fellowship that was more intimate and distinct. *Breaking bread from house to house.* The breaking of bread and eating of meat in this verse refer, not to the Lord's Supper, but to the happy social life they lived in their new fellowship, as shown in family visitation from home to home.

47. Praising God, and having favour with all the people. And the Lord added to the church daily such as should be saved.

Praising God, and having favour with all the people. They loved both God and man. The Christians were popular with the masses. In fact it was the leaders of the Jews, not the common people, who instigated the opposition to the church. Even as in the case of Jesus, the common people heard Him gladly until the religious leaders stirred them up against Him, so with the church. *And the Lord added to the church daily such as should be saved.* The Lord added to that group, already numbering thousands, "those that were being saved" (footnote, American Standard Version). Such was the fellowship of the early church. It was brotherly, each caring for the other's welfare. It was devout, recognizing God as the source of all their blessings. It was a happy fellowship, the numbers having found new joy in Christ. Small wonder then, that it was a growing fellowship.

CHAPTER 3

1. Now Peter and John went up together into the temple at the hour of prayer, being the ninth hour.

Peter and John. They had been companions in the "inner circle" of the twelve during Jesus' ministry. They seem now to have been partners in the preaching of the gospel. *Went up together.* The American Standard Version has "were going up" together. The imperfect, or incomplete, tense is used. Important events took place before they arrived within the temple area itself. *Into the temple.* It was a place of daily retreat for the apostolic group (Acts 2:46), apparently both for worship and for the preaching of the gospel. *The hour of prayer . . . the ninth hour.* Three o'clock in the afternoon was the time of burning the incense of evening sacrifice. Other special daily hours of prayer were at nine o'clock in the morning and at noon. These times would afford gatherings of devout, interested, and intelligent Jewish people who might be taught concerning their Messiah.

2. And a certain man lame from his mother's womb was carried, whom they laid daily at the gate of the temple which is called Beautiful, to ask alms of them that entered into the temple.

No better subject for the healing miracle could have been found. The people knew this man from long observation of his condition at the place of his daily begging. *Carried* and *laid* indicate the complete helplessness of his condition. *The gate . . . called Beautiful.* Officially named the gate of Nicanor, it marked the eastern entrance, leading to the Court of Israel from the Court of Women. The gate itself was sixty feet wide and seventy-five feet high. Its structure was of Corinthian brass, carved and ornamented, and "greatly excelled those that were only covered over with silver and gold" (Josephus, *War of the Jews,* 5:5:3). *To ask alms of them that entered into the temple.* No other source of livelihood seems to have been open to this man.

3. Who seeing Peter and John about to go into the temple asked an alms.

There is no indication here that the man knew the apostles or their Christ. However, the disciples had been assembling daily in the temple and were favorably known among "all the people" (Acts 2:46, 47). No doubt some of their miracles (Acts 2:43) were done in the temple. We can hardly believe this cripple knew nothing about them, since he too was in the temple daily (Acts 3:2).

4. And Peter, fastening his eyes upon him with John, said, Look on us.

Peter, always ready with words, was the spokesman, but John was none the less an active participant in the whole affair. *Fastening his eyes upon him.* In the man before them the apostles saw a matchless opportunity, both to meet a serious present human need, and especially to present the claims of Christ for the meeting of a still greater need in all men's lives. *Look on us.* The man was already appealing to them for a gift. These words indicate a deliberate focusing of attention, not only of the lame man but of all within earshot, on the event which was about to take place.

5. And he gave heed unto them, expecting to receive something of them.

The lame man was accustomed to having many of his appeals disregarded, or to having some stray small coin tossed to him by one in passing. Such a proclamation as Peter had made could hardly signify anything less than a handsome gift, worthy of the public attention being called to it.

6. Then Peter said, Silver and gold have I none; but such as I have give I thee: In the name of Jesus Christ of Nazareth rise up and walk.

Silver and gold have I none. Imagine the depth of the lame man's disappointment at this announcement. Led to expect much, he was

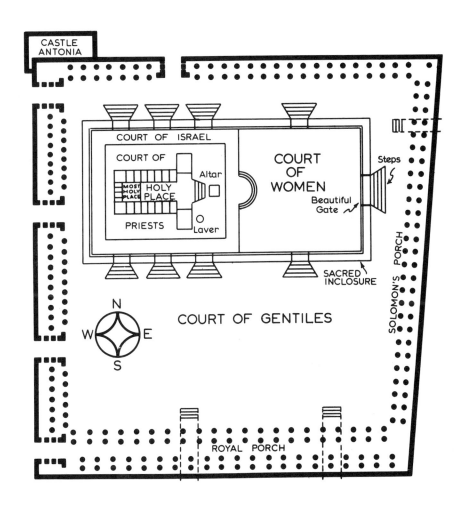

PLAN OF HEROD'S TEMPLE

now persuaded to expect nothing. *Such as I have.* "What I have, that give I thee" (American Standard Version). The moment must have been fraught with bewilderment for the lame man. Hope was stirred again, but for what? The apostles carried no parcels and displayed no finery which might become a gift. *In the name of Jesus Christ of Nazareth.* This is the center of the whole event. The name represents the authority, just as the signature of any man carries with it the full commitment of all that he is and has. *Rise up and walk.* The American Standard Version says simply, "Walk!" The lame man could not be expected to grasp its significance immediately. A thing so surprising, so unprepared for, could hardly be believed!

7. And he took him by the right hand, and lifted him up: and immediately his feet and ancle bones received strength.

And he took him by the right hand. The details of the event are most vividly and convincingly preserved in the inspired record. *Lifted him up.* The word was enforced by an assisting gesture. Peter helped the man up; he did not lift him bodily. And in responding to the touch of a human hand, the lame man responded also to the power of God. *Immediately his feet and ancle bones received strength.* In recording the event, Dr. Luke located the man's former weaknesses and his present healing.

8. And he leaping up stood, and walked, and entered with them into the temple, walking, and leaping, and praising God.

It is hard for those who are well to imagine the delight of this man who now could stand for the first time in his life. His vigorous activity expressed his joy and also demonstrated the completeness of his cure. Surely no worshiper in the temple was *praising God* more sincerely than this one.

9. And all the people saw him walking and praising God.

Someone has suggested that the customary worship got little attention that day, since all the worshipers must have been staring at this man. It seems likely, however, that the disciples and many others joined in praising God for the miracle of healing.

10. And they knew that it was he which sat for alms at the Beautiful gate of the temple: and they were filled with wonder and amazement at that which had happened unto him.

The people were the more amazed because they knew the man had been completely helpless. They had seen him at the gate day by day, for how long we do not know. We can hardly keep from wondering why he was healed at this time and not before. Possibly the reason lies in his own changing attitude. Jesus refused to do miracles for people who scorned Him (Matthew 12:38, 39), and probably the apostles followed His example.

11. And as the lame man which was healed held Peter and John, all the people ran together unto them in the porch that is called Solomon's, greatly wondering.

The lame man which was healed held Peter and John. The Living Oracles translation has, "While he kept fast hold of Peter and John." In the man's gesture there was enthusiastic gratitude, coupled perhaps with an unconscious fear that the miracle would depart with them if they were allowed out of his presence. *All the people ran together unto them in the porch that is called Solomon's.* The healed man had gone into the temple with Peter and John (v. 8). He came out again with them, perhaps when the time of prayer ended. The three made their way to Solomon's porch, a roofed colonnade at the east side of the outer court. There was room there for a huge crowd, and no doubt nearly everybody in the temple stopped there instead of going home.

12. And when Peter saw it, he answered unto the people, Ye men of Israel, why marvel ye at this? or why look ye so earnestly on us, as though by our own power or holiness we had made this man to walk?

When Peter saw it. The gathering of the throng was no surprise to Peter. It was the planned result and one of the prime purposes of the healing. The apostles desired to give the crowd something as much more important than physical healing as the healing was more important than silver or gold. *Why marvel ye at this?* The American Standard Version has, "Why marvel ye at this man?" The power of Christ and the mighty works done in His name were well known to Peter, and they might have been no occasion of surprise to any others who had known the Lord. *Or why look ye so earnestly on us, as though by our own power or holiness we had made this man to walk?* Peter desired as quickly as possible to turn to God and His Christ the attention which he and John had drawn to themselves by the event at hand. Any Jew should have known enough concerning the miracles of the Old Testament prophets to recognize the hand of God, rather than any innate power or divinity within any man, in the supernatural events which attended inspiration.

13. The God of Abraham, and of Isaac, and of Jacob, the God of our fathers, hath glorified his Son Jesus; whom ye delivered up, and denied him in the presence of Pilate, when he was determined to let him go.

Hath glorified his Son Jesus. God glorified Jesus in acknowledging Him at His baptism and transfiguration; by working through Him mighty miracles. But that was not all. He had further glorified the Son by working the present miracle of healing which had been called forth "in the name of Jesus Christ of Nazareth." *Whom ye delivered up.* The Jewish people had followed their leaders in delivering Jesus to the Roman authorities for crucifixion. *Denied him in the presence of Pilate, when he was determined to let him go.* The stories of the crucifixion make it plain that Pilate desired, and made several attempts, to dismiss the charges against Jesus, but that the Jews exerted political pressure to force the governor to order Him crucified.

14. But ye denied the Holy One and the Just, and desired a murderer to be granted unto you.

The Holy One and the Just. The American Standard Version has, "the Holy and Righteous One." Thus in the strongest possible terms Peter declared the sinlessness of Jesus. In the same words he declared that He is the Messiah. In Psalm 16:10 David speaks of the Messiah as the "Holy One"; the demon, of Mark 1:24, used the same term; and the apostles declared, "We have believed and know that thou art the Holy one of God" (John 6:69, American Standard Version). *Desired a murderer.* When Pilate sought to release Jesus as the prisoner customarily set free at the feast time, the crowd demanded that he release instead Barabbas, who "for sedition and murder was cast into prison" (Luke 23:25).

15. And killed the Prince of life, whom God hath raised from the dead; whereof we are witnesses.

The Jews did not themselves nail Jesus to the cross, but they brought about His death and they accepted the responsibility for it (Matthew 27:25). *Prince of life.* The author and ruler of life; compare John 14:6. *Whom God hath raised from the dead.* This was the climax of a powerful series of contrasts, beginning with verse 13. Your God glorified Jesus; you denied Him. You delivered Him to death; Pilate sought to release Him. You rejected the Holy One; you chose instead a murderer. You killed the Prince of life; God raised Him to rule. *Whereof we are witnesses.* Peter's hearers knew already that most of his assertions were true. He offered himself and John as witnesses of the resurrection (Acts 10:41), concerning which they might not know.

16. And his name through faith in his name hath made this man strong, whom ye see and know: yea, the faith which is by him hath given him this perfect soundness in the presence of you all.

Remembering that the name is equivalent to the authority of the person, we may paraphrase, "The power of Christ, appropriated through faithful obedience to His

authority, has accomplished this miracle." *Whom ye see and know.* The man, past forty years of age, was well known in Jerusalem, and the fact of his healing became an item of evidence which the Jewish authorities could not destroy (Acts 4:14-22). *The faith which is by him hath given him this perfect soundness in the presence of you all.* The American Standard Version has, "The faith which is through him. . . ." Christ, as the revelation of God, had acted before their eyes to accomplish the miracle they must now acknowledge. Here was no mere restoration of a function temporarily lost by disease; it was the giving of powers never before enjoyed. And it was not a gradual or partial process, but rather it was instantaneous and complete.

17. And now, brethren, I wot that through ignorance ye did it, as did also your rulers.

Brethren. Peter used this term because he was speaking to fellow Jews. *I wot.* I know. *Through ignorance ye did it.* They had not intended to kill the Messiah; they had not known who Jesus was. Some, of course, had not even known what was going on until the crucifixion was accomplished. *As did also your rulers.* The rulers certainly were more blameworthy than the people. They knew they had not sought the truth in Jesus' trial, but had tried only to convict Him. They knew they had hired false witnesses against Him (Mark 14:55-59). But they were so blinded by prejudice that they closed their minds to the evidence and did not know He was the Christ, the Son of God.

18. But those things, which God before had shewed by the mouth of all his prophets, that Christ should suffer, he hath so fulfilled.

The malice and selfishness of the rulers, the careless indifference and ignorance of the people—God had used these to accomplish His purpose. Through the prophets of Old Testament times He had foretold this. Doubtless many of the people now present had heard some of the apostles explaining prophecies at earlier times.

19. Repent ye therefore, and be converted, that your sins may be blotted out, when the times of refreshing shall come from the presence of the Lord.

To these people, as to those who heard him on the Day of Pentecost, Peter gave the call to *repent,* to turn from rejecting the Messiah and to accept Him, to be changed from disobedience to obedience. Then sin could be forgiven. *Times of refreshing* would come with the "gift of the Holy Ghost" mentioned in Acts 2:38.

20. And he shall send Jesus Christ, which before was preached unto you.

Probably the correct reading is *appointed* rather than *preached.* To those who repent and are forgiven, God will in due time again send Jesus, the Christ appointed for them.

21. Whom the heaven must receive until the times of restitution of all things, which God hath spoken by the mouth of all his holy prophets since the world began.

The Jews had expected that the Messiah would restore to them the kingdom of David and Solomon, triumphant over all the other nations of the world. Jesus had not done this, and so it was difficult for them to believe He was the Messiah. Peter said He was, and proved it

both by miracles done in His name and by His fulfillment of prophecy. He added that God would send Jesus again (v. 20). But first Jesus would remain in heaven until the proper time for the restoration, not of Solomon's glory, but of all that mankind has lost by sin. Such *restitution* has been promised in many ways through many prophecies, beginning with God's statement in Genesis 3:15.

22. For Moses truly said unto the fathers, A prophet shall the Lord your God raise up unto you of your brethren, like unto me; him shall ye hear in all things whatsoever he shall say unto you.

As an example of the many prophecies, Peter chose a statement of Moses from Deuteronomy 18:15-19. The Messiah was to be like Moses in many ways—a faithful representative of God who would lead from bondage to liberty. *Him shall ye hear.* Moses, the lawgiver, was recognized among the Jews as the ultimate authority, because the laws he gave were God's laws. Peter therefore noted that Moses foretold another like prophet, the Messiah, and commanded his people to give attention to what that prophet would say. Peter had heard that command confirmed by God himself (Matthew 17:1-5).

23. And it shall come to pass, that every soul, which will not hear that prophet, shall be destroyed from among the people.

Some of the Jews claimed to reject Jesus in favor of Moses (John 9:29). Peter used Moses' own word to show that to reject the Messiah was to reject Moses also. *Shall be destroyed from among the people.*

Our version of Deuteronomy 18:19 reads, "I will require it of him." Peter interpreted this to mean that the disobedient one would lose his place among God's people.

24. Yea, and all the prophets from Samuel and those that follow after, as many as have spoken, have likewise foretold of these days.

Not only Moses, but the later prophets—Samuel and those that followed him—foretold the days of Messiah's kingdom, the time that was beginning as the gospel of Jesus was proclaimed.

25. Ye are the children of the prophets, and of the covenant which God made with our fathers, saying unto Abraham, And in thy seed shall all the kindreds of the earth be blessed.

The Jews to whom Peter spoke were the proper inheritors of the prophetic messages. As descendants of Abraham, they were also heirs of the promise God made to him (Genesis 12:3).

26. Unto you first God, having raised up his Son Jesus, sent him to bless you, in turning away every one of you from his iniquities.

Since they had the law and the prophets and the old covenant to prepare them, the Jews were *first* given the opportunity to accept the gospel of Christ, to repent and find forgiveness in Him. Afterward the same opportunity would be given to Gentiles. *Having raised up his Son Jesus.* This phrase naturally calls to our minds the resurrection that was so prominent in Peter's preaching; but in this case that is not the meaning. Peter was alluding again to the prophecy quoted in verse 22. As used there, to "raise up" is to produce, or provide, or prepare. In this sense God raised up judges (Judges 2:16); He raised up David as well as Christ (Acts 13:22, 23); and He raised up the Chaldeans to punish His people (Habakkuk 1:6). In the verse before us the meaning seems to be this, "Having prepared the Messiah by bringing Him into the world in the form of man, God sent Him to bless you by turning you away from your sins, bringing you to repentance."

CHAPTER 4

1. And as they spake unto the people, the priests, and the captain of the temple, and the Sadducees, came upon them.

Not only Peter, but John also, preached. Both were probably speaking at the same time in different parts of Solomon's portico. The temple officials wasted no time. They had apparently met in haste upon seeing the stir among the people, and, having determined upon their course, they sent the arresting party to si- lence the apostles before they concluded their address. *The priests.* The "rulers" in the temple. *The captain of the temple.* The commander of the guard of Levites, who stood on duty at the gates and elsewhere, to keep order within the holy precincts. Luke 22:4 mentions more than one captain among those who conspired with Judas to betray Jesus. *The Sadducees.* They were the party in control of the priesthood and the temple. The Pharisees had been the principal opponents of Jesus, but now, probably because of the preaching of the resurrection, the Sadducees became the prime persecutors.

2. Being grieved that they taught the people, and preached through Jesus the resurrection from the dead.

"Being sore troubled" (American Standard Version). The preaching of Peter and John constituted an affront to each separate part of the Sanhedrin in a special way. The priests and scribes were offended that these ignorant Galileans were teaching at all in the temple; they considered that to be their own right exclusively. The captain was concerned lest the present enthusiasm of the people become a disturbance for which he would have to answer to the Roman authorities. The Sadducees were offended at the preaching of the resurrection. The whole Sanhedrin, and especially the high priestly pair, Annas and Caiaphas, were incensed at the preaching in the name of Jesus, whom they had condemned as a blasphemer and criminal (Matthew 26: 65; Mark 14:63, 64).

3. And they laid hands on them, and put them in hold unto the next day: for it was now eventide.

The overnight imprisonment of the apostles was calculated to serve the Sanhedrin well. It would give them a chance to frame a case against the offenders. It would cool the ardor both of the preachers and the people, so that measures of control would be both easier and safer; and it would serve to embarrass Peter and John in the eyes of the public.

4. Howbeit many of them which heard the word believed; and the number of the men was about five thousand.

Many . . . believed. Honest observers had heard and seen enough already to convince them that what the apostles had said was true, and they so committed themselves to that truth as to be numbered with the disciples. *"And the number of the men came to be about five thousand"* (American Standard Version). This indicates a net gain of at least two thousand since the day of Pentecost. There is no way of knowing how many women might have been counted besides the five thousand men.

5. And it came to pass on the morrow, that their rulers, and elders, and scribes.

Those members of the Sanhedrin who were not already in the temple precincts were in the city and were easily assembled for the trial of Peter and John. *Rulers, and elders, and scribes.* The Sanhedrin, indicated in the customary manner of Scripture, by listing the groups within it, rather than by naming the whole body. The American Standard Version concludes this verse, rather than the next one, with the words, "were gathered together in Jerusalem."

6. And Annas the high priest, and Caiaphas, and John, and Alexander, and as many as were of the kindred of the high priest, were gathered together at Jerusalem.

Annas, as the high priest still recognized among the Jews in spite of his ouster by the Romans, presided at the session. Caiaphas seconded Annas' actions. *John* and *Alexander*, apparently were well-known leaders of the Jews at the time of the writing. Nothing certain is known of their identity. *As many as were of the kindred of the high priest.* The Revised Standard Version has, "all who were of the high-priestly family." The whole ruling body was assembled for what was considered a very important action.

7. And when they had set them in the midst, they asked, By what power, or by what name, have ye done this?

By what power? Outraged officialdom was speaking. In the Sanhedrin were assembled the men who felt themselves divinely chosen and empowered to be the sole guardians and teachers of religion in Israel. Now in the sacred precincts of their temple, and without even a license, to say nothing of an ordination, these laymen from the back country of Galilee were presuming to teach and preach. What was worse, they were being accepted by the people. What right had they? It was an echo of the question which had been pressed upon Jesus himself: "By what authority doest thou these things? and who gave thee this authority?" (Matthew 21:23). *By what name?* The name represents the person. This was the Sanhedrin's key question. They knew well enough that Peter and John had been acting in the name of Jesus. But this same circle of judges, led by the same high priests, had only a few months previously condemned Jesus and secured His crucifixion. At that time Peter, the man now before them, had denied that he knew Jesus. How would he now be able to summon the courage to identify himself with the lost cause of

the discredited and crucified Nazarene? *Have ye done this?* What had the apostles done? Healed? Preached? The question was purposely vague. The Sanhedrin hoped, by a show of the power which had "destroyed" Jesus, and by the very vagueness of the question, to trap the overawed and confused Galileans into making damaging admissions from which to establish a case against them.

8. Then Peter, filled with the Holy Ghost, said unto them, Ye rulers of the people, and elders of Israel.

Peter is again and typically the spokesman. *Filled with the Holy Ghost.* This was in exact fulfillment of Jesus' command and promise: "When they shall lead you, and deliver you up, take no thought beforehand what ye shall speak, neither do ye premeditate: but whatsoever shall be given you in that hour, that speak ye: for it is not ye that speak, but the Holy Ghost" (Mark 13:11). *Ye rulers of the people, and elders of Israel.* Peter used the courteous and proper address to the Sanhedrin. His dignity and poise offered the first of many surprises to the court.

9. If we this day be examined of the good deed done to the impotent man, by what means he is made whole.

The healing of the lame man at the temple gate had started the whole incident. This reply furnished another surprise for the court! The Sanhedrin started with the authority and referred incidentally to the act. Peter took advantage of their vagueness, and started with the act, before introducing the authority. Immediately thereby he put the Sanhedrin in the unenviable position of arresting men for doing something that was not only innocent but praiseworthy.

10. Be it known unto you all, and to all the people of Israel, that by the name of Jesus Christ of Nazareth, whom ye crucified, whom God raised from the dead, even by him doth this man stand here before you whole.

By the name of Jesus Christ of Nazareth. There must be no chance for mistake in identity. The man of Nazareth was the Messiah expected by Israel. *Whom ye crucified.* They had readily accepted responsibility for the crucifixion, but now Peter presented proof that they had committed a wicked and senseless blunder. *Whom God raised from the dead.* Thus the Sanhedrin were arrayed in opposition to God, and He to them. *By him doth this man stand here before you whole.* This is the dramatic proof of the whole argument. The former cripple was "standing with them" (verse 14). We may be sure that the Sanhedrin had not themselves introduced a witness so damaging to their cause. The man had walked in of his own volition, either at the time the apostles were brought from the prison or afterward, and now supported their plea with his presence. The court was faced with a series of incontrovertible facts.

11. This is the stone which was set at nought of you builders, which is become the head of the corner.

Psalm 118:22 says, "The stone which the builders refused is become the head stone of the corner." Jesus quoted the verse as referring to himself (Matthew 21:42), and Peter here charged the Sanhedrin with casting aside Him whom God had provided as the chief cornerstone of spiritual creation.

12. Neither is there salvation in any other: for there is none other name under heaven given among men, whereby we must be saved.

The Holy Spirit led Peter to do a great deal more than to answer the question put to him. The name (that is, the person) of Jesus was not only the power behind the healing of the cripple, but it is equally, and for all time, the necessary power behind the salvation of all men.

13. Now when they saw the boldness of Peter and John, and perceived that they were unlearned and ignorant men, they marvelled; and they took knowledge of them, that they had been with Jesus.

The boldness of Peter and John. Contrast this with Peter's fear at the trial of Jesus before the crucifixion. See Mark 14:66-72. These men were on trial before very much the same group that had decided that Jesus must be put to death. Now, instead of trembling before them, Peter and John boldly preached that Jesus was the Christ and that these very men crucified Him. They also declared that God had raised Jesus from the dead, and thus had shown how wrong the rulers were in their condemnation of Him. *Unlearned and ignorant men.* These words do not mean what our modern use makes them mean. What the rulers realized was that these men did not have a theological education. They had not been taught in the schools that prepared men to preach or teach. More than this, they were not regular scribes or rabbis. They were men from one of the ordinary occupations of life. *Took knowledge of them.* "The Living Oracles" translates this, "Recollected their having been with Jesus." The rulers recognized that Peter and John had been Jesus' disciples.

14. And beholding the man which was healed standing with them, they could say nothing against it.

The crippled man, standing completely healed with Peter and John, was evidence of the power with which they spoke. In questioning the prisoners, the rulers had been careful not to mention the healing. They had asked, "By what power, or by what name, have ye done this?" While their question could have applied either to the teaching or the healing, Peter brought in the evidence of the healed man and connected it directly with the preaching of Jesus. The Sanhedrin had hoped, by a display of their authority, to reduce Peter and John to embarrassed silence. Now to their complete discomfiture, they discovered that the exact opposite had happened. The obvious facts and the evidence of divine favor were all on the other side.

15. But when they had commanded them to go aside out of the council, they conferred among themselves.

Perplexed by the problem stated in the next verse, the rulers thought best to discuss it privately. Their discussion no doubt was reported to the disciples later by some of the rulers who became Christians. See Acts 6:7.

16. Saying, What shall we do to these men? for that indeed a notable

miracle hath been done by them is manifest to all them that dwell in Jerusalem; and we cannot deny it.

The problem was a very delicate one. If they punished Peter and John for doing a good deed, the whole thing would be publicized throughout Jerusalem. But if they did not punish them, how could they stop them from preaching Jesus?

17. But that it spread no further among the people, let us straitly threaten them, that they speak henceforth to no man in this name.

J. B. Phillips translates, "Let us warn them that if they say anything more to anyone in his name it will be at their peril." They tried to frighten Peter and John.

18. And they called them, and commanded them not to speak at all nor teach in the name of Jesus.

The judges would have no more discussion. By the authority of their position, they simply ordered the apostles to say no more about Jesus. Thus, they hoped, the case was closed.

19. But Peter and John answered and said unto them, Whether it be right in the sight of God to hearken unto you more than unto God, judge ye.

Was it right to disobey God in order to obey the Jerusalem court? That was what the judges had to decide. Peter's choice was to obey God, even though this action could bring him under the condemnation of the court. He was risking the same condemnation that the court had given to Jesus when He was brought before it.

20. For we cannot but speak the things which we have seen and heard.

Their preaching was largely a narration of what Jesus had said and done and of the salvation that God had offered men through Him. Jesus ordered them to teach and preach as they did; the Holy Spirit empowered and guided them. They could not do otherwise.

21. So when they had further threatened them, they let them go, finding nothing how they might punish them, because of the people: for all men glorified God for that which was done.

All Jerusalem knew and praised the good deed of Peter and John. The judges could not punish them without losing popular support. They only threatened—but not with empty threats. Not much later, the apostles were arrested and beaten (Acts 5:17-40). Still later, Stephen was stoned to death for preaching the gospel (Acts 6:8—7:60). These accounts show the growing opposition and danger that threatened anyone who would tell the story of Jesus.

22. For the man was above forty years old, on whom this miracle of healing was shewed.

There was no possibility that this was a case of hysteria or temporary paralysis. The man had been born a cripple (Acts 3:2) and had lived as a cripple more than forty years. The miracle was unquestionable.

23. And being let go, they went to their own company, and reported all that the chief priests and elders had said unto them.

Associates of Peter and John naturally were anxious about them. As soon as the two were released, they hurried to relieve this anxiety. *Their*

own company probably means the apostles, since verse 31 says, "They were all filled with the Holy Ghost, and they spake the word of God with boldness." The whole band of believers then comes into the record in verse 32. To their fellow workers Peter and John reported the threats of the rulers.

24. And when they heard that, they lifted up their voice to God with one accord, and said, Lord, thou art God, which hast made heaven, and earth, and the sea, and all that in them is.

Threatened by the rulers of Jerusalem, the apostles immediately recognized a higher authority—the almighty Creator of all things.

25. Who by the mouth of thy servant David hast said, Why did the heathen rage, and the people imagine vain things?

The apostles were keenly aware of Old Testament prophecies because so many of them were now being fulfilled. They thought quickly of the opening lines of Psalm 2, recognizing them as God's own words. *People* means the chosen people, the people of Israel (v. 27). Both they and *the heathen* were arrayed against God's will.

26. The kings of the earth stood up, and the rulers were gathered together against the Lord, and against his Christ.

The psalmist pictured a huge alliance of earthly rulers with the purpose of overthrowing God's rule, but he visualized complete victory for God. Read the entire psalm.

27. For of a truth against thy holy child Jesus, whom thou hast anointed, both Herod, and Pontius Pilate, with

the Gentiles, and the people of Israel, were gathered together.

Jesus was the Lord's anointed mentioned in the psalm. ("Anointed" is "Messiah" in the Hebrew and "Christ" in the Greek of Acts 4:26). *Herod, and Pontius Pilate, with the Gentiles* who serve them, were the heathen arrayed against Him (Luke 23:1-25). *The people of Israel* were represented by the Jerusalem council and the mob obedient to it. These condemned Jesus in their own tribunal and insisted that Pilate sentence Him to death (Luke 22:66; 23:1, 13-25).

28. For to do whatsoever thy hand and thy counsel determined before to be done.

In their vicious effort to overthrow God's rule by destroying His anointed, the rulers succeeded only in establishing His kingdom as He had planned, for God promptly raised up the slain Christ and sent His message forth to win people, by thousands. Well might the inspired psalmist say, "He that sitteth in the heavens shall laugh: the Lord shall have them in derision" (Psalm 2:4).

29. And now, Lord, behold their threatenings: and grant unto thy servants, that with all boldness they may speak thy word.

The rulers who had killed Jesus were continuing their campaign, trying by threats to stop the spread of His message. For these rulers the apostles did not ask vengeance or destruction, but only God's notice; for themselves they did not ask safety or freedom from persecution, but boldness to go on with their appointed task.

30. By stretching forth thine hand to heal; and that signs and wonders may be done by the name of thy holy child Jesus.

The American Standard Version clarifies the first phrase: "While thou stretchest forth thy hand to heal." In addition to asking for boldness in their work, the apostles asked that God would continue to show His approval of their work by doing miracles through them, as He had done when the lame man was healed by the temple gate. Such miracles were signs of God's approval; they were *wonders* because they were beyond human power.

31. And when they had prayed, the place was shaken where they were assembled together; and they were all filled with the Holy Ghost, and they spake the word of God with boldness.

We need not suppose the Holy Spirit had departed from any of the apostles after His spectacular coming on the Day of Pentecost. Surely He had inspired Peter's defense before the rulers (v. 8). But now the shaking of the place gave tangible evidence of His presence and power. The apostles must have felt a renewed awareness and assurance of divine help as they continued to teach with undiminished *boldness.*

32. And the multitude of them that believed were of one heart and of one soul: neither said any of them that ought of the things which he possessed was his own; but they had all things common.

The church now numbered more than five thousand men in Jerusalem, besides women and children. *Of one heart and of one soul.* This emphasized the original unity of the church even more than the common phrase, "of one accord." The love of Christ and a whole-souled commitment to His cause dominated the life of each, so that the unity for which Christ prayed (John 17:11, 21, 22) was here a reality. All too soon the invasion of private opinions, jealousies, and human loyalties marred this perfect unity, so that the apostles had to give major emphasis in their preaching and teaching to the preservation and restoration of "the unity of the Spirit in the bond of peace" (Ephesians 4:3; compare 1 Corinthians 1:1-17; Philippians 2:2). *Neither said any of them that ought of the things which he possessed was his own.* The private possession of property was not done away, but Christians did not jealously guard their rights. They counted that their property, like their persons, belonged to God and should be held in trust only for His use. *They had all things common.* All belonged to the same Lord. The fact that no one was required to contribute (Acts 5:4), and that Mary the mother of Mark still owned a house some time later (Acts 12:12) is evidence that voluntary contribution to the common need, rather than the collective ownership of all possessions, is the thing here described in our text.

33. And with great power gave the apostles witness of the resurrection of the Lord Jesus: and great grace was upon them all.

The power was that which was promised as a result of the apostles' Holy Spirit baptism, plus the force which the unselfish devotion of the Christians gave to their message. Their audiences, having seen a sermon lived by the disciples, were pre-

pared to hear one preached by the apostles. *Witness of the resurrection of the Lord Jesus.* The apostles were the specially chosen observers and proclaimers of the resurrection. To tell of it was their chief assignment. *Great grace.* The Living Oracles translation has, "Great kindness was among them all." The evidence of God's favor was everywhere apparent.

34. Neither was there any among them that lacked: for as many as were possessors of lands or houses sold them, and brought the prices of the things that were sold.

The need of Christians far from home, and without possessions or business connections in Jerusalem, would be especially great. None was allowed to suffer want while another possessed anything that could be used to supply that want. *As many as were possessors of lands or houses sold them.* Their generosity went far deeper than giving from their surplus, or even the contribution of cash in hand. *Brought the prices of the things that were sold.* Their generosity was expressed in the name of Christ and through the leadership of the church, rather than by direct personal donation.

35. And laid them down at the apostles' feet: and distribution was made unto every man according as he had need.

Laid them down at the apostles' feet. Committed them to the care and authority of the apostles. Until the work became so heavy as to hamper them in their greater task of preaching, the apostles accepted the gifts of Christians and made the necessary distribution. This situation was changed with the choosing of the seven (Acts 6:1-4). *Distribution*

*was made unto every man according
as he had need.* The American Standard Version has, "Distribution was
made unto each, according as any
one had need." It was not a matter of
providing for the whole church, but
of supplying the needs of those who
lacked. The need was the key to the
whole arrangement: "That now at
this time your abundance may be a
supply for their want, that their
abundance also may be a supply for
your want: that there may be equal-
ity: as it is written, He that had
gathered much had nothing over;
and he that had gathered little had
no lack" (2 Corinthians 8:14, 15).

**36. And Joses, who by the apostles
was surnamed Barnabas, (which is,
being interpreted, The son of consolation,) a Levite, and of the country of
Cyprus.**

The inspired recorder introduced
here a specific example of the thing
he had described, choosing for his example a man who was later to become prominent in the advancement
of the church. *Joses.* Greek form of
the Hebrew name Joseph. This was
his real name, as Peter's name was
Simon. *By the apostles was surnamed
Barnabas.* This is the name by which
he was known. The giving of "honor
names" to fit the character of the person was a common and meaningful
custom followed by Jesus and His
disciples. (*Which is, being interpreted, the son of consolation*).
Barnabas is an Aramaic name, which
Luke translated for his Greek readers.

The name is elsewhere rendered
"Son of exhortation" (American
Standard Version). Barnabas was
known for helpful exhortation (Acts
11:23), and for the generous spirit
which consoled and encouraged
others in their needs (Acts 9:27; 15:
36-41). *A Levite.* A descendant of
Levi, and thus a member of the
priestly tribe in Israel. *Of the country of Cyprus.* From the time of Alexander the Great, many Jews had settled in Cyprus, a large and fertile island in the eastern Mediterranean,
not far removed from Cilicia, where
Paul was born and reared. Barnabas
evangelized in his homeland with
Paul on the first missionary journey
(Acts 13:4-12), and later returned
there with John Mark (Acts 15:39).

**37. Having land, sold it, and
brought the money, and laid it at the
apostles' feet.**

Having land. The phrase is variously rendered, "having a field"
(American Standard Version), "a
farm" (Moffatt), and "an estate"
(Living Oracles). The Levites did
not have a tribal inheritance in the
ancient economy (Deuteronomy 10:
8, 9), but the ancient order had been
disrupted with the Assyrian and
Babylonian captivities. *Sold it, and
brought the money.* Some have suggested that Barnabas was the one
who first suggested this means of
caring for the church's needs. It is in
harmony with his generous and helpful spirit.

CHAPTER 5

1. But a certain man named Ananias, with Sapphira his wife, sold a posession.

This case is set in contrast with that of Barnabas in the previous chapter.

2. And kept back part of the price, his wife also being privy to it, and brought a certain part, and laid it at the apostles' feet.

Apparently this couple did not want to seem different from their fellows: they wanted to be thought as generous as the rest. But on the other hand, they wanted to look out for themselves, to make sure they would not be impoverished. After selling their land, therefore, they kept part of the money for themselves, but they did this secretly.

3. But Peter said, Ananias, why hath Satan filled thine heart to lie to the Holy Ghost, and to keep back part of the price of the land?

The generosity of the church in those days was not taught by the apostles only, but by the Holy Spirit who filled the apostles and gave them their teaching. Therefore when Ananias thought he was lying to the apostles he was really lying to the Holy Spirit. Peter did not have to examine Ananias' books to find out what was going on. The Holy Spirit knew. He revealed it to Peter and told Peter what to say about it.

4. Whiles it remained, was it not thine own? and after it was sold, was it not in thine own power? why hast thou conceived this thing in thine heart? thou hast not lied unto men, but unto God.

It now becomes evident that Ananias' sin was not in keeping part of the money, but in lying. The land was his; he was not required to sell it. When he sold it, the money was his; he was not required to give all of it, or even a part of it. But he was required to tell the truth to God, and this he did not do. He was a hypocrite like those Jesus mentioned in Matthew 6:2: he did not wish to help the needy so much as he wished to be honored by his fellows. He was even worse than those Jesus mentioned, for he sought credit for more giving then he really did.

5. And Ananias hearing these words fell down, and gave up the ghost: and great fear came on all them that heard these things.

We are not told how many were present to witness the sudden death, but we can guess that they lost no time in telling others of the startling event. The disciples had become accustomed to the beneficial miracles; now they suddenly became aware that the divine power could punish as well as bless. This example warned all of them—and should warn all of us—not to try to deceive God.

6. And the young men arose, wound him up, and carried him out, and buried him.

Burial on the day of death was not unusual, but in this case it seems to have been especially quick and unceremonious. Ananias was buried before his wife heard of his death. Loud mourning was customary, but there seems to have been none. God had disposed of a liar; God's people disposed of his body as quickly as possible, and yet with proper decency. The young men *wound him up,* wrapped him in cloth, according to the usual custom. They carried him instead of dragging him as the carcass of an animal might be dragged, and they *buried him* instead of simply leaving him like garbage in the valley of Hinnom.

7. And it was about the space of three hours after, when his wife, not knowing what was done, came in.

There is no intimation of where she had been, but she now came into the presence of Peter and probably of some or all of the other apostles (v. 2).

8. And Peter answered unto her, Tell me whether ye sold the land for so much? And she said, Yea, for so much.

Sapphira repeated the same figure her husband had given, thus making it plain that she also was a liar.

9. Then Peter said unto her, How is it that ye have agreed together to tempt the Spirit of the Lord? behold, the feet of them which have buried thy husband are at the door, and shall carry thee out.

It was *the Spirit of the Lord,* not Peter, that Ananias and Sapphira put to the test with their attempted deceit. The Spirit met the test with divine knowledge and power. He recognized the lie, denounced it, and punished the liars. Peter was only His spokesman to expose the falsehood and pronounce the sentence.

10. Then fell she down straightway at his feet, and yielded up the ghost: and the young men came in, **and found her dead, and, carrying her forth, buried her by her husband.**

In addition to reemphasizing the power of God and the folly of trying to deceive Him, this second death must have kept anyone from supposing that Ananias had simply happened to have a heart attack at the same time Peter accused him.

11. And great fear came upon all the church, and upon as many as heard these things.

The awe produced by Ananias' sudden death (v. 5) was doubled by the similar end of his wife and accomplice.

12. And by the hands of the apostles were many signs and wonders wrought among the people; (and they were all with one accord in Solomon's porch.

By the hands of the apostles. The working of miracles was limited at this time to the apostles. Later, and by the laying on of the apostles' hands, the miracle-working power was given to certain others also. *Many signs and wonders.* The customary reference to miracles of all sorts. *They were all with one accord in Solomon's porch.* Solomon's portico, the vast colonnaded area along the east wall of the court of the Gentiles in the temple, had become the regular place of preaching and teaching for the apostles.

13. And of the rest durst no man join himself to them: but the people magnified them.

A large group of the Jews, priests, and others, closely associated with the temple rulers, were increasingly convinced of the truth of the gospel. But because they had too much to lose from the wrath of the high priests, they did not declare themselves. *But the people magnified them.* The Revised Standard Version says, "The people held them in high honor." The "people" were attracted by the same things which repelled "the rest." Here again, as in Acts 2:47, is indicated the respect with which the public observed the lives of the Christians. The admiration which they had for the apostles is indicated in verses 15, 16.

14. And believers were the more added to the Lord, multitudes both of men and women.)

Not all of those who held the apostles and their company in high regard became obedient believers, but a significant number did, and the day by day accessions to the church (Acts 2:47) were notably increased. Even though they were attracted by the miracles of the apostles and the purity of the church, it was not to the apostles nor to the church that they committed themselves; it was to Christ. *Multitudes.* The "five thousand" men, of Acts 4:4, is the last definite number indicated in Scripture. More than two thousand had been added within a few weeks, and now the rate was so increased that further numberings seem to have been impossible. *Both of men and women.* The church was discovering that in Christ there is "neither male nor female" but that all are one in Christ Jesus (Galatians 3:28). The membership in the apostolic church was of adult believers exclusively. Children below the age of responsibility could be neither "believers" nor "men and women "

15. Insomuch that they brought forth the sick into the streets, and laid them on beds and couches, that at the least the shadow of Peter passing by might overshadow some of them.

Having completed the parenthetical remarks concerning the regard with which the church was held by the people, the writer returns to the subject of verse 12—the healing miracles performed by the apostles. *They brought forth the sick into the streets.* The American Standard Version has, "They even carried out the sick into the streets." As the four had brought a palsied man to Jesus for healing (Mark 2:3-5), so now the people brought their friends to Peter, only in this case they laid them on pallets in the streets awaiting his passing. *The shadow of Peter passing by might overshadow some of them.* The record does not satisfy our curiosity as to how many cures were actually accomplished by this means. A touch of the hem of Jesus' garment was sufficient to heal some believers (Matthew 9:21; 14:36) and napkins carried to the sick from the person of Paul resulted in cures at Ephesus (Acts 19:12).

16. There came also a multitude out of the cities round about unto Jerusalem, bringing sick folks, and them which were vexed with unclean spirits: and they were healed every one.

As the multitudes had gone out from Jerusalem to hear John the Baptist in the wilderness, so now they came into the city from the outlying regions of Judea, to receive benefit of the apostolic miracles. *Vexed with unclean spirits.* Demon possession, or the control of one's personality by an evil spirit, was closely associated with physical and mental illness. *They were healed every one.* In later New Testament times, even such faithful folk as Paul, Timothy, Epaphroditus, and Trophimus were permitted to suffer illness without divine intervention to heal. But here in the earliest days of the church God used miracles freely to establish His word.

17. Then the high priest rose up, and all they that were with him, (which is the sect of the Sadducees,) and were filled with indignation.

The *Sadducees* were the liberal sect of that time, denying the existence of angels, spirits, and resurrection (Acts 23:8). Its leaders were *the high priest* and his associates. They of course had a special objection to the teaching of the resurrection of Jesus; but even without it they would have been *filled with indignation* at any teaching in Jesus' name, for they had specifically forbidden such teaching (Acts 4:18). The ruling council included Pharisees too, and most of these opposed the gospel as vigorously as the Sadducees did. The priests, however, were in charge of the temple, where the apostles often taught in Solomon's porch (Acts 5:12). Therefore they were the ones who brought the police to arrest the apostles.

18. And laid their hands on the apostles, and put them in the common prison.

As Peter and John previously had been arrested and imprisoned (Acts 4:1-3), so the whole group of apostles now was put *in the common prison* to be tried the next day.

19. But the angel of the Lord by night opened the prison doors, and brought them forth, and said.

We are not told why God sometimes delivered His messengers thus, but more often let them remain in jail. Possibly His purpose this time was to give the rulers additional evidence that He was with His apostles. This might lead some of the rulers to think seriously and even to moderate or give up their opposition. Note Acts 5:34-39; 6:7.

20. Go, stand and speak in the temple to the people all the words of this life.

The angel told the apostles to go on with their work, not seeking secrecy, but teaching in the temple under the noses of the priests as they had done before. *All the words of this life* means the gospel by which men are called to new life in Christ.

21. And when they heard that, they entered into the temple early in the morning, and taught. But the high priest came, and they that were with him, and called the council together, and all the senate of the children of Israel, and sent to the prison to have them brought.

Probably the apostles resumed their teaching as early as anyone was in the temple to listen. If the story of the apostles' release was being passed from person to person, no doubt a crowd gathered long before the mid-morning hour of prayer. While the teaching was going on, the high priest, knowing nothing of it, solemnly convened his court and sent his police to bring the prisoners. The council or Sanhedrin was the Jewish ruling body of about seventy men. The *Senate* or eldership may be another name for the same group. Some think additional elders were invited to this meeting.

22. But when the officers came, and found them not in the prison, they returned, and told.

The record is brief and factual, leaving us to imagine the excitement and dismay that must have prevailed when the prison was found to be empty.

23. Saying, The prison truly found we shut with all safety, and the keepers standing without before the doors: but when we had opened, we found no man within.

Apparently the guards did not know or even suspect there had been an escape. The angel must have put them to sleep or in a trance while he did his work.

24. Now when the high priest and the captain of the temple and the chief priests heard these things, they doubted of them whereunto this would grow.

The captain of the temple was in charge of the temple police. Naturally both he and the leading priests were much disturbed. It would be hard to maintain their authority if their jail would not hold prisoners. Under ordinary conditions they would have suspected the guards of permitting the escape; but in this case they were all too well aware of the many miracles involving the apostles, and this added to their perplexity and apprehension.

25. Then came one and told them, saying, Behold, the men whom ye put in prison are standing in the temple, and teaching the people.

It seems most likely that one of the police on duty in the temple brought this information, though of course any priest or caretaker could have reported.

26. Then went the captain with the officers, and brought them without violence: for they feared the people, lest they should have been stoned.

The Jews of Palestine were an excitable people, and violent riots were all too frequent among them. They were favorably impressed with the disciples (Acts 2:47; 5:13), and might have tried to rescue the apostles by mob violence if the officers had mistreated them. Therefore the police escorted them courteously to court.

27. And when they had brought them, they set them before the council: and the high priest asked them.

They set them before the council. The apostles were returned to the now-familiar place of the accused in the center of the circle of the Sanhedrin. See Acts 4:7. *The high priest asked them.* It is probable that Annas again took the lead in the examination, which was proper under the circumstances. It was right that the charge should be put in the form of a question, in order that the accused might have opportunity to speak in his own defense. The charge, which follows, takes the form of a direct statement, however, more than that of an inquiry.

28. Saying, Did not we straitly command you that ye should not teach in this name? and, behold, ye have filled Jerusalem with your doctrine, and intend to bring this man's blood upon us.

The American Standard Version has "We strictly charged you not to teach in this name." At the time of their former hearing, the council had forbidden further preaching in the name of Christ (Acts 4:18), but Peter had insisted that silence would be impossible. Peter later exhorted Christians to "submit . . . to every ordinance of man for the Lord's sake" (1 Peter 2:13-17), but where the human authority commands that which is in direct contradiction to the divine law, the Christian will obey God. *Ye have filled Jerusalem with your doctrine.* "Teaching" (American Standard Version) is clearer here than "doctrine." Even the council had to admit that their preaching had been effective and successful. *Intend to bring this man's blood upon us.* The Jews had said of Christ at the crucifixion, "His blood be on us, and on our children" (Matthew 27:25). Their leaders could hardly now avoid the responsibility they had then accepted.

29. Then Peter and the other apostles answered and said, We ought to obey God rather than men.

The American Standard Version has, "We must obey God." Peter was still the spokesman, but the whole body of the apostles concurred in the declaration. They simply reaffirmed the commitment Peter and John had made before (4:19).

30. The God of our fathers raised up Jesus, whom ye slew and hanged on a tree.

Raised up Jesus. The central fact of the gospel was here again declared. *Whom ye slew and hanged on a tree.* The American Standard Version has, "Whom ye slew, hanging him on a tree." The leaders' rejection of Christ was contrasted with God's glorification of Him. The "tree" is a poetic reference to the cross.

31. Him hath God exalted with his right hand to be a Prince and a Saviour, for to give repentance to Israel, and forgiveness of sins.

The exaltation and glory of Christ, whom the Sanhedrin had condemned, and the teaching that proud Israel, including the national leaders, needed to repent, enraged the Sanhedrin as much as the things with which they had formerly charged the apostles. *A Prince and a Saviour.* The authority of Christ to reign cannot be separated from the power of Christ to save. *To give repentance to Israel.* The privilege, opportunity, and incentives to repentance are all gifts from God. They are not limited to Israel, but the apostles made proper application of the gospel message to the people before them.

32. And we are his witnesses of these things; and so is also the Holy Ghost, whom God hath given to them that obey him.

The resurrection of Christ was a fact which the apostles had observed with their physical senses. The exaltation of Christ and His plan of salvation were known to them through His teaching and commission, together with the revelation that had come to them through the Spirit. The Sanhedrin could know, by means of the miracle of the apostles' deliverance from prison, that they had the revelation they claimed. *So is also the Holy Ghost.* The apostles boldly claimed supernatural confirmation ·of their declarations. *Whom God hath given to them that obey him.* Peter had declared the promise of the Holy Spirit to those who repented and were baptized into Christ (Acts 2:38). A continued lifelong obedience to God was naturally implied.

33. When they heard that, they were cut to the heart, and took counsel to slay them.

This is the response to Peter's bold reiteration of the apostles' former teaching, with the added call to repent of sins. *Cut to the heart.* The impression was the same as that on the hearers at Pentecost (Acts 2: 37), but the response was very different. The Living Oracles translation has, "They were enraged, and consulted to put them to death." Threats and imprisonments had failed to silence the apostles. More radical measures would be necessary.

34. Then stood there up one in the council, a Pharisee, named Gamaliel, a doctor of the law, had in reputation among all the people, and commanded to put the apostles forth a little space.

At least one in the Sanhedrin kept a cool head. The Pharisees had been Jesus' bitterest enemies, but now a Pharisee arose to the defense of the apostles against the Sadducees, who were in the majority in the council. *Had in reputation.* The Living Oracles translation has, "in great esteem among all the people." Gamaliel was known and respected for his wisdom and moderation. *Commanded to put the apostles forth a little space.* He evidently thought that the council would exercise more cool-headed judgment if the apostles, who stirred such fury in the high priests, were not present.

35. And said unto them, Ye men of Israel, take heed to yourselves what ye intend to do as touching these men.

Gamaliel used the same form of respectful address that Peter had formerly used (Acts 3:12). The American Standard Version has, "Take heed to yourselves as touching these men, what ye are about to do." They must not act in hasty passion, without considering the consequences.

36. For before these days rose up Theudas, boasting himself to be somebody; to whom a number of men,

about four hundred, joined themselves: who was slain; and all, as many as obeyed him, were scattered, and brought to nought.

The Living Oracles translation has, "Theudas arose, pretending himself to be a person of note." *As many as obeyed him, were scattered.* The Living Oracles translation has, "All who hearkened to him." Those who accepted Theudas' estimate of himself and became his followers were dispersed after he was put to death.

37. After this man rose up Judas of Galilee in the days of the taxing, and drew away much people, after him: he also perished; and all, even as many as obeyed him, were dispersed.

Judas of Galilee is named by Josephus as a member of the Zealot sect, who opposed the payment of taxes to Rome. The "days of taxing" ("days of enrollment" according to the American Standard Version) would offer a natural occasion for a popular revolt inspired by the Zealots.

38. And now I say unto you, Refrain from these men, and let them alone: for if this counsel or this work be of men, it will come to nought.

Arguing from the history of the abortive revolts just mentioned, Gamaliel asserted that a merely human uprising would fail because of its own inherent weakness and the natural opposition of the government. It would not be necessary for the Sanhedrin to take action against it.

39. But if it be of God, ye cannot overthrow it; lest haply ye be found even to fight against God.

The latter part of this verse completes the first part of the former one: "Refrain from these men, and let them alone: lest haply ye be found even to fight against God." Although he was evidently not thoroughly convinced that the apostles' mission was of God, he considered even that a definite possibility.

40. And to him they agreed: and when they had called the apostles, and beaten them, they commanded that they should not speak in the name of Jesus, and let them go.

The quick action of the Sanhedrin in beating and threatening the apostles was no part of Gamaliel's recommendation. The council yielded to him sufficiently that they did not carry out their former intention to kill Peter and the others. The beating, or scourging, was probably the flogging of "forty stripes save one" with a thonged lash, which Paul was later to suffer (2 Corinthians 11:24). Compare Acts 4:18-23.

41: And they departed from the presence of the council, rejoicing that they were counted worthy to suffer shame for his name.

Their stripes became badges of honor. This was the first severe physical persecution they had received. Jesus had warned them that it would come (John 15:20), and they had perhaps wondered if they would be able to endure it. Now that God had sustained them in their initiation to bloodshed, and they had been enabled to take it like veterans, they rejoiced, both in the fellowship they shared with Christ and in the power that upheld them. They knew the meaning of the final beatitude. "Blessed are ye, when men shall revile you, and persecute you . . . for my sake" (Matthew 5:11).

42. And daily in the temple, and in every house, they ceased not to teach and preach Jesus Christ.

The Living Oracles translation has, "Daily, in the temple, and from house to house, they ceased not to teach and to declare the good news, that Jesus is the Messiah." The temple was still available as a forum for all Jews, and because of the popularity of the apostles, the temple authorities did not dare to close it against them at this time. Christ had commanded His followers to declare the truth concerning Him. The temple authorities had now given an opposite command. Peter and his companions did not hesitate to obey the Lord's mandate to teach, daily and persistently, publicly and privately.

CHAPTER 6

1. And in those days, when the number of the disciples was multiplied, there arose a murmuring of the Grecians against the Hebrews, because their widows were neglected in the daily ministration.

Multiplied. Again a brief note in passing informs us that *the number of the disciples* was growing by leaps and bounds (Acts 2:41; 4:4; 5:14).

A murmuring. A grumbling, a muttering, an undertone of discontent and complaint. *Grecians.* Probably most of these were not Greeks by race, but Jews who had been born or had lived for some time in areas outside of Palestine, where Greek language and customs prevailed. *Hebrews.* Jews of Palestine. *Their widows were neglected in the daily ministration.* It seems that there were an unusual number of needy people among the disciples, probably because many neglected their work or business to gather every day and hear the apostles teach (Acts 2:46). The disciples who had more than they needed gave freely to care for those who did not have enough (Acts 2:44, 45; 4:33-37). As thousands were added to the fellowship, it was increasingly difficult to know about all who were in need. It may have been true that the widows and other needy among the Grecians were overlooked most often, since their families and friends were elsewhere and they were not well known in Jerusalem.

2. Then the twelve called the multitude of the disciples unto them, and said, It is not reason that we should leave the word of God, and serve tables.

The *twelve,* the apostles, called a meeting of the whole congregation to suggest a way of ending the difficulty. Jesus had especially appointed these twelve to teach others what He had taught them (Matthew 28:20). It would not be reasonable or proper for them to neglect that duty in order to manage the daily distribution of food to the needy; and now this daily ministration to the needy had become such a large task that they could not do it without neglecting their teaching.

3. Wherefore, brethren, look ye out among you seven men of honest report, full of the Holy Ghost and wisdom, whom we may appoint over this business.

The suggested solution was simple and democratic. The whole congregation was asked to choose a committee to take charge of distributing food. No reason is given for the number *seven.* Presumably the apostles judged that number would be needed to do the work.

4. But we will give ourselves continually to prayer, and to the ministry of the word.

The efforts of the new committee would leave the apostles free to give full attention to their appointed work.

5. And the saying pleased the whole multitude: and they chose Stephen, a man full of faith and of the Holy Ghost, and Philip, and Prochorus, and Nicanor, and Timon, and Parmenas, and Nicolas a proselyte of Antioch.

There is no hint of the procedure followed in the election, but the whole group promptly approved the idea and proceeded to choose the men. All the seven had Greek names. This does not necessarily mean that all of them were Grecians, but at least none were of families too narrowly Hebrew to use a Greek name. One of the seven, *Nicolas,* was not only a Grecian from *Antioch,* but also a *proselyte,* a convert instead of one born a Jew. These seven are often called the first deacons, since they were chosen to serve in a specified way and the word "deacon" means a servant. It is notable, however, that the record does not call them deacons. We can say with certainty only that they were men chosen for the task described.

6. Whom they set before the apostles: and when they had prayed, they laid their hands on them.

This seems to have been the usual way of appointing or ordaining one to a task (Acts 13:3; 1 Timothy 4:

14). Evidently the apostles were able to impart miraculous powers by laying their hands on others (Acts 8:17, 18). We are not told whether such power was now given to the seven or not; but Philip later had miraculous power (Acts 8:6), and Stephen is generally supposed to have been inspired in the great speech recorded in Acts 7.

7. And the word of God increased; and the number of the disciples multiplied in Jerusalem greatly; and a great company of the priests were obedient to the faith.

The word of God increased in influence and power as more and more people accepted it and *the number of the disciples multiplied.* Even among the most violent enemies of the gospel there were some who could not resist the truth, and *a great company of the priests were obedient to the faith.* Probably from some of these the historian was able to learn what took place in the secret sessions of the council (Acts 4:15-18; 5:34-40).

8. And Stephen, full of faith and power, did great wonders and miracles among the people.

Stephen was one of seven chosen to "serve tables," so that none of the needy should be neglected, and the apostles might be free to preach. *Full of faith and power.* This is the first indication of miracles worked by any except the apostles of the Lord Jesus.

This special power was given by the laying on of the apostles' hands (v 6; compare Acts 8:18)

9. Then there arose certain of the synagogue, which is called the synagogue of the Libertines, and Cyrenians, and Alexandrians, and of them of Cilicia and Asia, disputing with Stephen.

Certain of the synagogue. Some of the leaders took issue with the preaching of Stephen. Only one synagogue is described here. It was made up of various elements, all of which were of foreign and Hellenistic background. *Of the Libertines.* "Synagogue of the Freedmen," according to the marginal reading in the American Standard Version. Ptolemy had taken many Jewish slaves to Egypt, and Pompey had sold many into slavery in Rome. Some of these had been freed; hence this synagogue in which Hellenistic Jews from many nations worshiped had in it many former slaves. *Cyrenians.* Cyrene was a part of northern Africa opposite Greece. *Alexandrians.* The Jewish theologian Philo calculated that two-fifths of the population of Alexandria, the chief center of trade and learning in Egypt, were Jews. *Cilicia.* This was Saul's native province. Tarsus was one of its important cities. *Asia.* The western province of Asia Minor, centering around Ephesus. *Disputing with Stephen.* It seems that the opposition to Stephen here arose from among the congregation in the synagogue rather than from among the leaders.

10. And they were not able to resist the wisdom and the spirit by which he spake.

Jesus had been notably successful in silencing the objections of His critics, but the apostles had not yet been tried in this field of conflict, matching text with text, reason with reason, and argument with argument. If there were uncertainty as to the outcome of the first encounter, Stephen soon dispelled it. He had the studied knowledge of the Word, which, with divine assistance, made his reasoning irresistible.

11. Then they suborned men, which said, We have heard him speak blasphemous words against Moses, and against God.

The whole pattern of the opposition was reminiscent of the Pharisees' campaigns against Jesus. Unable to answer the teaching, the critics sought to destroy the teacher. To this end they began, not with physical force, but with a careful plan aimed to secure his condemnation and death on a charge of blasphemy. They would have witnesses, even if they had to bribe or coerce them into testifying. The testimony was the more vicious because it was near enough to the truth to be convincing. A statement lifted out of its context and twisted just enough to make it mean what the speaker did not intend would be sufficient.

12. And they stirred up the people, and the elders, and the scribes, and came upon him, and caught him, and brought him to the council.

They stirred up the people. In this the critics succeeded where the Sadducees had failed. "The people" had favored the apostles, but the persecutors this time chose as their victim, not the apostles, but one man who had only recently come into prominence. The charges of blasphemy were much better designed to stir popular sympathy than charges of disobedience to the temple authorities. *Came upon him, and caught him.* How like the arrest of Jesus! Having determined on their course, secured and coached their witnesses, and roused public opinion, they proceeded to the arrest and "trial."

13. And set up false witnesses, which said, This man ceaseth not to speak blasphemous words against this holy place, and the law.

The witnesses were false, not so much in telling out-right falsehoods, as in using facts and half-facts in a way to distort and destroy the truth. *This man ceaseth not to speak blasphemous words.* The witnesses' enthusiasm carried them beyond their original intention. They had agreed to testify that they had heard blasphemous words from Stephen (v. 11). Now they insisted that blasphemy poured from him without ceasing. Blasphemy is gross irreverence to sacred things—in this case the temple, and the law of Moses.

14. For we have heard him say, that this Jesus of Nazareth shall destroy this place, and shall change the customs which Moses delivered us.

With slight, but vicious, changes, the preaching of the apostles could be made to support this accusation. Concerning the coming destruction of Jerusalem Jesus himself had predicted, "There shall not be left here one stone upon another, that shall not be thrown down" (Matthew 24: 2). *Change the customs which Moses delivered us.* Jesus had said, "Think not that I am come to destroy the law, or the prophets: I am not come to destroy, but to fulfill" (Matthew 5:17). Jesus and the apostles did indeed change many of the Jewish customs, but they were not the customs delivered by Moses. They were the human traditions that had come to be accepted as authoritative, but which frequently nullified the plain teaching of the law.

15. And all that sat in the council, looking stedfastly on him, saw his

face as it had been the face of an angel.

This is the nearest thing we have to a physical description of one of the heroes of the New Testament. "Fastening their eyes on him" (American Standard Version.) The charge against Stephen had been made, and the witnesses had been heard. It was now his turn to speak, and they looked to see what he might do or say. *The face of an angel.* There may have been a supernatural change in Stephen's appearance as he manifested the divine presence in his looks as well as his speech. The intense emotions of the moment may have been sufficient, however, to effect the described appearance without any miracle.

CHAPTER 7

1. Then said the high priest, Are these things so?

The high priest himself had been involved in procuring false testimony against Jesus (Matthew 26: 59-62). He must have suspected that the accusers of Stephen had resorted to the same kind of trickery. Nevertheless he tried to preserve the appearance of a fair trial by giving Stephen a chance to speak in his own defense. He and the other council members, of course, would listen carefully, hoping Stephen would say something that could be misinterpreted and used against him.

2. And he said, Men, brethren, and fathers, hearken; The God of glory appeared unto our father Abraham, when he was in Mesopotamia, before he dwelt in Charran.

Stephen began by identifying himself with his hearers. He regarded his fellow Jews as *brethren;* the older ones he respected as *fathers.* He shared their pride in their ancestor *Abraham,* whom *the God of glory* called to be the founder of a new nation, God's own chosen. The record in Genesis 11:31—12:3 tells of Abraham's move to *Charran* or Haran before mentioning God's call; Stephen's address clarifies this, showing that God called him in *Mesopotamia,* where he lived in Ur, before he moved to Haran.

3. And said unto him, Get thee out of thy country, and from thy kindred, and come into the land which I shall shew thee.

This fact and those on the following verses were well known to all the Jews. Stephen's repetition of them served two purposes: it showed that he knew and treasured the history of his people just as his hearers did, and it laid a foundation for the unwelcome part of the message that was to come later.

4. Then came he out of the land of the Chaldaeans, and dwelt in Charran: and from thence, when his father was dead, he removed him into this land, wherein ye now dwell.

Note how Stephen emphasized the action of God in all of Israel's history. He did not say merely that Abraham went to Canaan, but that *he removed him:* that is, God moved Abraham.

5. And he gave him none inheritance in it, no, not so much as to set his foot on: yet he promised that he would give it to him for a possession, and to his seed after him, when as yet he had no child.

Abraham lived in Canaan, but he did not own any of it. He lived as a nomad, moving his tents from place to place to find pasture for his cattle and sheep (Hebrews 11:9). His faith is emphasized in this verse. He had no land and *he had no child*, yet he believed God's promise that all the land of Canaan would belong to his descendants.

6. And God spake on this wise, That his seed should sojourn in a strange land; and that they should bring them into bondage, and entreat them evil four hundred years.

This sojourn in Egypt began in the old age of Jacob, Abraham's grandson; but God told Abraham about it long before (Genesis 15: 13-16).

7. And the nation to whom they shall be in bondage will I judge, said God: and after that shall they come forth, and serve me in this place.

Thus briefly did God foretell the ten plagues and the exodus from Egypt.

8. And he gave him the covenant of circumcision: and so Abraham begat Isaac, and circumcised him the eighth day; and Isaac begat Jacob; and Jacob begat the twelve patri- archs.

Chapters 17 to 35 of Genesis are summarized in this one verse. *The twelve partriarchs* were the twelve sons of Jacob, from whom descended the twelve tribes of Israel.

9. And the patriarchs, moved with envy, sold Joseph into Egypt: but God was with him.

Thus Stephen approached the theme of his discourse so subtly that none of his hearers yet realized to what he was leading. As Joseph's brothers determined to get rid of him, so the Jews of a later genera- tion determined to get rid of Jesus.

10. And delivered him out of all his afflictions, and gave him favour and wisdom in the sight of Pharaoh king of Egypt; and he made him governor over Egypt and all his house.

See chapters 37 to 41 in Genesis. God brought Joseph to honor and power after his brothers sold him; God also brought Jesus to glory and power after His people killed Him. This was a frequent declaration of the apostles (Acts 2:23, 36; 3:13; 4: 10; 5:30, 31). Still it is not likely that any of the hearers yet realized that Stephen had this comparison in mind.

11. Now there came a dearth over all the land of Egypt and Chanaan, and great affliction: and our fathers found no sustenance.

Chanaan is Canaan, where Jacob and his family lived. The seven- year *dearth* or famine was severe both there and in *Egypt,* but Egypt had been divinely warned and had stored up wheat before the years of famine came. Consequently there was food enough there. In Canaan especially there was *great affliction* because the surplus of former years had not been stored, and in the famine years there were no crops. Jacob and his family *found no sustenance*: not enough food to sustain their lives.

12. But when Jacob heard that there was corn in Egypt, he sent out our fathers first.

Trading caravans like the one that took Joseph to Egypt were still mov- ing from that land to Canaan, Syria, and Mesopotamia, carrying news as well as goods. Naturally they told of

Egypt's vast stores. *Corn* means grain of any kind. *Egypt* was noted especially for its wheat. *First* here means the first time. Jacob sent his sons to Egypt twice (Genesis, chapters 42-45).

13. And at the second time Joseph was made known to his brethren; and Joseph's kindred was made known unto Pharaoh.

Joseph's brothers did not recognize him when they saw him as the ruler of Egypt; but on their second visit he told them who he was. Pharaoh then learned of their presence and authorized the moving of the family from Canaan to Egypt.

14. Then sent Joseph, and called his father Jacob to him, and all his kindred, threescore and fifteen souls.

With Pharaoh's consent, Joseph invited his father and his whole family to move to Egypt, and the invitation was accepted. Thus Joseph, once despised and rejected by his brothers, saved their lives (Genesis 45:5). In a larger sense, Jesus, despised and rejected by His people, became their Saviour. Our version of Genesis 46:27 gives the total number as seventy. Stephen apparently followed the Greek version commonly used in his time. This version adds grandsons of Joseph to the list, making a total of seventy-five.

15. So Jacob went down into Egypt, and died, he, and our fathers.

Since the family stayed in Egypt for centuries, Jacob and the twelve patriarchs (v. 8) all died there.

16. And were carried over into Sychem, and laid in the sepulchre that Abraham bought for a sum of money of the sons of Emmor the father of Sychem.

Even as they went to Egypt, Jacob and his people remembered that God had promised Canaan as their homeland. They wanted to be buried there. Jacob's body was returned soon after his death (Genesis 49:29, 30; 50:12, 13). Joseph's was kept in Egypt until the Exodus, when it was taken to a burial place at Sychem or Shechem (Genesis 50:24-26; Joshua 24:32). Josephus, a Jewish historian of the first century, says the remains of the other patriarchs also were returned to Canaan.

17. But when the time of the promise drew nigh, which God had sworn to Abraham, the people grew and multiplied in Egypt.

The time of promise here probably means the time at which God had promised that His people would return to their homeland in Canaan (Genesis 15:13-16). As they awaited that time, the Jews in Egypt constantly increased in numbers. The family of seventy (Genesis 46:27) became a nation with six hundred thousand fighting men (Numbers 2:32). The total population is variously estimated at one to three million.

18. Till another king arose, which knew not Joseph.

Probably this does not refer to a new king who inherited the throne from his father, but to a rebel who overthrew the old dynasty and made himself king. Since Joseph's people were favored by the former government, this new ruler regarded them as a menace to his rule.

19. The same dealt subtilly with our kindred, and evil entreated our fathers, so that they cast out their young children, to the end they might not live.

The new king feared the Hebrews might join with invaders or new rebels to overthrow him. He therefore planned *subtilly* or shrewdly to keep them from growing any more numerous. After other devices failed, he ordered that all newborn boys were to be thrown into the river (Exodus 1).

20. In which time Moses was born, and was exceeding fair, and nourished up in his father's house three months.

Moses' parents kept him hidden *three months*, but they realized they could not keep him out of sight forever. Finally his mother obeyed the letter of the king's order and put him into the river, but in a watertight basket that floated in the shallow water among the papyrus reeds (Exodus 2:1-4).

21. And when he was cast out, Pharaoh's daughter took him up, and nourished him for her own son.

No doubt this was a favorite story among Jews as it is among Christians. Stephen had only to mention the main facts very briefly.

22. And Moses was learned in all the wisdom of the Egyptians, and was mighty in words and in deeds.

Moses' education probably was as fine as could be obtained anywhere in the world. *The wisdom of the Egyptians* included history, government, literature, arts, science, business, and other fields. *Mighty in words and in deeds.* Josephus says Moses became general of the army and led in defeating the Ethiopians who had invaded Egypt and all but conquered it. His skill and daring, however, only made the envious Egyptians the more afraid of him and his people.

23. And when he was full forty years old, it came into his heart to visit his brethren the children of Israel.

This does not necessarily mean that Moses had never visited his own people before. His loyalty to them and to God seems to indicate that he had been in touch with them all along. But this visit merits special mention because of its far-reaching consequences.

24. And seeing one of them suffer wrong, he defended him, and avenged him that was oppressed, and smote the Egyptian.

Happening to come upon an Egyptian beating a Hebrew unjustly, Moses killed the Egyptian and buried his body in the sand (Exodus 2:11, 12).

25. For he supposed his brethren would have understood how that God by his hand would deliver them: but they understood not.

Here is another case in which God's people misunderstood and rejected the one whom God chose to deliver them. Their rejection of him is detailed in verses 26-28. Still Stephen did not declare that the rejection of Jesus was another case of the same kind, and possibly no one yet suspected that he was leading up to such a declaration.

26. And the next day he shewed himself unto them as they strove, and would have set them at one again, saying, Sirs, ye are brethren; why do ye wrong one to another?

This time Moses was merely trying to make peace between two Hebrews who were fighting with each other (Exodus 1:13, 14).

27. But he that did his neighbour

wrong thrust him away, saying, Who made thee a ruler and a judge over us?

One of the fighting Hebrews was clearly in the wrong. Knowing that any just judgment or arbitration would go against him, he wanted none of it—he wanted only to enforce his unrighteous will by force. Similar was the case of those who rejected Jesus.

28. Wilt thou kill me, as thou diddest the Egyptian yesterday?

Moses had thought the killing was unknown, but now he realized it was known and would be reported to the king. His position in the king's household would not protect him. If Josephus is correct, jealous Egyptians were eagerly looking for some excuse to kill him. If the man he killed was one of Pharaoh's appointed overseers, the killing would be considered the more intolerable.

29. Then fled Moses at this saying, and was a stranger in the land of Madian, where he begat two sons.

Read of Moses' flight and a little of his life in Midian in Exodus 2:15-22.

30. And when forty years were expired, there appeared to him in the wilderness of mount Sina an angel of the Lord in a flame of fire in a bush.

The event told in this and the following verses was thoroughly familiar to the Jews, as it is to Christians, but Stephen told it in some detail to emphasize the well-known fact that God intended for Moses to deliver His people. This call is recorded in more detail in Exodus 3:1—4:17.

31. When Moses saw it, he wondered at the sight: and as he drew near to behold it, the voice of the Lord came unto him.

The Jews were immensely proud of the assurance that God had personally directed Moses, their great national hero (John 9:29). They must have approved of Stephen's speech at this point, not yet seeing that he was laying the foundation for a devastating attack on them.

32. Saying, I am the God of thy fathers, the God of Abraham, and the God of Isaac, and the God of Jacob. Then Moses trembled, and durst not behold.

God is eternal, the same in all ages, and to be feared equally in the time of Abraham, the time of Moses, and the time of Stephen—also in our time.

33. Then said the Lord to him, Put off thy shoes from thy feet: for the place where thou standest is holy ground.

Again the glory of God is emphasized along with reverence for Him. It is no light thing to resist His will!

34. I have seen, I have seen the affliction of my people which is in Egypt, and I have heard their groaning, and am come down to deliver them. And now come, I will send thee into Egypt.

After stressing the grandeur and glory of God, Stephen laid emphasis on His determination to deliver His people. This too must have been popular with Stephen's hearers, for they were longing for deliverance from the Romans.

35. This Moses whom they refused, saying, Who made thee a ruler and a judge? the same did God send to be a ruler and a deliverer by the hand of the angel which appeared to him in the bush.

Now appears the point of the story, the purpose of Stephen in telling it. This one whom the people angrily rejected was the very one God sent to deliver them. This was added to the story of Joseph, whom his brothers rejected but God chose to save their lives. Did some of the more perceptive hearers now begin to guess where Stephen was leading? Did any begin to wonder if the Jesus they had rejected might possibly be God's chosen Redeemer?

36. He brought them out, after that he had shewed wonders and signs in the land of Egypt, and in the Red sea, and in the wilderness forty years.

God used miracles to show His approval of Moses. He showed His approval of Jesus in the same way (Acts 2:22).

37. This is that Moses, which said unto the children of Israel, A prophet shall the Lord your God raise up unto you of your brethren, like unto me; him shall ye hear.

Moses himself, the inspired, the infallible, whose word was honored by all the Jews, had told them to expect another prophet and to give honor to Him and His word (Deuteronomy 18:15, 18, 19).

38. This is he, that was in the church in the wilderness with the angel which spake to him in the mount Sina, and with our fathers: who received the lively oracles to give unto us.

The church in the wilderness is the congregation of Israel in the desert between Egypt and the promised land. Moses led them, but not Moses alone: the very Presence that spoke from the burning bush spoke again when Moses returned to Sinai with the people rescued from Egypt.

At Sinai God delivered to Moses and to all the people His *lively oracles,* His living law.

39. To whom our fathers would not obey, but thrust him from them, and in their hearts turned back again into Egypt.

With increasing force Stephen came back to the recurring theme of his address: Not only once, but many times, the Jews of Moses' time had rejected the deliverer and leader God had sent.

40. Saying unto Aaron, Make us gods to go before us: for as for this Moses, which brought us out of the land of Egypt, we wot not what is become of him.

Here is an outstanding example. Even while Moses was upon Mount Sinai receiving God's law for them, the people gave him up and demanded that Aaron provide idols to lead them (Exodus 32:1-7).

41. And they made a calf in those days, and offered sacrifice unto the idol, and rejoiced in the works of their own hands.

In turning away from God's chosen leader they turned away from God also—and so does everyone who rejects God's Son.

42. Then God turned, and gave them up to worship the host of heaven; as it is written in the book of the prophets, O ye house of Israel, have ye offered to me slain beasts and sacrifices by the space of forty years in the wilderness?

Gave them up cannot be taken to mean that God took His law away from His people in the wilderness or ceased to offer His guidance; but in some cases He allowed them to follow their own inclination for a time, even into idolatry or worship of the stars, *the host of heaven.* Later, through *the book of the prophets,* God questioned the sincerity of the people's devotion to Him through the *forty years in the wilderness* (Amos 5:25-27).

43. Yea, ye took up the tabernacle of Moloch, and the star of your god Remphan, figures which ye made to worship them: and I will carry you away beyond Babylon.

This continues the quotation from Amos. God answers His own question asked in the preceding verse: "Have you offered to me? Yes, but you have also worshiped Moloch and Remphan, idols you made. Because you have continued in idolatry I will cause you to go into captivity." This prophecy was given centuries after the exodus and probably refers to false worship in the promised land and not in the wilderness only. Moloch was one of the most brutal and barbarous false gods of Old Testament times; Remphan or Rephan probably was the same as Saturn. As in other quotations, Stephen followed the Greek version commonly used in his time, and therefore the passage is not exactly as it appears in our version of Amos.

44. Our fathers had the tabernacle of witness in the wilderness, as he had appointed, speaking unto Moses, that he should make it according to the fashion that he had seen.

The idolatry of Israel was the more inexcusable because all the time they had before them the witness of the tabernacle, designed and built for the pure worship of Jehovah. It was constructed exactly to the specifications God gave to Moses (Exodus 25:8, 9), and so stood as a constant re-minder that worship also should be according to God's revealed will.

45. Which also our fathers that came after brought in with Jesus into the posession of the Gentiles, whom God drave out before the face of our fathers, unto the days of David.

For the proper meaning of this verse, read "Joshua" instead of *Jesus.* These represent Hebrew and Greek forms of the same name, but reference here is to the Joshua who led Israel into the promised land after Moses died. The Israelites had the tabernacle before them not only in the wilderness, but also in the land of promise, the land that had been *the possession of the Gentiles* until God drove them out and gave the land to Israel. The tabernacle was kept until *the days of David.*

46. Who found favour before God, and desired to find a tabernacle for the God of Jacob.

David, a man specially favored of God, made a place in Jerusalem for the sacred ark of the covenant, which had long been separated from the ancient tabernacle (2 Samuel 6:12, 17). He wished to build a magnificent temple, but that privilege was reserved for his son, Solomon (2 Samuel 7:1-13).

47. But Solomon built him an house.

Solomon built a magnificent temple to replace the tabernacle. It was larger and made of stone and timber instead of fabrics and leather, but it followed the pattern of the original tabernacle, and so held before Israel the same testimony to the will of God in worship.

48. Howbeit the most High dwelleth not in temples made with hands; as saith the prophet.

The Jews had sadly misinterpreted the testimony of the temple. The leaders and teachers seemed to think it meant only that the prescribed ceremonies should be conducted, not that lives should be holy and good (Luke 11:42). Jesus brought a new covenant in which the temple lost its importance. God's people worship Him wherever they are (John 4:21-24).

49. Heaven is my throne, and earth is my footstool: what house will ye build me? saith the Lord: or what is the place of my rest?

The Jews would resent any slighting reference to the temple, so Stephen hastened to show that he was not advancing any new or heretical thought. Long before, God himself had said no temple could be adequate for His dwelling place. He is everywhere; He fills all creation.

50. Hath not my hand made all these things?

The people of Israel did well to build as God directed, but the temple was designed to meet their need rather than His. He who made the whole universe does not need a house built by men. The significance of the temple faded, partly because the Jewish teachers misunderstood and misinterpreted it, but even more because the new covenant brought in the worldwide kingdom of Christ. Assembly of all God's people in one place became impossible even then, with membership multiplying daily.

51. Ye stiffnecked and uncircumcised in heart and ears, ye do always resist the Holy Ghost: as your fathers did, so do ye.

Now comes the application of Stephen's address. Jews of former generations had rejected God when they rejected Joseph and Moses; those of the present generation were rejecting God when they rejected Jesus. They exalted the temple and declared their loyalty to Moses, but they would not accept God's will for their time and themselves.

52. Which of the prophets have not your fathers persecuted? and they have slain them which shewed before of the coming of the Just One; of whom ye have been now the betrayers and murderers.

The Jews all knew their ancestors had been delivered into captivity because they had resisted God's will and persecuted His prophets. Stephen declared that their own resistance to God was even worse: they had murdered the Messiah whom the prophets had foretold.

53. Who have received the law by the disposition of angels, and have not kept it.

God used angels in delivering the law of Moses (Galatians 3:19), in just what way we do not know. Stephen's hearers had received that law and they pretended to honor it greatly, but Stephen bluntly declared that they did not obey it.

54. When they heard these things, they were cut to the heart, and they gnashed on him with their teeth.

When they heard these things. The council, never weary at hearing a recital of the story of their nation, followed along, not knowing where they were being led, until Stephen, by deliberate announcement of their sin and God's judgment, showed them the conclusion to which his whole sermon had been designed. This touched off the explosion. When they were accusing

Stephen of disrespect to God, the law, and the temple, they could maintain a calm and judicial composure, but when they found Stephen disrespectful to themselves, they flew into a violent rage. *They were cut to the heart.* To the tearing of Stephen's words they reacted with the most violent emotion. The staid and dignified court very speedily became a mob, with all the uncontrolled and unreasoning passion that is characteristic of mobs everywhere. *They gnashed on him with their teeth.* They ground their teeth together in animal-like, impotent rage, and perhaps even frothed at the mouth.

55. But he, being full of the Holy Ghost, looked up stedfastly into heaven, and saw the glory of God, and Jesus standing on the right hand of God.

The evidence of Stephen's spiritual nature is seen in the fact that, when indignities and danger pressed closest around him, his thought was of God rather than of himself. *Saw the glory of God.* This was a preview of glory. *And Jesus standing on the right hand of God.* Jesus, in the moment of His being condemned for blasphemy by this same court, had declared, "Hereafter shall ye see the Son of man sitting on the right hand of power, and coming in the clouds of heaven" (Matthew 26:64). See also Acts 2:34; Ephesians 1:20; Colossians 3:1; Hebrews 1:3.

56. And said, Behold, I see the heavens opened, and the Son of man standing on the right hand of God.

This bold assertion of divine approval served only to infuriate the members of the council more. They might have reasoned that they were in danger of "fighting against God" (Acts 5:39), but they were now beyond reason.

57. Then they cried out with a loud voice, and stopped their ears, and ran upon him with one accord.

They would do anything to avoid hearing further the searching, condemning, maddening words of this man. Until they could silence him, they would drown out his voice with their outcries and stop their ears so as not to hear him. "Rushed upon him with one accord" (American Standard Version). Already encircled by the Sanhedrin, Stephen had no chance of escape as the circle closed in with their blood-curdling cries of hatred.

58. And cast him out of the city, and stoned him: and the witnesses laid down their clothes at a young man's feet, whose name was Saul.

The action had long since ceased to be orderly or legal, but even in their mob violence the council retained two items of lawful procedure. They might not stone a man inside the city walls, and those who testified against him were to cast the first stones (Deuteronomy 17:6, 7). Thus the *witnesses* laid off the outer garments that might have hindered their stone-throwing. This is the first mention which Scripture makes of Saul of Tarsus, but it describes a scene which burned itself indelibly into the mind of this young man (Acts 22:20).

. 59. And they stoned Stephen, calling upon God, and saying, Lord Jesus, receive my spirit.

The stoning continued as long as there was life in the body. Still no word of personal complaint came from Stephen, although the present act demonstrated with horrible force the charge he had already made against the Jewish people, that they rejected and destroyed the messengers of God. In his prayer Stephen made no distinction between "God" and "Lord Jesus." He prayed a prayer most appropriate to the occasion.

60. And he kneeled down, and cried with a loud voice, Lord, lay not this sin to their charge. And when he had said this, he fell asleep.

The kneeling may have been in weakness or in prayer. Stephen's outcry told the persecutors, and a whole world besides, that ill-will and vengefulness had no part in his being. The prayer was genuine. *When he had said this.* Stephen was ready for God's presence when he prayed for his persecutors. *He fell asleep.* What a peaceful conclusion to a turbulent event! "Precious in the sight of the Lord is the death of his saints" (Psalm 116:15). He who was faithful unto death had discovered that death was not to be dreaded.

CHAPTER 8

1. And Saul was consenting unto his death. And at that time there was a great persecution against the church which was at Jerusalem; and they were all scattered abroad throughout the regions of Judaea and Samaria, except the apostles.

Saul was a student of Gamaliel, (Acts 22:3) who had advised moderation in the treatment of the apostles (Acts 5:34-39). Evidently the student did not follow his teacher in this respect, but favored an attempt to silence Christian teachers by death if necessary. Having failed to silence the apostles, Saul and others now turned their attention to the rank and file of the church, punishing its members with *a great persecution*. The members therefore left Jerusalem and *scattered* into the villages of *Judaea and Samaria*, where the persecution reached them more slowly. In later chapters we shall see that some of them soon scattered much farther from Jerusalem (Acts 11:19). *The apostles*, however, remained in Jerusalem for the time being. Thus the scattered members could send to them

for counsel and encouragement when necessary.

2. And devout men carried Stephen to his burial, and made great lamentation over him.

This is in marked contrast to the burial of Ananias and Sapphira (Acts 5:1-10). The brethren honored their first martyr, although in so doing they doubtless marked themselves as members of the same group and so made themselves targets of the continuing persecution.

3. As for Saul, he made havock of the church, entering into every house, and haling men and women committed them to prison.

The vigorous and determined young Saul now took the lead in persecuting the disciples. It seems that all who could be found were imprisoned, and Acts 26:10 suggests that Stephen was not the only one who was killed.

4. Therefore they that were scattered abroad went every where preaching the word.

Therefore. The journeys and the

sojournings of Christians in outer parts of Judea and in Samaria were occasioned by the persecution in which Saul of Tarsus was a central figure. *They that were scattered abroad.* The Christians generally; not the apostles, according to verse 1. *Went every where preaching the word.* These Christians did not leave Jerusalem with the deliberate purpose of evangelizing Judea and Samaria, but they carried the gospel with them and shared it with others wherever they went.

5. Then Philip went down to the city of Samaria, and preached Christ unto them.

Jesus had paved the way for evangelizing in Samaria by the ministry that began with the woman at the well of Sychar (John 4). Samaria was next in order after Jerusalem and Judea in the program of world-wide evangelism (Acts 1:8). The proclamation of Christ included the declaration of His life, teaching, death, and resurrection, with the terms by which believers might be brought into fellowship with Him.

6. And the people with one accord gave heed unto those things which Philip spake, hearing and seeing the miracles which he did.

Philip, like Stephen, worked miracles by the special power of the Holy Spirit conveyed through the laying on of the apostles' hands (Acts 6:6; 8:18; 19:6). The purpose was that the hearers might know the divine source of the gospel.

7. For unclean spirits, crying with loud voice, came out of many that were possessed with them: and many taken with palsies, and that were lame, were healed.

Philip's miracles were much like those of Jesus. He drove out demons that had taken possession of people; he healed the sick and crippled. *Palsies* are various kinds of paralysis.

8. And there was great joy in that city.

The people were happy not only in the healing of the sick and lame, but also in the good news that salvation through the Messiah now was available to them as well as to the Jews (v. 12).

9. But there was a certain man, called Simon, which beforetime in the same city used sorcery, and bewitched the people of Samaria, giving out that himself was some great one.

Sorcery probably consisted of pretended fortune-telling and tricks of supposed magic. By claiming supernatural abilities, *Simon* could gain both money and prestige as he sold his advice in matters of business, politics, health, and romance.

10. To whom they all gave heed, from the least to the greatest, saying, This man is the great power of God.

Apparently Simon was a capable advertising man as well as a clever magician and shrewd adviser. He had the attention and confidence of the whole town.

11. And to him they had regard, because that of long time he had bewitched them with sorceries.

Simon was not a cheap fraud who had to make a quick "killing" and get out of town. He was clever enough to hold the confidence of the people for a long time.

12. But when they believed Philip preaching the things concerning the kingdom of God, and the name of

Jesus Christ, they were baptized, both men and women.

As in Jerusalem, many promptly accepted and obeyed the gospel.

13. Then Simon himself believed also: and when he was baptized, he continued with Philip, and wondered, beholding the miracles and signs which were done.

Simon was quick to see that Philip's miracles were totally different from his own pretended magic. Knowing well the limitations of trickery, he accepted the explanation that Philip's works were done by divine power—done by God and not by Philip. With such evidence before him he soon became a disciple.

14. Now when the apostles which were at Jerusalem heard that Samaria had received the word of God, they sent unto them Peter and John.

The purpose is not stated here, but it seems natural to suppose that Peter and John went to help the work in Samaria in the way described in the following verses.

15, 16. Who, when they were come down, prayed for them, that they might receive the Holy Ghost: (For as yet he was fallen upon none of them: only they were baptized in the name of the Lord Jesus.)

Does this mean the Samaritans had not received the gift of the Holy Spirit that Peter had promised as he spoke earlier in Jerusalem (Acts 2: 30)? Or does it mean they had received their gift when they were baptized, that they now had the Holy Spirit dwelling within as all Christians do (1 Corinthians 6:19), but had not yet received any miraculous powers of the Spirit such as Philip had and the apostles had shown when the Spirit came upon them (Acts 2:1-

4)? We shall watch for an answer in the following verses.

17. Then laid they their hands on them, and they received the Holy Ghost.

Whatever gift the Samaritans lacked, it was supplied when the apostles prayed and laid their hands on them.

18. And when Simon saw that through laying on of the apostles' hands the Holy Ghost was given, he offered them money.

Here we find an answer to the question raised by verse 17. The Spirit was bestowed in a visible way or with visible results: *Simon saw* that He *was given*. We conclude that the Samaritans now received miraculous power perhaps to speak with tongues or heal the sick, or both. If such powers had not been evident, Simon could not have seen that the Spirit was given, nor would he have *offered them money* for power to make such a bestowal himself.

19. Saying, Give me also this power, that on whomsoever I lay hands, he may receive the Holy Ghost.

Simon's old worldly greed laid hold on him again. If he could buy the power Peter and John had, surely he could enrich himself by selling power such as they had bestowed on the Samaritans.

20. But Peter said unto him, Thy money perish with thee, because thou hast thought that the gift of God may be purchased with money.

Peter indignantly spurned not only the offer, but the whole mistaken idea that money could have anything to do with God's spiritual gifts. Many who were blessed by miracles did contribute money to the Lord's work, but no one ever bought a miracle or miraculous power.

21. Thou hast neither part nor lot in this matter: for thy heart is not right in the sight of God.

A greedy heart not only cannot buy God's gifts; it cannot even receive them when they are offered free.

22. Repent therefore of this thy wickedness, and pray God, if perhaps the thought of thine heart may be forgiven thee.

Here is good advice for any Christian who falls into the devil's trap of greed or lust or malice or envy or hatred. He must repent, shake himself free from the grip of evil motives, turn to the Lord, and pray for forgiveness.

23. For I perceive that thou art in the gall of bitterness, and in the bond of iniquity.

Simon had previously accepted Christ (v. 13), but now sin had captured and bound him again.

24. Then answered Simon, and said, Pray ye the Lord for me, that none of these things which ye have spoken come upon me.

Since "the gall of bitterness" and "the bond of iniquity" had already come upon Simon, we suppose *those things which ye have spoken* refers to the apostles' teaching, about future punishment. Presumably Simon accepted Peter's word and prayed for forgiveness; he asked Peter to pray for him as well.

25. And they, when they had testified and preached the word of the Lord, returned to Jerusalem, and preached the gospel in many villages of the Samaritans.

Peter and John added their testimony to that of Philip in the city where he had been working. Then,

journeying back toward Jerusalem, they stopped to spread the gospel in the villages along the way.

26. And the angel of the Lord spake unto Philip, saying, Arise, and go toward the south unto the way that goeth down from Jerusalem unto Gaza, which is desert.

God used supernatural means to accomplish the conversion recorded in the following verses, but the special acts of God were limited to bringing the preacher and the prospect together. From that point onward the conversion followed the normal, universal pattern of hearing, believing, and obeying the gospel. *Go toward the south.* The place of meeting the Ethiopian has been estimated to be fifty to seventy miles south of the city of Samaria, depending on the routes chosen. *The way that goeth down from Jerusalem unto Gaza.* McGarvey tells of having seen and traced remnants of a paved Roman road covering this route, extending approximately fifty miles from city to city. *Which is desert.* That is, uninhabited, or deserted.

27. And he arose and went: and, behold, a man of Ethiopia, an eunuch of great authority under Candace queen of the Ethiopians, who had the charge of all her treasure, and had come to Jerusalem for to worship.

The timing of this event is of great interest. Philip would need to leave Samaria sometime before the eunuch left Jerusalem in order to meet him at the place indicated. *A man of Ethiopia.* The queen of Sheba had come to Jerusalem to visit Solomon from this same kingdom south of Egypt in Africa. The distance was well over a thousand miles. *An eunuch of great authority.* It was not uncommon to make eunuchs of slaves. Even so, many such slaves gained positions of prominence and respect through superior intelligence and dependability. *Candace queen of the Ethiopians.* The title Candace appears many times as the name of queens reigning at Meroe, capital of Ethiopia. *Had come to Jerusalem for to worship.* He may have attended one of the great feasts. In any case his making a journey of this extent is evidence of his devotion.

28. Was returning, and sitting in his chariot read Esaias the prophet.

The American Standard Version has, "And he was returning and sitting in his chariot, and was reading the prophet Isaiah." It has been suggested that the eunuch may have purchased the scroll of Isaiah while he was in Jerusalem. If so, he was losing no time in examining his new treasure, to have read so far by the time Philip met him.

29. Then the Spirit said unto Philip, Go near, and join thyself to this chariot.

The mission that had begun by the angel was continued by direct intervention of the Holy Spirit. Philip knew now for the first time why he had been brought from Samaria. He did not yet know the details about the Ethiopian. The ensuing conversation would reveal them.

30. And Philip ran thither to him, and heard him read the prophet Esaias, and said, Understandest thou what thou readest?

Philip had to move quickly or lose his opportunity. He did not need to listen long to identify the words he heard being read. *Understandest thou what thou readest?* With this one quick, skillful question, and

without being offensive or embarrassingly personal, Philip learned all he needed to know of his prospect's religious standing. The passage being read by the Ethiopian is understood as referring to Christ, or it is not understood at all.

31. And he said, How can I, except some man should guide me? And he desired Philip that he would come up and sit with him.

The eunuch's answer showed why God had thought it worthwhile to bring Philip from Samaria to teach him. Here was a thoughtful and reverent student of the Word, seeking for truth. He was untaught in the gospel, but he was anxious to learn. With true humility he was willing to accept help from whatever source it might come.

32. The place of the scripture which he read was this, He was led as a sheep to the slaughter; and like a lamb dumb before his shearer, so opened he not his mouth.

The passage is found in Isaiah 53: 7, 8. The whole chapter in Isaiah forms an unmistakable picture of the sufferings of Jesus. *As a sheep to the slaughter.* The sheep does not resist violence. Neither did Christ. *A lamb dumb before his shearer.* There is no sound of complaint.

33. In his humiliation his judgment was taken away: and who shall declare his generation? for his life is taken from the earth.

Justice was denied to Him, and He received instead the extremes of undeserved humiliation. *Who shall declare his generation?* Either, how shall we even talk about a generation of people who will be guilty of so great evil? or, because He is untimely removed by death, who will declare that He will have any spiritual posterity to continue His work? *His life is taken from the earth.* That is, He is slain by violence.

34. And the eunuch answered Philip, and said, I pray thee, of whom speaketh the prophet this? of himself, or of some other man?

A most natural question. The Isaiah passage names its subject only as God's "servant." Neither Isaiah nor any other known person did the things or endured the things that are written in this chapter.

35. Then Philip opened his mouth, and began at the same scripture, and preached unto him Jesus.

The pattern of the sermon was evidently very similar to that which Peter preached at Pentecost, and that which Paul preached at Antioch of Pisidia (Acts 13:14-41). It began with the Old Testament prophecies of Christ, continued with the facts of His earthly life, emphasizing His atoning death and resurrection, and concluded by showing Christ's program for man's redemption. The eunuch's response in word and deed make this clear.

36. And as they went on their way, they came unto a certain water: and the eunuch said, See, here is water; what doth hinder me to be baptized?

On the route they traveled toward Gaza, they would cross the brook in the Valley of Elah, where David met Goliath; they would cross the larger Wady el Hasy in the Philistine plain, and they would pass innumerable artificial pools in which rainwater was caught and stored. Any of these would answer the description and serve the purpose. *Here is water; what doth hinder me to be baptized?* Philip had obviously taught the Ethi-

opian concerning Christian baptism, that it is in water; that it is a part of one's acceptance of Christ; and that faith and repentance are required on the part of the one who would be baptized. The teaching concerning baptism is not a thing separated from and additional to the preaching of Christ; it is a part of it.

37. And Philip said, If thou believest with all thine heart, thou mayest. And he answered and said, I believe that Jesus Christ is the Son of God.

This verse does not appear in the most ancient New Testament manuscripts, and is therefore omitted from the American Standard Version and others. Dummelow calls the verse a "very early and trustworthy marginal addition, which was ultimately incorporated into the text." It was quoted by Irenaeus, whose writing dates from A.D. 170 to 210. It is in harmony with known New Testament practice as indicated in Romans 10:8, 9; 1 Timothy 6:13; and 1 Peter 3:21, indicating the spoken response of faith associated with one's baptism. The simple statement of fact, like the confession of Peter at Caesarea Philippi, is true to the genius of apostolic preaching and practice.

38. And he commanded the chariot to stand still: and they went down both into the water, both Philip and the eunuch; and he baptized him.

This is the most graphic description of the act of baptism to be found in Scripture, and it accords completely with the meaning of the word *baptize,* from the Greek *baptizo,* to "dip, plunge, or immerse." Philip and the eunuch stopped immediately on their way, although there were not many witnesses, and probably neither

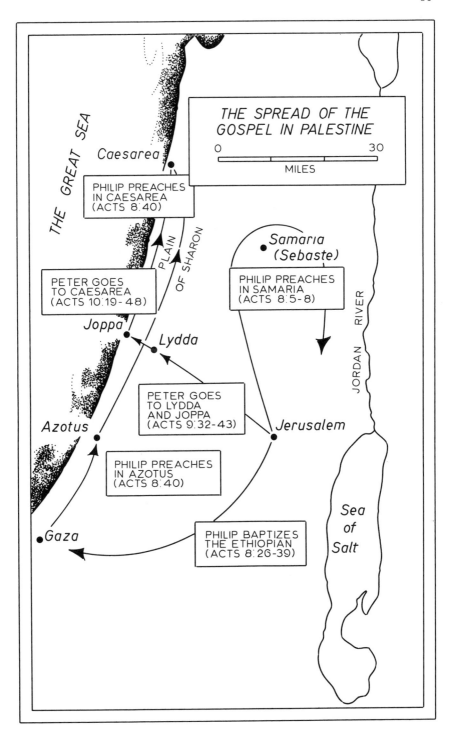

THE SPREAD OF THE GOSPEL IN PALESTINE

0   30
MILES

THE GREAT SEA

Caesarea

PHILIP PREACHES
IN CAESAREA
(ACTS 8:40)

PLAIN OF SHARON

Samaria
(Sebaste)

PHILIP PREACHES
IN SAMARIA
(ACTS 8:5-8)

PETER GOES
TO CAESAREA
(ACTS 10:19-48)

Joppa

Lydda

JORDAN RIVER

PETER GOES
TO LYDDA
AND JOPPA
(ACTS 9:32-43)

Jerusalem

Azotus

PHILIP PREACHES
IN AZOTUS
(ACTS 8:40)

Sea
of
Salt

Gaza

PHILIP BAPTIZES
THE ETHIOPIAN
(ACTS 8:26-39)

man had a change of raiment. The matter was too important to admit of delay. The act required that both candidate and administrator descend into the water. The baptizing— burial, according to Romans 6:3, 4 and Colossians 2:12—took place while both were in the water.

39. And when they were come up out of the water, the Spirit of the Lord caught away Philip, that the eunuch saw him no more: and he went on his way rejoicing.

The Spirit of the Lord caught away Philip. Some take this to mean that the Holy Spirit led Philip to walk away immediately. Others think the Spirit miraculously transported Philip to Azotus (v. 40). Lenski says, "If Philip was merely induced to say good-by and to tear himself away,

Luke chose a strange way in which to tell us this." Note 2 Corinthians 12:2, 4 and 1 Thessalonians 4:17 where the same word for *caught away* is used. In any case, we know that Philip was divinely taken on to other work, while the new disciple *went on his way rejoicing* in the new life and new hope that were his. This man may have been the first to take the gospel to Ethiopia.

40. But Philip was found at Azotus: and passing through he preached in all the cities, till he came to Caesarea.

This shows that Philip worked his way north along the Mediterranean shore, teaching in the coastal towns as he previously had done in Samaria. Luke records no more about him at the time, but notes that he had a home in Caesarea some twenty years later (Acts 21:8).

CHAPTER 9

1. And Saul, yet breathing out threatenings and slaughter against the disciples of the Lord, went unto the high priest.

Saul had taken a rather active part in the opposition and final death sentence against Stephen. Now he pursued an even more violent course of persecution. *Threatenings and slaughter.* Moffatt's translation has "threats of murder," and Goodspeed has, "murderous threats." News of Christian activity in such far cities as Damascus had come back to Jerusalem. The knowledge that previous persecutions had failed to wipe out the upstart sect, but had succeeded only in spreading its influence, seems to have gendered a feeling of frustrated exasperation that knew no bounds. *Went unto the high priest.* Saul the

Pharisee would have been glad to accomplish his purpose without the humiliation of seeking help from a Sadducee, but he would endure even that if it was necessary to the accomplishment of his purpose.

2. And desired of him letters to Damascus to the synagogues, that if he found any of this way, whether they were men or women, he might bring them bound unto Jerusalem.

"Asked of him letters" (American Standard Version). Acts 26:10 speaks of "authority from the chief priests." The official seal of the Sanhedrin was apparently on the letters given. *Damascus* lay east of Mount Hermon, approximately 140 miles northward from Jerusalem. Saul, who had been influential in causing the Christians to flee to this distant city, now pursued them even there. *To the synagogues.* Damascus had a large Jewish population and numerous synagogues. *If he found any of this way.* The "way" is used as a specific term to describe the Christian faith and life. *Whether they were men or women.* There would be no special favors shown to women as the weaker sex. They shared the faith and the promises of Christ (Galatians 3:28); they shared also in the persecutions attendant upon the faith. *He might bring them bound unto Jerusalem.* This was evidently not the first such errand on which Saul had gone (see Acts 26:10-12). Since the "offense" of the believers was religious rather than civil or criminal, they would have to be tried before the religious court, the Sanhedrin, at Jerusalem. The letters to the synagogues would carry no civil authority, but Aretas the governor could be expected to accede to the synagogue rulers' request for permission to remove the offenders. See 2 Corinthians 11:32.

3. And as he journeyed, he came near Damascus: and suddenly there shined round about him a light from heaven.

The record passes over the four or five days of the journey without notice. The event about to be narrated is the important item. *Near Damascus.* He may even have been within sight of the city. *Suddenly there shined round about him a light.* Acts 26:13 says that the events happened about midday and that the light was "above the brightness of the sun." Travelers say that the sun is no brighter anywhere than on the sandy plain near Damascus. *From heaven.* By some means not recorded here

Saul knew that this light came from the presence of God.

4. And he fell to the earth, and heard a voice saying unto him, Saul, Saul, why persecutest thou me?

He fell to the earth. Acts 26:14 says "we were all fallen to the earth." Reverence for the divine presence would have caused Saul to prostrate himself, but a greater demonstration of power would be necessary to account for the falling of the others to the ground. Acts 22:9 says that they saw the light and were afraid. *Heard a voice saying unto him.* Acts 26:14 recounts that the voice spoke in the Hebrew language. Saul's companions heard the sound (9:7), but they did not understand the words. *Saul, Saul, why persecutest thou me?* The form of the question, with its double address to Saul by name, followed with the insistent and personal query, is such as to convey gentle remonstrance in a most remarkable degree. No word is wasted. The Lord searched the heart of Saul with the word "why." He must have reason for his actions. What reason could he give? Saul had thought of his work as a rendering of justice and a service to God; but Jesus called it persecution. Saul had considered himself as a somewhat impersonal agent of the Jewish authorities; but Jesus viewed the persecution as the work of Saul himself. Most amazing of all was the word, "me." Saul had thought of his efforts as being directed against the members of an outlaw sect; now the heavenly presence indicated himself as the victim.

5. And he said, Who art thou, Lord? And the Lord said, I am Jesus whom thou persecutest: it is hard for thee to kick against the pricks.

Who art thou, Lord? This is apparently the moment when Saul looked into the heavenly glory and saw Jesus in person, as Ananias declared (v. 17), and Barnabas testified (v. 27), and Saul himself later avowed (1 Corinthians 15:8). That he did not recognize the heavenly personage as Jesus may be due to the fact that he had not seen the Lord during His earthly ministry. *I am Jesus.* A more astounding revelation could not have been made. The celestial one identified himself as the prophet of Nazareth—not a false messiah as Saul had maintained, but the King of glory; not a missing corpse, but a living Lord. *Whom thou persecutest.* Whether or not he had heard the words before, Saul knew now what Jesus meant when He said, "Inasmuch as ye have done it unto one of the least of these my brethren, ye have done it unto me" (Matthew 25:40). *It is hard for thee to kick against the pricks.* These words do not appear in this verse in the most ancient manuscripts, and so are omitted from the American Standard Version and other late translations. They appear, however, in Acts 26:14: "It is hard for thee to kick against the goad." The claims of Christ were such that, by resisting them, Saul could only injure himself, as an ox would injure himself by lashing out against the driver's sharp prod.

6. And he trembling and astonished said, Lord, what wilt thou have me to do? And the Lord said unto him, Arise, and go into the city, and it shall be told thee what thou must do.

The American Standard and othe¹ late translations omit the former part of this verse as being introduced from Acts 22:10. The facts it records are clearly true, none the less, as related by Paul himself in that chapter. He was in the same situation as Peter's hearers on the Day of Pentecost. Divine revelation had shown him to be wrong in such a way as to make him an enemy of God. To a sincere man this was an intolerable situation, and one to be remedied by even the most drastic means. *Arise, and go into the city, and it shall be told thee what thou must do.* Saul's conversion was not yet completed. It could not be completed until, according to the commission of Christ and the pattern everywhere followed in Scripture, a human messenger had conveyed the gospel terms of pardon and they had been met: "He that believeth and is baptized shall be saved" (Mark 16:16). That was soon to take place in the city of Damascus.

7. And the men which journeyed with him stood speechless, hearing a voice, but seeing no man.

Saul's companions are not identified. Their principal importance in the Scripture record lies in their capacity as witnesses to establish the facts. They saw the light (22:9) and were prostrated with Saul (26:14). They heard the sound of the voice that spoke to him, although they did not comprehend words or meaning. They did not see the Lord, but they saw the effect of the vision on Saul. *Stood speechless.* After they arose from the ground.

8. And Saul arose from the earth; and when his eyes were opened, he saw no man: but they led him by the hand, and brought him into Damascus.

Saul arose from the earth. Saul, the one most affected by the experience was last to rise to his feet. *When his eyes were opened.* The blinding

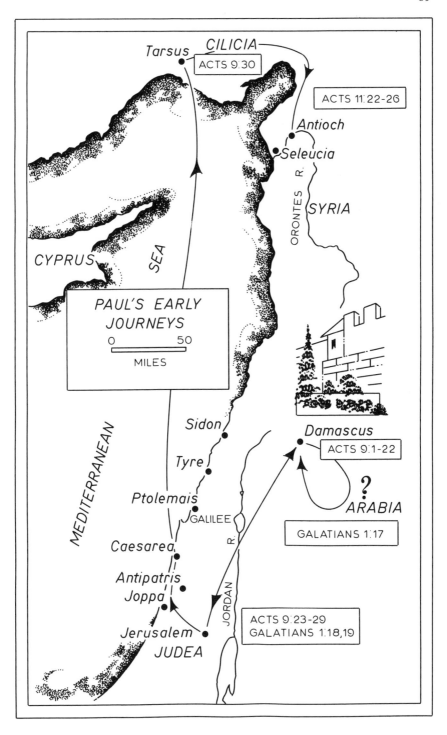

PAUL'S EARLY JOURNEYS

0   50
MILES

Tarsus
CILICIA
ACTS 9:30

ACTS 11:22-26

Antioch
Seleucia

ORONTES R.

SYRIA

CYPRUS
SEA

Sidon
Tyre
Ptolemais
GALILEE

Damascus
ACTS 9:1-22

?
ARABIA

GALATIANS 1:17

MEDITERRANEAN

Caesarea
Antipatris
Joppa

JORDAN R.

Jerusalem
JUDEA

ACTS 9:23-29
GALATIANS 1:18,19

glory of the heavenly vision had probably caused him to close his eyes, after viewing the person of Jesus. The Lord was the last person he saw until three days later. *He saw no man.* The American Standard Version has, "He saw nothing." Paul himself later said that he could not see "for the glory of that light" (22: 11). *But they led him by the hand, and brought him into Damascus.* Saul experienced a swift plunge from ecstatic communion with heaven to the blind following of his human companions.

9. And he was three days without sight, and neither did eat nor drink.

The three days of blindness probably included the afternoon of the day of his vision, the following day, and a substantial part of the third day. *Neither did eat nor drink.* As Jesus fasted for forty days upon the assumption of his ministry, so Saul fasted the briefer time upon being called to the apostleship. In the case of Saul there was the added burden of remorseful brooding.

10. And there was a certain disciple at Damascus, named Ananias; and to him said the Lord in a vision, Ananias. And he said, Behold, I am here, Lord.

A certain disciple at Damascus. There is nothing in the record to distinguish Ananias from others whom Saul had come to Damascus to arrest, and no Scriptural evidence to support the late tradition that he was the leader of the Christian community in that city. *Ananias.* The name means "Jehovah is gracious." Paul later described him as "a devout man according to the law, having a good report of all the Jews which dwelt there" (Acts 22:12). The di-

vision between believing Jews like Ananias and unbelieving Jews was not yet so sharp in Damascus as it was in Jerusalem. *To him said the Lord in a vision, Ananias.* "The Lord" refers to Jesus, whom Ananias acknowledged. *And he said, Behold, I am here, Lord.* Ananias' reply, so like that of Samuel (1 Samuel 3:1-10) and of Isaiah (Isaiah 6:8), indicated that he could be depended upon for prompt obedience, and shows why the Lord chose him for this mission.

11. And the Lord said unto him, Arise, and go into the street which is called Straight, and enquire in the house of Judas for one called Saul, of Tarsus: for, behold, he prayeth.

Straight Street is easily identified in Damascus today. *The house of Judas.* Of this Judas nothing more is known. He may have been a prominent member of the Jewish community in Damascus. *One called Saul, of Tarsus.* The words make it clear that Saul and Ananias had not previously met. The identification is precise in its detail. *He prayeth.* This should have reassured Ananias. A praying man is not usually a violent man.

12. And hath seen in a vision a man named Ananias coming in, and putting his hand on him, that he might receive his sight.

The Lord introduced each of the two men to the other in the same ways—a vision. *A man named Ananias.* A spoken message from the Lord evidently accompanied the vision to Saul, even as to Ananias. *And putting his hand on him, that he might receive his sight.* This explains that the imposition of hands was for healing, and not for the conveying of the Holy Spirit, as verse 17 alone might lead some to suppose. The indication of Saul's blindness should have further reassured Ananias that he was now harmless.

13. Then Ananias answered, Lord, I have heard by many of this man, how much evil he hath done to thy saints at Jerusalem.

The name of Saul stirred such fear in Ananias that both reason and obedience fell away from him. Saul's reputation had come to Damascus ahead of him on the lips of every Christian arriving from Jerusalem. *Thy saints.* This is the first appearance of the word "saint" to describe a Christian. A saint is one set apart to God.

14. And here he hath authority from the chief priests to bind all that call on thy name.

How did Ananias know of Saul's mission? Had some secret believer within the Sanhedrin—perhaps Joseph of Arimathea—conveyed word to the Christians in Jerusalem so that they were able to send a messenger to Damascus ahead of Saul? At any rate, an exceptionally efficient "grape vine" had in some way conveyed amazingly accurate information. *All that call on thy name.* Equivalent to "saints." Jesus was the one addressed.

15. But the Lord said unto him, Go thy way: for he is a chosen vessel unto me, to bear my name before the Gentiles, and kings, and the children of Israel.

Go thy way. The Lord knew His own purposes, and His command was not to be changed by man's demurring. Ananias's "way" was to lead to the house of Judas in Straight Street, as the Lord first directed. *He is a chosen vessel unto me.* He was

to bear the treasure of the gospel as a vessel, or casket, bears a precious jewel. "We have this treasure in earthen vessels, that the excellency of the power may be of God, and not of us" (2 Corinthians 4:7). *To bear my name before the Gentiles.* It is amazing that Christ should have chosen a "dyed-in-the-wool" member of the central sect of the Jews—"a Hebrew of the Hebrews"—as His special emissary to the Gentile world. Saul's education was such that he could reach out to all men, and his zeal guaranteed the faithful accomplishment of the task, once it was fully accepted (See Acts 22:21; 26:17; Romans 1:5; 11:13; Galatians 2:7, 8). *And kings.* Felix, Agrippa, and the household of Caesar were to hear the gospel from this remarkable world citizen. *And the children of Israel.* Mentioned last in this commission, the Jews were still first to be given the gospel.

16. For I will shew him how great things he must suffer for my name's sake.

The American Standard Version has, "How many things he must suffer." Ananias was to fear no evil at the hands of Saul. The former circumstances were to be reversed, as the persecutor tasted the bitterness of persecution. High honor and distinguished usefulness nearly always entail suffering. That suffering, in this instance, was to be for the sake of the name that Saul had hitherto despised. In 2 Corinthians 11:23-30 one may read the fulfillment of this declaration.

17. And Ananias went his way, and entered into the house; and putting his hands on him said, Brother Saul, the Lord, even Jesus, that appeared

unto thee in the way as thou camest, hath sent me, that thou mightest receive thy sight, and be filled with the Holy Ghost.

Entered into the house. Depending fully on Christ's word, Ananias put himself in a position where he would be helpless if Saul were minded to take him. *Putting his hands on him.* This was to heal Saul's blindness (v. 12). *Brother Saul.* Ananias' fear and reluctance fell away at the sight of the penitent blind man—a fellow Jew, and a fellow believer in Christ. *The Lord, even Jesus, that appeared unto thee in the way as thou camest, hath sent me.* A more careful identification could not be given. Acting under the same divine authority that had spoken to Saul, Ananias proceeded to the mission that Jesus had promised (v. 6). No other credentials were necessary. *That thou mightest receive thy sight.* This was a ministry to the flesh, a release from the burden of the recent days. *And be filled with the Holy Ghost.* The Scripture indicates that only the apostles had power to impart the Holy Spirit to others. See Acts 8:15-17. Hence, the filling with the Holy Spirit here probably refers to the gift of the Holy Spirit that all receive after being baptized (Acts 2:38, 39), though the Spirit did at some time empower Saul to perform miracles.

18. And immediately there fell from his eyes as it had been scales: and he received sight forthwith, and arose, and was baptized.

Dr. Luke writing! The scaly substance may have resulted from the irritation of the dazzling light on his eyes. The plain, vivid recounting of details furnishes good evidence of the factual nature of the miracle. *And arose, and was baptized.* Jesus had said that in Damascus Saul would be told what he must do. Paul's own words recall what he was told: "And now why tarriest thou? arise, and be baptized, and wash away thy sins, calling on the name of the Lord" (22:16). The "arising" signifies the active nature of the baptism, which Paul described to the Romans as a burial (Romans 6:3, 4). The river Abana would furnish ample accommodations for baptism at Damascus, either in its own course or in one of the artificial pools in the courts of large buildings in the city.

19. And when he had received meat, he was strehgthened. Then was Saul certain days with the disciples which were at Damascus.

Having partaken of the assurance given by Jesus—"He that believeth and is baptized shall be saved" (Mark 16:16)—Saul had no further cause for fasting. "And he took food and was strengthened" (American Standard Version). *Certain days.* A short period of time. *With the disciples which were at Damascus.* Saul joined in fellowship with those whom he had come to prosecute. His place of dwelling was evidently no longer the house of Judas.

20. And straightway he preached Christ in the synagogues, that he is the Son of God.

The synagogues received a vastly different message than the undelivered one Saul had brought in his letters. He was not disobedient to the heavenly vision (26:19, 20). *He is the Son of God.* This phrase is not used elsewhere in Acts. The circumstances give it tremendous force here. The Jews would find in this phrase a fulfillment of the Messianic promise in Psalm 2:7.

21. But all that heard him were amazed, and said; Is not this he that destroyed them which called on this name in Jerusalem, and came hither for that intent, that he might bring them bound unto the chief priests?

Saul's coming to Damascus was no surprise. Both Jews and Christians had heard of what he had done in Jerusalem and that he was coming to Damascus to continue the same bitter persecution against Christians. His sudden about-face was amazing.

22. But Saul increased the more in strength, and confounded the Jews which dwelt at Damascus, proving that this is very Christ.

The Jews in the Damascus synagogues did not listen to Paul's teaching without contradicting it, but his teaching was so sure and so well supported by the Scriptures that opposition served only to establish the truth of it more securely.

23. And after that many days were fulfilled, the Jews took counsel to kill him.

From Galatians 1:15-18 we learn that Saul went to Arabia for some time, and then returned to Damascus. The many days added up to about three years before he returned to Jerusalem. The record says nothing of what he did in Arabia. He was a tentmaker (Acts 18:1-3), and among the tent-dwelling Arabs he no doubt could make a living by that trade. Certainly he was thinking constantly of Christ, and probably he was telling of Him at every opportunity. Perhaps he spent much time in restudying the Scriptures in the light of his new knowledge of Jesus;

we cannot tell to what extent divine guidance made such study unnecessary. After he went back to Damascus, he no doubt resumed his teaching, and the Jews who opposed him became so angry they *took counsel to kill him.*

24. But their laying await was known of Saul. And they watched the gates day and night to kill him.

Many of the Jews had become Christians, and many others were sympathetic to them. The hostile Jews therefore found it impossible to keep their assassination plans secret. Probably Paul went into hiding. It would be almost impossible to find him by searching the city house by house, so the enemies guarded the gates, hoping to seize him as he tried to leave. They had enough influence to secure the help of the governor and his troops in this (2 Corinthians 11:32).

25. Then the disciples took him by night, and let him down by the wall in a basket.

In an ancient city a house just inside the wall might have an upper story resting on top of the city wall. Perhaps one such house belonged to a disciple or sympathizer. Thus a large *basket* with Saul in it could be put out through a window (2 Corinthians 11:33) and lowered by ropes outside *the wall.*

26. And when Saul was come to Jerusalem, he assayed to join himself to the disciples: but they were all afraid of him, and believed not that he was a disciple.

When Saul was come to Jerusalem. He had left the city three years before as a persecutor of Christians. He returned as a fugitive from the same kind of persecution. "He attempted to associate with the disciples" (Living Oracles translation), in the same way in which he had made himself a part of the Christian community in Damascus. "And they were all afraid of him, not believing that he was a disciple" (American Standard Version).

27. But Barnabas took him, and brought him to the apostles, and declared unto them how he had seen the Lord in the way, and that he had spoken to him, and how he had preached boldly at Damascus in the name of Jesus.

Barnabas again demonstrated how appropriate was the name (son of consolation) given him by the apostles. Barnabas' home on the island of Cyprus was not far removed from Saul's home at Tarsus of Cilicia. It is possible that the two men had known each other before. *Took him, and brought him to the apostles.* From Galatians 1:18, 19 we learn that Saul came to Peter and to James, the Lord's brother. These leaders of the church would be best able to determine the genuineness of Saul's conversion, and their acceptance would quiet the fears of the disciples generally. *Declared unto them how he had seen the Lord in the way.* Motivated by his characteristic generosity of spirit, Barnabas had taken the trouble to learn the facts, whether from Christians at Damascus, from Saul himself, or by prophetic revelation.

28. And he was with them coming in and going out at Jerusalem.

Coming in and going out. A Hebrew idiom indicating daily intimate contact. Even this contact, however, added nothing new to the gospel preached by Saul; it came by revelation (Galatians 2:6).

29. And he spake boldly in the name of the Lord Jesus, and disputed against the Grecians: but they went about to slay him.

The preaching career that had begun in Damascus was continued in the Jewish capital. It was made possible by the friendly help of Barnabas, without whom Saul would have been a lonely and futile figure. But his preaching had the same result in Jerusalem as in Damascus. Some of the Jews were determined to resist the truth. Unable to overthrow it by argument, they determined to silence it by killing Saul. The *Grecians* in Jerusalem, Jews who had been born abroad, were the ones who had led the opposition to Stephen (Acts 6:9). Saul himself was a Grecian, so probably members of his own synagogue were plotting his murder.

30. Which when the brethren knew, they brought him down to Caesarea, and sent him forth to Tarsus.

As in Damascus, the would-be assassins could not keep their secret. Someone reported their plot to the disciples. A group of them went with Saul to Caesarea to prevent a secret murder on the way. Probably they made some investigation to be sure none of the plotters were aboard the ship on which Saul then sailed to his home in Tarsus.

31. Then had the churches rest throughout all Judaea and Galilee and Samaria, and were edified; and walking in the fear of the Lord, and in the comfort of the Holy Ghost, were multiplied.

The furious persecution now ceased, and the churches had a time of *rest,* or peace, in which they were *edified,* or built up. Luke does not pause to explain all the reasons for this. Certainly the persecutors could see that their efforts were ineffective. Instead of stamping out the teaching of Christ, they were spreading it all over the country. They must have been tired of such wasted effort. With the flight of Paul they could claim a minor victory, and perhaps thought that was a good time to drop their persecution. Perhaps the disciples, having given their testimony strongly to all the Jews, now ceased to dispute in the synagogues controlled by their enemies, and thus reduced the friction. They continued to testify in other places, however, both in word and by living righteously *in the fear* of the Lord, with the result that the number of disciples continued to be multiplied.

32. And it came to pass, as Peter passed throughout all quarters, he came down also to the saints which dwelt at Lydda.

As Peter passed throughout all quarters. Apparently Peter was visiting the disciples in other places as he and John had visited those in Samaria (Acts 8:14-17). *The saints.* The New Testament writers often call Christians by this name. It means dedicated people, those set apart. As applied to Christians, of course, it means they are dedicated to Christ and therefore obedient to Him. *Lydda.* A town a little more than twenty miles northwest of Jerusalem, where the foothills give way to the coastal plain.

33. And there he found a certain man named Aeneas, which had kept his bed eight years, and was sick of the palsy.

Palsy is paralysis. There are num-

erous kinds, but any kind that kept a man helpless for *eight years* would be thought to be permanent.

34. And Peter said unto him, Aeneas, Jesus Christ maketh thee whole: arise, and make thy bed. And he arose immediately.

No doubt hundreds of miracles were done through the apostles (Acts 5:12-16). Luke chose a few for special mention, perhaps because they had especially notable results. In this case, the one miracle seems to have been unusually effective in winning favorable attention and bringing people to obey the gospel.

35. And all that dwelt at Lydda and Saron saw him, and turned to the Lord.

This is the notable result that made this miracle more notable than many others. *Saron,* or Sharon, is the name of the coastal plain extending from Lydda northward to the foot of Mount Carmel.

36. Now there was at Joppa a certain disciple named Tabitha, which by interpretation is called Dorcas: this woman was full of good works and almsdeeds which she did.

Joppa. A city along the seacoast northwest of Jerusalem. *A certain disciple.* The word "disciple" is used in exactly the same sense as "Christian." The followers of Jesus were known as "disciples" before they came to be known as "Christians." See Acts 11:26. The word "disciple" is used as both masculine and feminine. *Tabitha, which by interpretation is called Dorcas.* "Tabitha" is an Aramaic or Hebrew word meaning a gazelle. This was the name by which this woman was known to her Jewish friends who did not habitually speak

Greek. "Dorcas" is the Greek word having the same meaning. Since he was writing this record in Greek, Luke gave this translation of the name for readers who would not understand the Hebrew or Aramaic word. *Full of good works.* We would say that her life was full of good deeds, or that she was always doing good things. *Almsdeeds.* Our modern term would be "acts of charity."

37. And it came to pass in those days, that she was sick, and died: whom when they had washed, they laid her in an upper chamber.

In those days. While Peter was at Lydda. *When they had washed.* This was part of the preparation for burial. After being washed, the body was enclosed in a wrapping of linen cloth, sometimes with spices to retard decay. For illustrations of this, see the accounts of Jesus' burial (Mark 15:46; John 19:38-43; 20:6, 7) and the appearance of Lazarus when he came forth from the tomb (John 11:43, 44). It seems that Dorcas' body was not yet wrapped in the linen. *In an upper chamber.* The upper rooms of houses often were used for special occasions. The family would live in the room below. If the upper room was in Dorcas' own house it may indicate that she was a person of some wealth, as does her generous help to the poor. A poor family would have only a one-room house, in which they might even keep their animals at night.

38. And forasmuch as Lydda was nigh to Joppa, and the disciples had heard that Peter was there, they sent unto him two men, desiring him that he would not delay to come to them.

And forasmuch as. We would say

simply "because" or "since." *Lydda.* Use your map to locate this town. Peter had been there for some time. *The disciples.* That is, the Christians. *Peter.* This statement shows the respect in which Peter and the other apostles were held. Jesus had made them His special witnesses (Acts 1: 8), with miraculous guidance (John 16:13) and miraculous power (Acts 2:4, 43). This gave them a special place in the church, even though their miraculous power was shared with certain others, such as Philip (Acts 8:6). *Two men.* The sending of two men on missions seems to have been the custom. Jesus sent the disciples out two by two (Mark 6: 7; Luke 10:1); Peter and John were sent together to Samaria by the church at Jerusalem (Acts 8:14); Barnabas and Saul were sent out together by the church at Antioch (Acts 13:2, 3), though Mark went along to help (Acts 13:5). The custom of sending two was not rigid or invariable, of course, Barnabas seems to have been sent to Antioch alone (Acts 11:22), and Cornelius added a soldier escort to the two he sent to Peter (Acts 10:7). *Desiring him.* We would say "requesting him" or "asking him." *He would not delay.* Their need was urgent and they wished him to come immediately.

39. Then Peter arose and went with them. When he was come, they brought him into the upper chamber: and all the widows stood by him weeping, and shewing the coats and garments which Dorcas made, while she was with them.

Peter arose and went. We do not know just what the disciples had in mind in asking Peter to come. They probably had heard of the miraculous healing of Aeneas, for Lydda was near to Joppa, as noted in verse 38. It may be that they hoped Peter would even now restore Dorcas. However, the raising of the dead was so rare and the early Christians so seldom expected a miracle to be performed that there is some doubt that this was in their mind. J. W. McGarvey wrote that they probably wanted the presence of one to comfort the distressed little band rather than hoping that he would raise Dorcas from the dead, "for it was not the custom of the apostles to bring back to life their deceased brethren and sisters merely because they had been useful in their lives; otherwise Stephen and others who had been cruelly slain in the midst of their usefulness would have been resuscitated." *The widows stood by him weeping, and shewing the coats and garments which Dorcas made, while she was with them.* These probably were some of the poor whom Dorcas had befriended. As a tribute to her, they were showing the clothing that she had made for them, perhaps with her own hands.

40. But Peter put them all forth, and kneeled down, and prayed; and turning him to the body said, Tabitha, arise. And she opened her eyes: and when she saw Peter, she sat up.

Put them all forth. Notice the similarity between Peter's actions and those in other cases of the raising of the dead recorded in the Bible: Elijah (1 Kings 17:19-23); Elisha (2 Kings 4:33); Jesus with the son of the widow at Nain (Luke 7:11-15), Jesus with Lazarus (John 11:41-44); and Jesus with Jairus' daughter (Mark 5:40-42). *Tabitha, arise.* Peter used her Aramaic name. See

explanation of verse 36 above. The call is much like that of Jesus in raising Jairus' daughter.

41. And he gave her his hand, and lifted her up, and when he had called the saints and widows, presented her alive.

Lifted her up. He helped her to arise, though the restoration to life and health was immediate and total. *The saints.* This is another name for the Christians or disciples. The word "saint" is used throughout the book of Acts and the Epistles to mean those who have consecrated themselves to Christ. They are holy ones, not because they are sinlessly perfect, but because they have accepted Christ as Saviour and Lord. See Paul's use of the term in 1 Corinthians 1:2, where he speaks of his readers as "sanctified" and as "saints" though their lives were far from perfect. Their failures are stated very pointedly in the early chapters of 1 Corinthians. *The widows.* Probably most of the widows Dorcas had helped were saints, but perhaps there were some who were not.

42. And it was known throughout all Joppa: and many believed in the Lord.

It was known . . . many believed. The effect of the raising of Dorcas was to call the attention of the community to the Christian and the Christian message. They were then subjects for evangelism. Much of the preaching probably was done by Peter.

43. And it came to pass, that he tarried many days in Joppa with one Simon a tanner.

He tarried many days. Peter's continued teaching was one reason that "many believed in the Lord" (v. 42). *Simon a tanner.* Jewish teachers were scornful of tanners, probably because their trade was accompanied by unpleasant odors as well as because they might become "unclean" under the law by skinning dead animals. Peter's staying with this Simon in-dicates that his Jewish outlook, and that of the Jews in Joppa, was not so strictly narrow as that of the rabbis. But still it took a vision sent by God to enable him to see clearly that God was concerned equally with Jews and Gentiles. See the account of the vision in Acts 10:9-16.

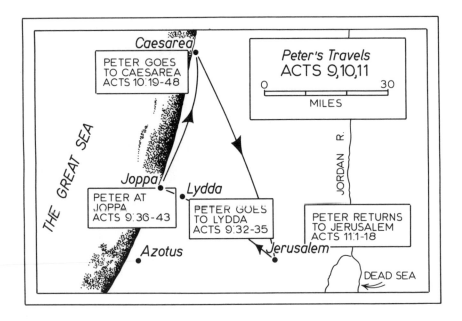

CHAPTER 10

1. There was a certain man in Caesarea called Cornelius, a centurion of the band called the Italian band.

Caesarea was on the seacoast some twenty miles south of Mount Carmel and sixty miles northwest of Jerusalem. It was the headquarters of the Roman governor of Judea and Samaria, and doubtless many troops were stationed there. A *band,* or cohort, normally had about six hundred men and therefore would have six centurions. This cohort may have taken the name *Italian* because it was composed of men recruited in Italy rather than in provinces farther from Rome.

2. A devout man, and one that feared God with all his house, which gave much alms to the people, and prayed to God alway.

Cornelius was not a Jew, but *one that feared God:* that is, a Gentile who had forsaken paganism to worship the one true God whom the Jews worshiped. *All his house,* probably including relatives (v. 24) as well as servants and soldiers who "waited on him continually" (v. 7), had come to the same faith. Apparently Cornelius' religion was obvious and attractive. *Gave much alms.* The centurion put his religion into practice by contributing generously to the poor. *To the people.* This means the Jewish people, many of whom hated the Romans on their soil and found many ways of making their hatred known. Nevertheless, Cornelius gave generously to the needy among them. *Prayed to God alway.* His habit of prayer was as notable as his good life.

3. He saw in a vision evidently about the ninth hour of the day an angel of God coming in to him, and saying unto him, Cornelius.

Evidently means openly. Apparently Cornelius saw the angel quite clearly. *The ninth hour* was mid-afternoon. If Cornelius followed the custom of many devout Jews, this was one of his daily prayer times (Acts 3:1).

4. And when he looked on him, he was afraid, and said, What is it, Lord? And he said unto him, Thy prayers and thine alms are come up for a memorial before God.

To be *afraid* is the normal reaction of a man in the presence of a superhuman being. *Lord* was a term of respect and honor. In the New Testament it is most often used of God or Jesus, but in respectful address to men it was used almost as freely as "Sir" is with us. Cornelius regarded the angel as his superior, not necessarily as God. The angel's first words were reassuring: Cornelius' *prayers* and *alms,* his worship and good deeds, were remembered *before God.*

5. And now send men to Joppa, and call for one Simon, whose surname is Peter.

If Cornelius would know more of God's will, he could learn from Peter, one of Jesus' chosen apostles.

6. He lodgeth with one Simon a tanner, whose house is by the sea side: he shall tell thee what thou oughtest to do.

The houses were not numbered as ours are, but it would not be too difficult to find Simon's home by inquiring along the waterfront in Joppa. *He shall tell thee what thou oughtest to do.* Why send for Simon? God's angel was already in Caesarea; why didn't he tell Cornelius what to do? No explanation is given, but it seems evident that Jesus has committed this task to man and does not intend to relieve him of it. An angel sent Philip to an Ethiopian, but Philip told the man what to do (Acts 8:26-38). Jesus himself appeared to Saul, but Ananias told Saul what to do (Acts 22:6-16). An angel told Cornelius to send for Peter, but it remained for Peter to tell the man what he ought to do.

7. And when the angel which spake unto Cornelius was departed, he called two of his household servants, and a devout soldier of them that waited on him continually.

As messengers to Peter, Cornelius chose one of his military aides and two civilians in his employ. Evidently the centurion had a home that required considerable service.

8. And when he had declared all these things unto them, he sent them to Joppa.

Cornelius knew a Jew would not welcome a summons to his house. He told the messengers what had happened so they could explain to Peter that an angel of God, not merely a centurion of Rome, invited him.

9. On the morrow, as they went on their journey, and drew nigh unto the city, Peter went up upon the housetop to pray about the sixth hour.

The scene now shifts to the home in Joppa where Peter was staying. It was the noontime hour of prayer, and Peter sought solitude on the flat roof of the home.

10. And he became very hungry, and would have eaten: but while they made ready, he fell into a trance.

Peter's hunger gives point to the account that follows. He was hungry, but not hungry enough to disregard his teaching about diet. His *trance* apparently was a condition God imposed to make him less sensitive to his physical surroundings and more sensitive to the vision about to be given to him.

11. And saw heaven opened, and a certain vessel descending unto him, as it had been a great sheet knit at the four corners, and let down to the earth.

The vision showed *a great sheet* like the sail of a ship. It was held by the four corners, allowing it to sag in the middle and form a *vessel* or basin. This was lowered from above.

12. Wherein were all manner of fourfooted beasts of the earth, and wild beasts, and creeping things and fowls of the air.

Birds and animals of all kinds filled the hollow of the sheet.

13. And there came a voice to him, Rise, Peter; kill, and eat.

The opportunity was offered for Peter to satisfy his pressing hunger.

14. But Peter said, Not so, Lord; for I have never eaten any thing that is common or unclean.

Peter gave the answer that had been drilled into him since childhood. Many of the animals shown were *unclean* according to law; they must not be eaten. The others were contaminated, made *common*, by contact with the unclean.

15. And the voice spake unto him again the second time, What God hath cleansed, that call not thou common.

Whatever Peter had been taught before, he should know that the sheet let down from heaven and the voice accompanying it were from God. Therefore he should accept its instructions even if he had to change some ideas he already held and treasured.

16. This was done thrice: and the vessel was received up again into heaven.

The repetition emphasized the message. The fact that all the animals came from heaven and returned to heaven emphasized the thought that they were clean in God's sight and man should not call them defiled.

17. Now while Peter doubted in himself what this vision which he had seen should mean, behold, the men which were sent from Cornelius had made enquiry for Simon's house, and stood before the gate.

Doubted in himself. Peter was wondering about the meaning of the vision. It was plain enough that he should not call anything defiled when God called it clean. He rightly surmised that he should make some practical application of this principle, but as yet he did not know what that application was to be. *Had made enquiry for Simon's house.* The messengers had inquired of people they met and had been directed to the house they were seeking. *Stood before the gate.* A large house might be built around a central courtyard or patio, which was closed off from the street by a gate. Simon's house was likely large, to serve as tannery as well as residence.

18. And called, and asked whether Simon, which was surnamed Peter, were lodged there.

Getting the attention of someone within, the men sent by Cornelius inquired for the man for whom they had come.

19. While Peter thought on the vision, the Spirit said unto him, Behold, three men seek thee.

In order to give infallible guidance to the church in its beginning, Peter and the other apostles were inspired in such a way that they could recognize the Holy Spirit's message unquestionably.

20. Arise therefore, and get thee down, and go with them, doubting nothing: for I have sent them.

The same strict Jewish teaching that made Peter extremely careful about his diet (v. 14) made him shun Gentiles. The strength of this prejudice is evident when we see the extraordinary methods God used to overcome it: first the vision, now a special message of the Spirit—and there is more to come.

21. Then Peter went down to the men which were sent unto him from Cornelius; and said, Behold, I am he whom ye seek: what is the cause wherefore ye are come?

Knowing Peter's impetuous disposition, we can imagine that he was now almost bursting with curiosity. Obviously some unusual event was in the making. What was it? Where was God leading, and why? If Peter had suddenly been told to go into a Gentile home and invite Romans to become Christians, probably he would have reacted as uncompromisingly as he did to the order to eat some of the unclean animals of his vision (v. 14). Instead of giving a sudden order, God was leading His apostle gently, step by step.

22. And they said, Cornelius the centurion, a just man, and one that feareth God, and of good report among all the nation of the Jews, was warned from God by an holy angel to send for thee into his house, and to hear words of thee.

The messengers were careful to represent their master in the most favorable way to overcome Peter's Jewish prejudice. Some soldiers might extort money by means of false accusations and threats of violence (Luke 3:14), but this man was *just,* upright, fair. He was *one that feareth God:* that is, a worshiper of the true God and not the pagan gods of Rome. He had a *good report,* a favorable reputation even among the Jews. All this Peter could readily check by inquiry among the Jews in Caesarea. The messengers added that God himself had sent His angel to tell Cornelius to send for Peter. This could not be checked so easily, but events that had happened and would happen surely would convince Peter that it was true.

23. Then called he them in, and lodged them. And on the morrow

Peter went away with them, and certain brethren from Joppa .accompa-
nied him.

Respecting the Jewish prejudice,
the men had not asked permission
to come in. They were still standing
in the street. In the light of his 'vision
and the Spirit's special message, however, Peter now relaxed his prejudice
enough to invite them in for the
night, probably with the consent of
his host, the owner of the house. The
next day he *went away with them* as
the Spirit had told him to do, perhaps torn between his reluctance and
his eagerness to see what all this was
leading to. Well knowing he would
be criticized for going to a Gentile
home, Peter induced six *brethren*
(Acts 11:12) *from Joppa* to go with
him. Whatever happened, Peter's
critics would not have to depend on
his unsupported word for a report
of it.

**24. And the morrow after they en-
tered into Caesarea. And Cornelius
waited for them, and had called together his kinsmen and near friends.**

The distance from Joppa to Caesarea is not much more than thirty
miles. After spending a night at
some village on the way, the travelers could reach Caesarea long before
night on the following day. Cornelius
knew about when they would arrive,
either because they had planned the
trip in detail before it began or because one of the messengers had
hurried on ahead of the rest. The
centurion had full confidence that
what he would hear would be God's
own message. In keeping with his
godly and generous nature, he
wanted to share it. He had invited
his kinsmen and near friends to hear
it with him.

**25. And as Peter was coming in,
Cornelius met him, and fell down at
his feet, and worshipped him.**

In the New Testament *worshipped*
usually refers to honoring God, but
the word can be used also of honour-
ing a man. Since the centurion knew
the one true God, it is not likely that
he thought of Peter as a god, but he
recognized him as a superior and did
homage by kneeling or prostrating
himself.

**26. But Peter took him up, say-
ing, Stand up; I myself also am a man.**

Peter did not know just what was
in Cornelius' mind; a person with a
Roman heathen background might
mistake a man for a god. Peter therefore made it clear that he was no
more than human and was not seeking any special reverence for himself.

**27. And as he talked with him,
he went in, and found many that
were come together.**

Cornelius evidently had gone to
the gate to meet Peter, and together
they came into the house where the
guests were waiting.

**28. And he said unto them, Ye
know how that it is an unlawful thing
for a man that is a Jew to keep company, or come unto one of another
nation; but God hath shewed me that
I should not call any man common or
unclean.**

Peter began by frankly recognizing
the barrier between him and his
hearers. What he was doing was not
specifically forbidden in God's law,
but it was against the accepted
teaching that supposedly interpreted
the law and was generally given the
force of law. This was well known to
Romans as well as to Jews. Peter was

violating the custom of his people, he explained, because *God hath shewed me that I should not call any man common or unclean.* With the help of the Spirit's word in verses 19, 20, Peter now made this application of the lesson of his vision.

29. Therefore came I unto you without gainsaying, as soon as I was sent for: I ask therefore for what intent ye have sent for me?

This preacher of the gospel did not yet realize that he was there to preach the gospel. If this seems absurd to us, it is because we fail to realize the depth and width of the gulf between Jew and Gentile. Peter knew God had sent him, but it would take further leading to convince him that Gentiles could come into God's kingdom as readily as Jews. At this point he may have been wondering if his duty was to persuade Cornelius and his friends to accept circumcision and become Jews, keeping the entire Old Testament law. Peter had heard briefly that an angel had directed Cornelius to send for him (v. 22). Perhaps he hoped that fuller information would help him know what to do.

30. And Cornelius said, Four days ago I was fasting until this hour; and at the ninth hour I prayed in my house, and, behold, a man stood before me in bright clothing.

We now have our first statement of what the angel looked like. He was in the form of *a man,* but his *bright clothing* marked him as heavenly messenger. See Luke 24:4; Acts 1:10.

31. And said, Cornelius, thy prayer is heard, and thine alms are had in remembrance in the sight of God.

Cornelius' sincere worship and good life were not enough to secure his salvation without Jesus. Nevertheless God made special arrangements for him to hear of Jesus, and used him to help show the Jews that salvation was for all the world.

32. Send therefore to Joppa, and call hither Simon, whose surname is Peter; he is lodged in the house of one Simon a tanner by the sea side: who, when he cometh, shall speak unto thee.

In answer to Peter's question in verse 29, Cornelius could only recount what had happened. He had sent for Peter because that was what God's angel had told him to do.

33. Immediately therefore I sent to thee; and thou hast well done that thou art come. Now therefore are we all here present before God, to hear all things that are commanded thee of God.

Peter had had a struggle within himself and later would have a struggle with his fellow Jews over what he was doing. Cornelius understood this and expressed his appreciation briefly: *Thou hast well done.* He went on to place himself and his friends at the disposal of God and God's man: they were gathered in the sight of God to hear whatever God wanted them to hear. This may have been just the word Peter needed to make his next duty clear. *All things that are commanded thee of God* must have called to mind his commission to "preach the gospel to every creature" (Mark 16:15; Matthew 28:19, 20).

34. Then Peter opened his mouth, and said, Of a truth I perceive that God is no respecter of persons.

Peter had long been familiar with this principle (2 Chronicles 19:7; 2

Samuel 14:14), but now he was forced to apply it in a new way. Probably he had taken it to mean that God would not favor one of the chosen people above another; now he was beginning to see that God would not even favor a Jew above a Gentile.

35. But in every nation he that feareth him, and worketh righteousness, is accepted with him.

God does not respect persons, but He does respect character and devotion. Cornelius' worship and goodness were so sincere and unfailing that God was not only willing but eager to accept him into His kingdom.

36. The word which God sent unto the children of Israel, preaching peace by Jesus Christ: (he is Lord of all).

Being persuaded that God willed it, Peter now proceeded to announce the *word* or message that he had been commissioned to teach—the gospel. The divine purpose was to send it to all the world; but *God sent* it first *unto the children of Israel,* and as yet it had been given only to them. *Preaching peace by Jesus Christ.* This is a beautiful summary of the gospel, the good news. Through Jesus men find peace— peace with God and peace with each other. The disjointed structure of the sentence here suggests that perhaps the Spirit who inspired Peter was teaching Peter along with Peter's hearers. Possibly now for the first time Peter began to grasp the idea that peace in Jesus could even abolish the enmity between Jew and Gentile (Ephesians 2:11-22). Thus he was moved to interrupt himself and declare, *He is Lord of all,* of Jew and Gentile alike.

37. That word, I say, ye know, which was published throughout all Judaea, and began from Galilee, after the baptism which John preached.

Cornelius' situation among family and friends suggests that he had been stationed in Caesarea a long time, perhaps throughout the ministry of Jesus. Jesus' ministry had been sensational, and so had the ministry of the apostles. The Roman forces charged with keeping the peace had watched closely, knowing riots were possible whenever Jews gathered in large crowds. They must have admired the consummate skill with which Jesus prevented such disturbances. Peter could say with confidence that word of Jesus had already come to Cornelius and his friends. Such word had been spread to almost everyone *throughout all Judaea,* and Caesarea was the Roman capital of that province. Jesus' early ministry in Judea had been comparatively obscure, and only John records it (John 2:13—4:3). His more spectacular work and greater fame *began from Galilee after the baptism which John preached* (Matthew 4:12-25).

38. How God anointed Jesus of Nazareth with the Holy Ghost and with power: who went about doing good, and healing all that were oppressed of the devil; for God was with him.

Peter may have said more than is recorded, recalling some of the tremendous miracles of Jesus. It was not necessary to dwell at length on these, however; Cornelius and his friends already knew about them. Peter's aim was rather to emphasize the conclusion to be drawn: Jesus could do mighty miracles because

God had endowed Him *with the Holy Ghost and with power*: the miracles were evidence that *God was with him.*

39. And we are witnesses of all things which he did both in the land of the Jews, and in Jerusalem; whom they slew and hanged on a tree.

Peter was one of the apostles specially chosen to testify of Jesus. That was why God sent him to Cornelius. In sharp contrast with Jesus' divine power and goodness is the fact that He was killed by crucifixion, and of this also Peter and his fellow apostles were witnesses. This too needed only to be mentioned briefly, for Cornelius was well aware of it and probably aware also of the malicious plotting that had brought about such an injustice. "This thing was not done in a corner" (Acts 26:26).

40, 41. Him God raised up the third day, and shewed him openly; Not to all the people, but unto witnesses chosen before of God, even to us, who did eat and drink with him after he rose from the dead.

Cornelius knew that Jesus' resurrection had been proclaimed by some and hotly denied by others. He had been neutral in that dispute, interested only in making sure it did not lead to rioting. Now Peter declared himself to be one of the witnesses who could testify with absolute certainty that Jesus had truly risen. This was additional proof that God was with Jesus—and proof that Jesus, despite His death, was alive and to be reckoned with.

42. And he commanded us to preach unto the people, and to testify that it is he which was ordained of God to be the Judge of quick and dead.

Here is the fearsome fact to those who oppose Jesus, and the blessed assurance to those who obey Him. He will judge everyone living and dead, for the dead must be raised to face the consequences of what they did before death. This message of assurance and solemn warning Peter and the other apostles were commanded to deliver faithfully.

43. To him give all the prophets witness, that through his name whosoever believeth in him shall receive remission of sins.

Peter may well have spent some time explaining how Jesus fulfilled prophecies of the Old Testament. Jesus had instructed the apostles carefully on this point (Luke 24:44-48), and they often made use of it. See examples in Peter's sermon in Acts 2. The climax of the whole message to Cornelius came in the declaration that *whosoever believeth in him shall receive remission of sins.*

44. While Peter yet spake these words, the Holy Ghost fell on all them which heard the word.

If Peter had not done so already, the mention of remission of sins must lead him soon to say, "Repent, and be baptized." (See Acts 2:38.) This would bring him face to face with a question that apparently was not even yet settled in Peter's own mind. To baptize Gentiles would be to bring them into the fellowship of God's church. Was this permissible? God seemed to be leading in that direction, but Peter's presuppositions were contrary. But God settled the question beyond any doubt when He bestowed the Holy Spirit upon the Gentiles. If they were fit for fellowship with God's Spirit, who would say they were unfit for fellowship with God's people?

45. And they of the circumcision which believed were astonished, as many as came with Peter, because that on the Gentiles also was poured out the gift of the Holy Ghost.

They of the circumcision which believed were the Jewish believers in Jesus, the six brethren who *came with Peter* from Joppa to Caesarea They shared Peter's presuppositions and prejudices. Probably he had told them of his vision and the Spirit's leading, but still they were not prepared for the idea that Gentiles could be as acceptable to God as could Jews.

46. For they heard them speak with tongues, and magnify God. Then answered Peter.

This speaking *with tongues* was like that of the apostles recorded in Acts 2. It was the evidence that proved God had poured out the Holy Spirit on these Gentiles as He had upon the apostles. The Spirit led them to *magnify God* as the apostles had done (Acts 2:11).

47. Can any man forbid water, that these should not be baptized, which have received the Holy Ghost as well as we?

It seems that Peter's last doubts vanished and he was ready to follow God's leading even to the extent of receiving Gentiles into the fellowship of God's people. The question of this verse probably was directed to the brethren who came with him. If any of them had an objection, Peter wanted to know it now.

48. And he commanded them to be baptized· in the name of the Lord. Then prayed they him to tarry certain days.

Apparently no one voiced any objection: the six brethren were convinced just as Peter was. Cornelius therefore was baptized, along with his relatives and friends. Quite naturally they asked Peter to stay and continue teaching them for some time. Recalling the commission recorded in Matthew 28:20, he probably was glad to do as they asked.

CHAPTER 11

1. And the apostles and brethren that were in Judaea heard that the Gentiles had also received the word of God.

The apostles and brethren that were in Judæa. The dispersion recorded in Acts 8:1 did not remove the entire Christian community from Jerusalem. Many remained also in the outlying villages of Judaea. "Heard that the heathen had also accepted God's message" (Goodspeed). The English words "Gentiles," "nations," and "heathen" are all translations of the same New Testament Greek word. It signified any who were not Jews. Thus when the "Gentiles" were at last evangelized, the commission to preach the gospel to the "nations" began to be fulfilled. News of Peter's visit to Cornelius traveled rapidly from Caesarea to Jerusalem.

2. And when Peter was come up to Jerusalem, they that were of the circumcision contended with him.

Peter had remained "certain days" with the disciples at Caesarea. "The advocates of circumcision took him to task" (Goodspeed). The other apostles were probably not among the objectors. To the strict Judaizers, it was bad enough that members of a mixed nation, like the Samaritans, and proselytes, like the Ethiopian eunuch, should be included among the Christians, but these at least had received the covenant symbol of circumcision. But for one as prominent among them as Peter to fraternize with uncircumcised Gentiles was more than they could bear.

3. Saying, Thou wentest in to men uncircumcised, and didst eat with them.

The law and the traditions had no precedent to forbid preaching to Gentiles, for the law and the traditions did not deal with gospel preaching. But the traditions—not the law—were strict and explicit in forbidding the kind of fraternization of which Peter had been guilty in accepting the familiar hospitality of a Gentile home. The traditional prejudice against eating with Gentiles was so strong that Peter himself later reverted to it on at least one occasion (Galatians 2:12).

4. But Peter rehearsed the matter from the beginning, and expounded it by order unto them, saying.

Peter himself had so recently been of the same mind with them that he could take no offense at their rebuke. He did the only sensible thing, recounting for their information the same events that had convinced him of God's will for the Gentiles.

5. I was in the city of Joppa praying: and in a trance I saw a vision, A certain vessel descend, as it had been a great sheet, let down from heaven by four corners; and it came even to me.

In his narrative Peter omitted many details that are recorded in Acts 10. There the narrator was concerned with the conversion of Cornelius.

Here Peter was concerned with the evidence that God had directed him to preach to Gentiles and to have fellowship with them. Hence he emphasized the events that would show the hand of God in the whole procedure. *In a trance I saw a vision.* This was not an uncommon means by which God revealed His will to prophets and apostles. It was not a natural dream. "Something like a great sheet descending from heaven" (Living Oracles). Peter recognized that whatever this was, it came from God (see v. 8). *It came even to me.* The approach was direct and personal. There was no avoiding it.

6. Upon the which when I had fastened mine eyes, I considered, and saw fourfooted beasts of the earth, and wild beasts, and creeping things, and fowls of the air.

"And looking attentively on it, I observed. . . ." (Living Oracles). The gesture of heaven in his direction challenged Peter's complete attention. He wanted to know what it was all about. "Quadrupeds, wild animals, reptiles and wild birds" (Goodspeed). What a collection of creatures to come from heaven! There may not have been one in the lot that would be acceptable for food under the laws written in Leviticus 11. It was a most amazing vision.

7. And I heard a voice saying unto me, Arise, Peter; slay and eat.

The message was as unmistakably direct and personal as the vision had been. *Arise.* The prelude to prompt obedience to a divine command. *Slay and eat.* This was in direct contradiction to the Levitical law.

8. But I said, Not so, Lord: for nothing common or unclean hath at any time entered into my mouth.

"By no means, Lord" (Living Oracles). Peter recognized the command as from God, but it was so contrary to his whole nature that he could not entertain the thought. "Nothing that was not ceremonially cleansed has ever passed my lips" (Goodspeed). Peter objected, not because the command was contrary to God's revealed law, but because it was contrary to his own established practice. His record was clear and he intended to keep it that way.

9. But the voice answered me again from heaven, What God hath cleansed, that call not thou common.

The reply was addressed directly to Peter's objection. *What God hath cleansed.* These were not beasts in their natural state. These had the touch of God upon them. Peter was to learn that the touch of God through Calvary's sacrifice was enough to lift every man out of the ranks of the "unclean."

10. And this was done three times: and all were drawn up again into heaven.

There was to be no forgetting the message. Just as the dreams of Joseph (Genesis 37:5-11) and of Pharaoh (Genesis 41:1-7) were variously repeated and established, so this was established by threefold repetition. Acts 10:17-19 relates that Peter was much perplexed to know the meaning of the vision.

11. And, behold, immediately there were three men already come unto the house where I was, sent from Caesarea unto me.

The messengers from Cornelius had traveled thirty miles, evidently starting in the afternoon of the second day before this. That Peter's vision came to its conclusion in the moment when they stood at the gate inquiring for him is a further demonstration of the hand of God in the whole affair.

12. And the spirit bade me go with them, nothing doubting. Moreover these six brethren accompanied me, and we entered into the man's house.

The spirit bade me go with them. Acts 10:19, 20 indicate that Peter learned of the men's presence through the revelation of the Spirit, who indicated that they also had come by revelation. Only then did he go forth to meet them. "Making no distinction" (American Standard Version). This was the first application of the vision-lesson. Peter was not to despise the company of the Gentile messengers. *These six brethren accompanied me.* Peter wisely provided himself with witnesses among the believing Jews, probably knowing that he would face just such objections as he was now answering. *And we entered into the man's house.* This was the charge against Peter. He acknowledged it freely, but showed that it was of God.

13. And he shewed us how he had seen an angel in his house, which stood and said unto him, Send men to Joppa, and call for Simon, whose surname is Peter.

See Acts 10:1-8. The angel came in remembrance of Cornelius's prayers and his benevolence. These things won the favor of God, but they did not win Cornelius's salvation. That required his hearing and believing.

14. Who shall tell thee words, whereby thou and all thy house shall be saved.

Cornelius' sincere piety and upright generosity were not sufficient to save him. The words whereby he was to be saved included telling him what he ought to do (10:6). Peter told him only one thing to do, and that came after the preaching of Christ and the coming of the Spirit. Peter told him to be baptized (10:47, 48). *Thou and all thy house* (American Standard Version). The terms of salvation were the same to each member of the household as to himself (compare Acts 16:31-34).

15. And as I began to speak, the Holy Ghost fell on them, as on us at the beginning.

Acts 10:34-43 gives the record of what Peter said before he was interrupted. *The Holy Ghost fell on them.* This was a special manifestation, designed to show Peter and his Jewish friends that the Gentiles also were included in God's plan. *As on us at the beginning.* Peter refers to the Day of Pentecost, the beginning of the church, when he and the others had received the same miraculous outpouring of the Spirit with a similar expression in the speaking with tongues.

16. Then remembered I the word of the Lord, how that he said, John indeed baptized with water; but ye shall be baptized with the Holy Ghost.

See Acts 1:5. The baptism of the Holy Spirit is the work of Christ (Matthew 3:11), coming as a special gift for special reasons. The apostles did not preach concerning it, and its coming on this occasion was a surprise both to Peter and to the Christians from Joppa who had accompanied him.

17. Forasmuch then as God gave them the like gift as he did unto us, who believed on the Lord Jesus Christ; what was I, that I could withstand God?

"When we believed on the Lord Jesus Christ" (American Standard Version). The outpouring of the Spirit did not come on the apostles when they first acknowledged Jesus as Messiah, but rather when their faith became active in obedience to the great commission, as it did on the Day of Pentecost. "Who was I, that I could withstand God?" (American Standard Version). God's acceptance of the Gentiles on equal terms with the Jews was abundantly clear. If God had indicated His acceptance of them, how could Peter take it upon himself to reject them?

18. When they heard these things, they held their peace, and glorified God, saying, Then hath God also to the Gentiles granted repentance unto life.

Peter succeeded in his purpose. The forthright recounting of facts supported by the witnesses that had been with him, accomplished what long arguments would never have done. The Judeans apparently gave complete and ungrudging acknowledgement of having been convinced. *Granted repentance to life.* Removed the barriers in the ways of Gentiles' repenting and finding new life in Christ Jesus.

19. Now they which were scattered abroad upon the persecution that arose about Stephen travelled as far as Phenice, and Cyprus, and Antioch, preaching the word to none but unto the Jews only.

The record goes back to Acts 8:1-4, which tells of the persecution in which Saul was a key figure, and in which "they were all scattered abroad

throughout the regions of Judaea and
Samaria, except the apostles." *Travelled as far as Phenice*. They went
beyond Samaria and Galilee northwestward to Phoenicia, the long fertile plain between the Lebanon
mountains and the Mediterranean
Sea. Its principal cities were Tyre
and Sidon, of ancient heathen no-
toriety, which Jesus had said would
receive the gospel more readily than
Capernaum did (Matthew 11:21,
22.) These cities did receive the gospel (Acts 15:3), and churches were
established there (21:3, 4; 27:3).
Cyprus, principal island of the eastern Mediterranean, was the ancestral
home of Barnabas (Acts 4:36),
Christianity spread by the principal
trade routes over land and sea. *Antioch*, a sort of "Oriental Rome," was
the starting place for the first great
missionary enterprise of the church.

**20. And some of them were men of
Cyprus and Cyrene, which, when they
were come to Antioch, spake unto the
Grecians, preaching the Lord Jesus.**

Cyrene was a city of north Africa,
having Greek culture and a large
Jewish population. *When they were
come to Antioch*. The record does
not tell whether or not they came for
the purpose of preaching; but going
into all the world, they did preach
where they went. Antioch had the
first specifically named church outside Palestine. "Spake unto the
Greeks also" (American Standard
Version). The men of Cyprus and
Cyrene were, like Barnabas and Saul,
themselves Grecians—that is, Jews
with Greek-speaking background.
Because of their wider environment,
they would naturally be quicker to
associate with Gentiles than would
the Palestinian Jews.

**21. And the hand of the Lord was
with them: and a great number believed, and turned unto the Lord.**

"A great number that believed
turned unto the Lord" (American
Standard Version). The believing
and turning were obviously not the
same thing. The nature of the "turning to the Lord" is indicated in a
parallel passage concerning the Corinthians: "Many of the Corinthians
hearing believed, and were baptized"
(Acts 18:8).

**22. Then tidings of these things
came unto the ears of the church which
was in Jerusalem: and they sent forth
Barnabas, that he should go as far
as Antioch.**

"And the report concerning them
came to the ears of the church which
was in Jerusalem" (American Standard Version). The apostles were still
the core of the church. It was natural
that any significant activity, especially of an unusual nature, should
be reported to them, even without
any official arrangement, and that
they should be interested in knowing
of every important development.
They sent forth Barnabas, just as
they had sent Peter to observe and
help in Philip's work at Samaria
(Acts 8:14). Here was a severe test
of the genuineness with which the
Jerusalem church had received the
acceptance of the Gentiles by Peter
(11:18).

**23. Who, when he came, and had
seen the grace of God, was glad, and
exhorted them all, that with purpose
of heart they would cleave unto the
Lord.**

It became immediately apparent
that the apostles had sent the right
man—one whose firm faith and generous spirit would fit him perfectly to

work with these new Christians. He was firm and bold as well as gentle and generous. His exhortation was addressed to Jew and Gentile alike.

24. For he was a good man, and full of the Holy Ghost and of faith: and much people was added unto the Lord.

Scripture is powerful in its simplicity. What a glorious tribute to any man! To be good, Spirit-filled, and faithful is better than to be great, clever, and famous. "A considerable number were added to the Lord" (Living Oracles).

25. Then departed Barnabas to Tarsus, for to seek Saul.

Acts 9:30 tells that Saul went to Tarsus in Cilicia when the Jews would have slain him in Jerusalem. Galatians 1:21 speaks of his coming into Syria and Cilicia. Paul was the best choice for the work.

26. And when he had found him, he brought him unto Antioch. And it came to pass, that a whole year they assembled themselves with the church,. and taught much people. And the disciples were called Christians first in Antioch.

When he had found him. Barnabas knew only that Saul was at Tarsus. Some search was involved. *And taught much people.* Barnabas and Saul carried on the same sort of teaching program in Antioch that the apostles had conducted in Jerusalem when the first converts met with them daily in Solomon's porch of the temple (Acts 5:12). *And the disciples were called Christians first in Antioch.* In effect, they "did business under the name of Christians." A new name for the disciples came into use, with the implication that it was immediately and widely adopted, al-though it appears in Scripture only in Acts 26:28 and 1 Peter 4:16 besides this verse. In both of those references it appears as used by outsiders. The name "Christian" is a Latinized derivation from the Greek word meaning Messiah. The Jews would not naturally use it, for they did not admit that Jesus was the Messiah. It might have been chosen by the Gentile believers themselves, or it might have been applied to them by the Gentiles. Some hold that the Greek word *chrematisai*, translated here "were called," carries with it the suggestion of divine calling. Thus they look upon this as a fulfillment of the prophecy in Isaiah 62:2. In any case, the appearance of this new name marked a point at which the followers of Christ were no longer considered a mere sect of the Jews.

27. And in these days came prophets from Jerusalem unto Antioch.

Prophets were men or women specially inspired to give messages from God—messages not learned in ordinary ways, but given to them by revelation. Through them God provided guidance for the churches before the New Testament was done.

28. And there stood up one of them named Agabus, and signified by the spirit that there should be great dearth throughout all the world: which came to pass in the days of Claudius Caesar.

Signified by the spirit. Spake as the Holy Spirit directed him. *Great dearth.* A severe famine. *All the world.* This term means the Roman Empire. The rest of the world was almost unknown to the people living under Roman dominion. *Claudius Caesar.* Roman emperor from A.D. 41 to 54.

29. Then the disciples, every man according to his ability, determined to send relief unto the brethren which dwelt in Judaea.

Though the famine was world-wide, the Christians in Judea were in greater need than those in Antioch. They had given up their regular work to listen daily to Christian teaching and to get the church strongly established (Acts 2:46). The wealthy among them had already sacrificed their wealth (Acts 4:34-37). They had been further impoverished by persecution (Acts 8:1). Because of their suffering the gospel had come to Antioch (Acts 11:19, 20), and now in gratitude the Christians of Antioch moved to relieve the suffering of the brethren in Judea. Each Christian made an offering *according to his ability*: the wealthy gave much, the poor gave little.

30. Which also they did, and sent it to the elders by the hands of Barnabas and Saul.

At first the apostles had been the leaders of the church in Jerusalem, but now there were recognized elders to supervise it, as became the custom in other congregations (Acts 14:23). Perhaps they were ended because the apostles were now working much of the time outside of Jerusalem. Acts 9 and 10 tell something of Peter's work in other places. The apostles still kept in touch with the Jerusalem church and were influential along with the elders (Acts 15:2), but the offering was sent *to the elders* for distribution to the needy. *Barnabas and Saul,* outstanding leaders in Antioch, were chosen to deliver it.

CHAPTER 12

1. Now about that time Herod the king stretched forth his hands to vex certain of the church.

This event probably occurred in A.D. 44. The church had by this time passed through the first decade of its triumphant history. Amid bitter persecution that sought first to silence and then to destroy, the disciples had with amazing boldness effectively proclaimed the gospel to the high and the low. Verses 1-19 of this chapter reveal how Peter and John and the others met the tidal wave of persecution. Following the healing of the lame man and the sermon that Peter preached on that occasion, Peter and John were arrested and tried before the Sanhedrin. But to these fearless messengers of Christ, this was the very sort of opportunity they desired—the opportunity to preach to these wicked leaders of the nation. These Sadducees and Pharisees decided to threaten them if they did not cease their proclamation of Jesus: "And they called them, and commanded them not to speak at all nor teach in the name of Jesus" (Acts 4:18). "But Peter and John answered and said unto them, Whether it be right in the sight of God to hearken unto you more than unto God, judge ye. For we cannot but speak the things which we have seen and heard" (verses 19, 20).

Now after more than ten years *Herod the king,* who was Herod Agrippa I, the grandson of Herod the Great, determined to gain favor with Jewish religious and political leaders by giving to them some decisive assistance. *To vex certain of the church.* Imprisonment and death give a very dark meaning to the word "vex."

2. And he killed James the brother of John with the sword.

The extreme brevity of the account reveals a divine restraint. All the details of the arrest, summary trial, and execution are omitted. James was beheaded, becoming the first of the apostles to suffer death for Christ. Years before this, they had declared they were ready to die for Christ, but they had not left an enviable record in their behavior in Gethsemane and at the trials and death of Christ. But they now faced death for Christ without flinching

3. And because he saw it pleased the Jews, he proceeded further to take Peter also. (Then were the days of unleavened bread.)

He saw it pleased the Jews. The approval and praise of the Jewish leaders now led Herod to go a step further and arrest the leader of the church. The days of unleavened bread immediately followed the Passover. James and Peter must have reflected that their death was occurring as had that of Jesus at the Passover.

It seems likely that Herod had heard of the mysterious fashion in which the apostles had earlier escaped from prison and had been found the next morning preaching in the temple (Acts 5:19-21), and so he was determined that there would be no escape this time. He therefore assigned four soldiers to guard Peter at a time: Peter was chained to two, and the other two guarded the doors inside and out-

side. But God sent an angel to deliver Peter from prison (verses 6-10). Like Stephen, James was expendable. But the church still needed the leadership of Peter. Therefore God intervened to save him from death at this time.

4. And when he had apprehended him, he put him in prison, and delivered him to four quaternions of soldiers to keep him; intending after Easter to bring him forth to the people.

When he had apprehended him. Some little difficulty is indicated. At the death of James, the church may have taken precautions to protect the other apostles from a similar fate. *Four quaternions of soldiers to keep him.* Herod knew that on a former occasion this same Peter, with others of the apostles, had been arrested and put in the common prison, only to disappear, so that he was found the next morning preaching in the market place (Acts 5:17-25). No satisfactory explanation of the escape had been forthcoming. Herod was taking no chances on its happening again. He authorized a guard of four groups of four soldiers each, relieving each other at three-hour intervals. Peter was chained between two of the soldiers (v. 6), and two others were on guard at spaced intervals before the doors (v. 10), probably to forestall any attempt of the church to rescue him.

5. Peter therefore was kept in prison: but prayer was made without ceasing of the church unto God for him.

The contrast is powerfully drawn, with Herod and the Jews on one side responsible for the imprisonment, and the church and God on the other working in Peter's behalf "Earnest and continued prayer was made to God on his account, by the congregation" (Living Oracles). Two things seem to indicate that the church was not praying for Peter's release. In the prayer recorded in Acts 4:23-30 there is no petition for the apostles' comfort or safety. When Peter was released the church was surprised and incredulous (vv. 13-15). The prayer of faith would not have been thus amazed at its fulfillment. In the spirit of their former prayers, therefore, it seems likely that they prayed that he might remain faithful. The services of prayer were going on in several places at the same time. James the brother of Jesus was in some group other than the one meeting at the house of Mary (v. 17).

6. And when Herod would have brought him forth, the same night Peter was sleeping between two soldiers, bound with two chains: and the keepers before the door kept the prison.

"And when Herod was ready to have brought him out, even that very night" (Living Oracles). This was to have been Peter's last night. Probably both he and the church knew it. Their prayers persisted to the end. *Peter was sleeping.* The prayers of the church were already answered. Far from denying the faith, Peter was serene in the face of death. He remembered, no doubt, the prophecy of Jesus that at the end of his days "another shall gird thee, and carry thee whither thou wouldest not" (John 21:18). He understood, as John did, that Jesus thus signified "by what death he should glorify God," and he was prepared for it. *Between two soldiers, bound with two chains: and the keepers before*

the door kept the prison. One is reminded of the care with which the Jews made the tomb of Jesus as sure as they could (Matthew 27:65).

7. And, behold, the angel of the Lord came upon him, and a light shined in the prison: and he smote Peter on the side, and raised him up, saying, Arise up quickly. And his chains fell off from his hands.

"An angel of the Lord stood by him, and a light shined in the cell" (American Standard Version). The description of angelic visitation is characteristic (Compare Luke 2:9): the standing of the heavenly messenger in the company of the person visited, and the light accompanying. "He smote Peter on the side, and awoke him, saying, Rise up quickly" (American Standard Version). Both the blow and the word were designed to arouse Peter from his slumber. *And the chains fell off from his hands.* A vivid detail, but without further explanation, in a whole series of miracles.

8. And the angel said unto him, Gird thyself, and bind on thy sandals. And so he did. And he saith unto him, Cast thy garment about thee, and follow me.

Peter had prepared himself for sleeping by removing, and perhaps covering himself with, his outer garment, loosening his tunic, and taking off his sandals. The angel did not do for Peter what he could do for himself: hence he commanded Peter to clothe himself. The release was effected with dispatch, but without undue haste. Nothing was left behind, and Peter was ready for travel when he got outside.

9. And he went out, and followed him; and wist not that it was true

which was done by the angel; but
thought he saw a vision.

Went out, and followed. Still half
asleep, Peter obeyed and acted without full comprehension. "And knew
not that it was true which was done
by the angel" (American Standard
Version). Roused suddenly from
deep slumber, he needed time and
full awakening to realize that the experience was not a dream.

10. When they were past the first
and the second ward, they came unto
the iron gate that leadeth unto the
city; which opened to them of his
own accord: and they went out, and
passed on through one street; and
forthwith the angel departed from
him.

"Past the first and second guard"
(American Standard Version). Probably Peter's private guard of soldiers,
placed to forestall any attempt to rescue him (v. 4). Scripture does not
satisfy our curiosity by explaining the
miracle that brought Peter past these
watchmen without being challenged.
They went out. One of the ancient
manuscripts adds what is probably an
authentic detail: "Down the seven
steps" to the iron gate. *Which opened
to them of his own accord.* The last
of the miracles by which the release
was accomplished, it is like the opening of the doors of the prison at
Philippi (Acts 16:26). *Passed on
through one street; and forthwith the
angel departed from him.* Having
brought Peter about a block down
the darkened street from the prison,
the angel was needed no longer, and
so he left the apostle to his own devices.

11. And when Peter was come to
himself, he said, Now I know of a
surety, that the Lord hath sent his

angel, and hath delivered me out of
the hand of Herod, and from all the
expectation of the people of the Jews.

Peter must have stood for a moment to think the matter through and
come to a realization of what had
happened. *The Lord hath sent his
angel.* The angel had not identified
himself as being different from any
man; but the circumstances were
enough to show Peter the source of
his rescue. *Out of the hand of
Herod.* Herod could not say as Jesus
said of His followers, "Neither shall
any man pluck them out of my hand"
(John 10:28). "And [from] all that
the Jewish people were expecting"
(Goodspeed). Some enemies of
Christ and the church had anticipated a repetition of the grisly amuse-
ment they had enjoyed at Calvary.
Others had looked forward at least to
seeing the church crippled by the
loss of its most prominent leader.

12. And when he had considered
the thing, he came to the house of
Mary the mother of John, whose surname was Mark; where many were
gathered together praying.

The angel guide had departed
without giving further directions.
Peter had to decide for himself,
quickly, on the spot, where he would
go and what he would do. He determined, it seems, to leave Jerusalem
and withdraw to some place of comparative safety (v. 17). But first he
would put the minds of the brethren
at rest by telling them of the amazing result of their prayers. *He came
to the house of Mary the mother of
John, whose surname was Mark.*
John Mark became a companion to
Peter (1 Peter 5:13), and incorporated many of the personal recollec-
tions of Peter in the Gospel he wrote.

Mark's mother was a sister of Barnabas (Colossians 4:10). Her house, large enough to have a gate to its courtyard and a door within the gate, and a portress attending the door (v. 13), seems to have been a place of regular meeting for the church. One tradition says that it was the site of Jesus' last supper with the apostles. "Where many were gathered together and were praying" (American Standard Version). How remarkable that a prayer meeting should be interrupted with the news that God had already granted all they asked and much more besides!

13. And as Peter knocked at the door of the gate, a damsel came to hearken, named Rhoda.

Without interrupting the prayer meeting, this girl came to see who was at the door.

14. And when she knew Peter's voice, she opened not the gate for gladness, but ran in, and told how Peter stood before the gate.

Presumably the girl asked who was there, and Peter responded. Recognizing his voice, she was too excited to think or act logically. Apparently her first thought was for the anxious people in the house. Without even opening the door, she rushed to tell them Peter had come.

15. And they said unto her, Thou art mad. But she constantly affirmed that it was even so. Then said they, It is his angel.

"You're crazy," the people said to Rhoda. It seemed simply unbelievable that Peter was free. But Rhoda knew what she had heard. We can imagine how excitedly almost hysterically, she kept declaring *that it was even so.* Trying to quiet her, the people suggested, *It is his angel.* To us this brings immediately the thought of a heavenly being. We must remember, however, that *angelos* was an ordinary Greek word for a messenger, whether heavenly or earthly. This word is used for messengers sent by John the Baptist (Luke 7:24) and of John himself (Luke 7:27). It seems likely that the people were saying to the excited Rhoda, "It can't be Peter; perhaps it is a messenger from him. Perhaps you misunderstood what he said through the door. Instead of 'I am Peter' he must have said, 'I have word from Peter.'"

16. But Peter continued knocking: and when they had opened the door, and saw him, they were astonished.

The argument with Rhoda could hardly have lasted more than a minute or two. While it was still going on, perhaps, some of the people hastened to settle it in the obvious way—by opening the door. To their amazement it really was Peter.

17. But he, beckoning unto them with the hand to hold their peace, declared unto them how the Lord had brought him out of the prison. And he said, Go shew these things unto James, and to the brethren. And he departed, and went into another place.

Peter's first care was to relieve the anxiety of his brethren. They would rejoice to know that he not only was free, but had been freed miraculously by a heavenly angel. This he told to the group at Mary's house and asked them to give the news to the rest of the believers, among whom *James,* the brother of Jesus (Galatians 1:19), was a leader. Peter's next care was to avoid bringing any further anxiety to his friends. Herod's men would soon be searching for him, and Herod's wrath might fall on any who were found with him. He therefore went to *another place*. Evidently it was a place where the police could not find him, and perhaps none of his Christian friends knew where it was.

18. Now as soon as it was day, there was no small stir among the soldiers, what was become of Peter.

The angel who managed Peter's escape must have brought a sleep or a trance upon the guards so that they did not know what happened, else a turmoil would have arisen before daybreak. No small *stir* sounds like a classic understatement. There must have been a terrific stir when it was known that a prisoner had escaped from "maximum security."

19. And when Herod had sought for him, and found him not, he examined the keepers, and commanded that they should be put to death. And he went down from Judaea to Caesarea, and there abode.

What an exciting chapter Luke could have written—the soldiers turning the city upside down, Herod in fury questioning the guards, the sentence of violent death! This was the usual punishment of guards who allowed a prisoner to escape. But Peter was not found, and Herod finally retired to *Caesarea*, where he probably had a magnificent home. He had been in Jerusalem for the Passover feast (Acts 12:3), perhaps both to gain favor with the Jews and to be at hand to give orders in case rioting broke out, as it sometimes did when great crowds were in Jerusalem for a feast.

20. And Herod was highly displeased with them of Tyre and Sidon: but they came with one accord to him, and, having made Blastus the king's chamberlain their friend, desired peace; because their country was nourished by the king's country.

Herod Agrippa I was now king of all Palestine. For some reason now unknown, he was hostile to the neighboring Phoenician land, where Tyre and Sidon were the chief cities. People of that area were mostly seamen and traders, not farmers. King Herod's country was the most convenient place for them to buy foodstuffs, and so *their country was nourished by the king's country*. Consequently they were much concerned about Herod's hostility. By persuasion or bribery they got *Blastus the king's chamberlain* to intercede for them; and when opportunity was given, a large number of them came to seek the king's favor.

21. And upon a set day Herod, arrayed in royal apparel, sat upon his throne, and made an oration unto them.

The historian Josephus adds that Herod arranged a great show at Caesarea and appeared in a garment all of silver. He was making the most of an opportunity to parade his royal splendor.

22. And the people gave a shout, saying, It is the voice of a god, and not of a man.

Josephus attributes this cry to flatterers scattered throughout the crowd. As the shout arose in various places, no doubt it was taken up by others until it seemed that the whole multitude in the great stadium was shouting praises to Herod as divine.

23. And immediately the angel of the Lord smote him, because he gave not God the glory: and he was eaten of worms, and gave up the ghost.

"Whosoever exalteth himself shall be abased" (Luke 14:11). In His own way and His own time God crushes the arrogance of rulers who would give His place to themselves. Josephus says Herod lingered in great pain for five days before he died.

24. But the word of God grew and multiplied.

Herod's persecution died with him, and still the message of God increased its influence and effectiveness as His people proclaimed it.

25. And Barnabas and Saul returned from Jerusalem, when they had fulfilled their ministry, and took with them John, whose surname was Mark.

Acts 11:27-30 explains why Barnabas and Saul were in Jerusalem. They had gone there with gifts from the brethren in Antioch to help the famine-stricken disciples in Judea. *Barnabas* was a relative of John Mark. In the King James Version of Colossians 4:10, included in the latter part of our text, Mark is called "sister's son to Barnabas," indicating that Barnabas was a brother of Mary. The same Greek word is used of a cousin as well as a nephew, however, so we cannot be sure what the relationship was. Barnabas was not one of the twelve apostles, but was a noteworthy Christian in Jerusalem (Acts 4:36, 37; 9:26, 27). He had gone to Antioch to assist in the church-planting venture there (Acts 11:19-24). *Saul*, of course, was the former persecutor of the church who later became Paul, the great missionary-evangelist. At Barnabas' urging, he too had gone to help at Antioch.

CHAPTER 13

1. Now there were in the church that was at Antioch certain prophets and teachers; as Barnabas, and Simeon that was called Niger, and Lucius of Cyrene, and Manaen, which had been brought up with Herod the tetrarch, and Saul.

This is Antioch of Syria, not to be confused with Pisidian Antioch mentioned in verse 14. The emphasis here is on the city. This may indicate that more than one congregation of Christians met there. *Certain prophets and teachers.* Leaders who spoke with direct inspiration from God (1 Corinthians 14:1-40), and who had the facts of the gospel by which they conveyed the teaching of the apostles. *Barnabas* had been sent by the apostles from Jerusalem. He had already earned the admiration, confidence, and affection of the brethren for his generosity (4:36, 37), fairmindedness (9:27), and power as an encourager of the saints (11:22-24). *Simeon that was called Niger.* The name "Simeon" was common among the Jews. This man was probably called Niger (black) because of his dark hair and swarthy complexion. *Lucius of Cyrene.* See Acts 11:20. Lucius may have been one of those from the "parts of Libya about Cyrene" who were present in Jerusalem on the Day of Pentecost (Acts 2:10). "Manaen the foster brother of Herod the tetrarch" (American Standard Version). This was not the first invasion of the royal household by Christian influence, however. Joanna, wife of Chuzas, Herod's steward, was one of the women who gave financial support to the ministry of Jesus (Luke 8:3). It is small wonder, then, that Agrippa, another of the same household, was curious to hear the gospel from Paul (Acts 26). *And Saul.* The newest addition to the corps of leaders at Antioch is named last. How soon the order was to be reversed (verse 13)!

2. As they ministered to the Lord, and fasted, the Holy Ghost said, Separate me Barnabas and Saul for the work whereunto I have called them.

Service in the name of Christ was a "ministry to the Lord." *And fasted.* Fasting was a normal accompaniment to prayer. No ritual fasting is necessarily implied. *The Holy Ghost said.* So prominent is the personal activity of the Holy Spirit in the events recorded in Acts that the book is often called "the gospel of the Holy Spirit." See 8:29, 39; 10:19; 11:12; 16:6. *The work whereunto I have called them.* Saul had already been called to be the apostle to the Gentiles (26:16). Scripture does not tell just when Barnabas received the special commission here referred to, and by which he was called an apostle (14:4, 14).

3. And when they had fasted and prayed, and laid their hands on them, they sent them away.

The solemnity of the occasion made prayer with fasting appropriate *Laid their hands on them.* It is impossible to say just who participated in the laying on of the hands. No hierarchal installation is indicated. It seems unlikely that special powers were conferred, since the ones on whom hands were laid had already received appointments and powers of apostleship beyond the possession of those who participated in this "ordi-

nation." The gesture indicated the conveyance of a task and a responsibility, together with the participants' pledge of fellowship in the doing of the work. "They dismissed them" (Living Oracles translation). From such "sending away" we derive the terms *mission* and *missionary* to describe the work.and the person of the one sent. The significance of this dismissal involves more than seeing them aboard the ship and bidding them farewell. They were going to a heathen country. There was no church there to support them. Traveling costs and expense of daily living all had to be met by the church at Antioch. The church was obligated thus to support them as their "living link" to carry the gospel to the ends of the earth. It seems that for a time Antioch faltered in its obligations. Paul at Corinth was compelled to resort to his trade to support himself and helpers until Philippi and Thessalonica came to the rescue.

4. So they, being sent forth by the Holy Ghost, departed unto Seleucia; and from thence they sailed to Cyprus.

The church at Antioch had acted as the Holy Spirit's agent in commissioning the party. "Went down to Seleucia" (American Standard Version). Seleucia, the seaport of Antioch, was their port of embarkation. *They sailed to Cyprus,* the principal island of the eastern Mediterranean, nearly a hundred miles southwest from Seleucia. In going there, Barnabas was approaching his own people (4:36), as Saul had already done in going to Tarsus (11:25). Cyprus had a large Jewish population, to which the missionaries·could address themselves.

5. And when they were at Salamis, they preached the word of God in the synagogues of the Jews: and they had also John to their minister.

Of special interest in this lesson is the fact that young John Mark went with the two evangelists. No reason is given except the one seen in this verse. From the use of the word "minister," we may conclude that he served as their assistant. Thus he had a wonderful opportunity for on-the-job training with these two seasoned evangelists. If he did not help with preaching and teaching from the start, we can imagine he made himself useful by taking care of the baggage, securing food and lodging, and so on. *Salamis* was probably the city where they landed on Cyprus.

6. And when they had gone through the isle unto Paphos, they found. a certain sorcerer, a false prophet, a Jew, whose name was Bar-jesus.

Salamis was at the east end of the island; Paphos was near the west end. Barnabas and Saul may have preached in some of the towns between, but the brief record omits them and gives an unusual incident in Paphos. This *sorcerer,* like the one we read about in Acts 8, probably used sleight of hand and other "magical" methods to convince people that he had supernatural power. A *false prophet* was one who falsely claimed to be a spokesman for God. The name *Bar-jesus* means son of Jesus. Probably it has no reference to Jesus of Nazareth, but merely indicates that the · magician's father also was named Jesus. This name is the Greek form of "Joshua."

7. Which was with the deputy of the country, Sergius Paulus, a prudent man; who called for Barnabas and Saul, and desired to hear the word of God.

This *deputy* was what the Romans called a proconsul: he was the governor, or chief man, *of the country.* He was prudent, which means intelligent or wise. If it seems strange to us that such a man would have a sham magician among his counselors, we need to remember that it takes considerable intelligence and perception to be a good magician. It is quite likely that this man had given the proconsul good advice on various occasions. Apparently Sergius Paulus was open-minded as well as intelligent. Upon hearing that teachers of a new religion were in town, he invited them to tell him about their faith.

8. But Elymas the sorcerer (for so is his name by interpretation) withstood them, seeking to turn away the deputy from the faith.

In the Jewish language of the time, *Elymas* was the word for *sorcerer.* This magician opposed Barnabas and Saul, probably fearing they would undermine his influence with the proconsul.

9. Then Saul, (who also is called Paul,) filled with the Holy Ghost, set his eyes on him.

Thus is introduced the name *Paul,* by which Saul is called through the rest of the book. In the Greek it is *Paulus,* the same as the surname of the proconsul; but as to why it is now used of Saul we have no explanation. Saul, or Paul, now turned his full attention upon the magician who was opposing his message. The punishment described in the following verses was not Paul's vengeance but God's warning, for Paul was *filled* and controlled by *the Holy Ghost.*

10. And said, O full of all subtilty and all mischief, thou child of the devil, thou enemy of all righteousness, wilt thou not cease to pervert the right ways of the Lord?

Subtilty is craftiness, or deceit; *mischief* is guile, or villainy. "Son of Jesus" was no proper name for this deceiver, said Paul; he was better called *child of the devil.* He was gifted with intelligence, but he was misusing it to *pervert,* twist, misrepresent *the right ways of the Lord,* which Paul was teaching truthfully.

11. And now, behold, the hand of the Lord is upon thee, and thou shalt be blind, not seeing the sun for a season. And immediately there fell on him a mist and a darkness; and he went about seeking some to lead him by the hand.

At Paul's word, or more properly, at the Holy Spirit's word spoken through Paul, the magician became blind. *For a season* implies that his sight was later restored, but we are not told how soon.

12. Then the deputy, when he saw what was done, believed, being astonished at the doctrine of the Lord.

If the proconsul was wavering between Paul's word and the magician's, he now wavered no longer. It was evident that Paul represented a power superior to all of Elymas' magic. We are not told whether any other miracles were done in Paphos, but this one was decisive. Somewhat surprisingly, the record does not say the proconsul was *astonished* at the Lord's power or work, but at His *doctrine* or teaching. Obviously the teaching given through Paul was closely allied with the

power manifested through Paul. Sergius Paulus *believed* that both were of God, and so he accepted the gospel.

13. Now when Paul and his company loosed from Paphos, they came to Perga in Pamphylia: and John departing from them returned to Jerusalem.

Paul and his company. Paul's bold answer to the opposition of Bar-Jesus had established him as the natural leader of the group, a position which he held from that time on. It is much to the credit of Barnabas that he surrendered his leadership with no sign of jealousy or waning enthusiasm. "Set sail from Paphos" (American Standard Version). The capital city was also the western seaport of the island. *Perga in Pamphylia,* the capital city on the southern coast of Asia Minor about 250 miles west of Tarsus. Paul was no doubt well acquainted with the territory. *John departing.* We are not told why John Mark withdrew, but it is clear from later reference to the incident (15:37-40) that Paul considered his motives unworthy. Mark may have resented the eclipse of his kinsman Barnabas in leadership; he may have objected to the acceptance of Gentile converts; he may have feared to go among the "wild and lawless clans" for which the Pisidian highlands were noted; or he may simply have lacked the perseverance needed for continued strenuous labors. Whatever the cause, he later proved his worth, not only to Barnabas, but also to Paul (Colossians 4: 10; 2 Timothy 4:11).

14. But when they departed from Perga, they came to Antioch in Pisidia, and went into the synagogue on the sabbath day, and sat down.

Scripture gives no explanation for Paul's leaving Perga without any indication of having preached there. Some have suggested, from Galatians 4:13, that Paul was forced by reasons of health to leave the malarial plains about Perga for the higher and more healthful uplands of south Galatia. Pisidian Antioch was a center of military and civil authority. *Went into the synagogue on the sabbath day, and sat down.* This was the natural place to secure a hearing for the preaching of Christ as the Jews' Messiah. It seems probable from verse 15 that Paul and Barnabas had approached the ruler of the synagogue before the service and asked permission to speak.

15. And after the reading of the law and the prophets the rulers of the synagogue sent unto them, saying, Ye men and brethren, if ye have any word of exhortation for the people, say on.

It seems to have been the custom to invite visiting teachers to speak in the synagogue. Jesus had spoken thus in many places and at many times (Mark 1:39).

16. Then Paul stood up, and beckoning with his hand said, Men of Israel, and ye that fear God, give audience.

Men of Israel of course were Jews, and of course they feared God. However, *ye that fear God* probably was Paul's address to Gentiles in the audience. Where Jewish influence was felt, many of them had forsaken paganism and accepted the true God, although they had not been circumcised and formally inducted into the Jewish race. Such a one was Cornelius of Caesarea (Acts 10:2). In many places these god-fearing Gentiles worshiped in the synagogues along with the Jews.

17. The God of this people of Israel chose our fathers, and exalted the people when they dwelt as strangers in the land of Egypt, and with an high arm brought he them out of it.

The history of their nation was familiar to all the Jews. Probably parts of it were repeated nearly every Sabbath so that it was well known also to Gentiles who attended the synagogue meetings. The deliverance from Egypt was especially clear to Jews who lived in Gentile lands as did these in Antioch. Many of them were fervently hoping that God would repeat that deliverance, bringing them again to the land of promise with a leader like Moses (Deuteronomy 18:15).

18. And about the time of forty years suffered he their manners in the wilderness.

Some ancient manuscripts have "he nourished them in the wilderness," which is a very fitting summary of God's care during the wanderings recorded in Exodus and Numbers. It is true, however, that God did *suffer* or tolerate a great deal of bad *manners* on the part of His people during those *forty years.*

19. And when he had destroyed seven nations in the land of Chanaan, he divided their land to them by lot.

The history recorded in the book of Joshua is thus summarized in a sentence. It is possible that Paul spoke at greater length and Luke abbreviated his address; but even so the speech must have greatly abbreviated the history. By recalling this history, however briefly, Paul was identifying himself with his hearers. He was one of them; he shared their pride in the past and their hope for the future.

20. And after that he gave unto them judges about the space of four hundred and fifty years, until Samuel the prophet.

Thus another single sentence summarizes the book of Judges and part of 1 Samuel.

21. And afterward they desired a king: and God gave unto them Saul the son of Cis, a man of the tribe of Benjamin, by the space of forty years.

So the kingdom of Israel had its beginning. The name of King Saul's father, *Cis*, appears as "Kish" in our version of the Old Testament. Such differences in spelling come about because the letters of the alphabet are not exactly the same in Hebrew and Greek and English.

22. And when he had removed him, he raised up unto them David to be their king; to whom also he gave testimony, and said, I have found David the son of Jesse, a man after mine own heart, which shall fulfil all my will.

The kingdom of Israel made its most spectacular advance under the rule of David, and this king was specially honored also for his godliness. He was a man after God's own heart (1 Samuel 13:14).

23. Of this man's seed hath God according to his promise raised unto Israel a Saviour, Jesus.

The Old Testament has many references to God's *promise* that David's descendants would rule forever (2 Samuel 7:12-16; Psalm 89:20-29). The coming *Saviour*, the Messiah or Christ, the great deliverer of Israel, the prophet like Moses, was to be the son of David (Matthew 22:42). Paul announced that God's promise was now fulfilled: the Messiah had come.

24. When John had first preached before his coming the baptism of repentance to all the people of Israel.

No doubt Paul told much more than is recorded here about the work of John the Baptist and Jesus. Luke had already written much about this in his Gospel; he therefore summarized Paul's address very briefly. Among other things, Paul probably pointed out that John fulfilled the closing prophecy of the Old Testament (Malachi 4:5, 6).

25. And as John fulfilled his course, he said, Whom think ye that I am? I am not he. But, behold, there cometh one after me, whose shoes of his feet I am not worthy to loose.

Paul emphasized the greatness of Jesus by recalling that He was incomparably greater than John, even though John came in the spirit and power of Elijah.

26. Men and brethren, children of the stock of Abraham, and whosoever among you feareth God, to you is the word of this salvation sent.

Even before he finished the story of Jesus, Paul broke in excitedly to tell his hearers that God's message of salvation was for them personally —not only the Jews, *children of the stock of Abraham,* but also the Gentiles worshiping with them, *whosoever among you feareth God.*

27. For they that dwell at Jerusalem, and their rulers, because they knew him not, nor yet the voices of the prophets which are read every sabbath day, they have fulfilled them in condemning him.

With unerring precision Paul

pointed out the failure of the Jewish leaders in Jerusalem—he knew it well because it had been his own! They studied *the prophets* and read them publicly *every sabbath*—the prophets that declared the Messiah would be despised and rejected—but they did not know them. Led astray by their own selfish desires, they saw only the prophecies of triumph and majesty. Consequently they did not know the Messiah when He came. They themselves despised and rejected Him, thus fulfilling the prophecies they had failed to know.

28. And though they found no cause of death in him, yet desired they Pilate that he should be slain.

Volumes might be written on the innocence of Jesus and the injustice of His death, but again a single sentence tells the story.

29. And when they had fulfilled all that was written of him, they took him down from the tree, and laid him in a sepulchre.

Again comes the reminder that the vengeful enemies of Jesus brought about the fulfillment of God's promise and God's purpose. They accomplished what His hand and His counsel had determined (Acts 4:28).

30. But God raised him from the dead.

Thus God himself continued the accomplishment of His purpose, overruling the malice of the vengeful enemies and presenting life after death as an accomplished fact.

31. And he was seen many days of them which came up with him from Galilee to Jerusalem, who are his witnesses unto the people.

In any time and place a story of rising from the dead is apt to be doubted. Paul hastened to say that this report was verified by many competent witnesses. The fact was established beyond any doubt.

32, 33. And we declare unto you glad tidings, how that the promise which was made unto the fathers, God hath fulfilled the same unto us their children, in that he hath raised up Jesus again; as it is also written in the second psalm, Thou art my Son, this day have I begotten thee.

"Good news!" said Paul. "The ancient promise to our fathers is fulfilled in our time by the resurrection of Jesus to live forever." He cited *the second psalm,* in which God promised eternal dominion to His Son.

34. And as concerning that he raised him up from the dead, now no more to return to corruption, he said on this wise, I will give you the sure mercies of David.

Still dwelling on the theme that Jesus was raised to die no more, Paul called to mind the fifty-fifth chapter of Isaiah, in which *the sure mercies of David* are linked with "an everlasting covenant." This joyous Messianic song calls to mind the promise that David's Son, the Messiah, would rule forever. Even death could not end His reign.

35. Wherefore he saith also in another psalm, Thou shalt not suffer thine Holy One to see corruption.

This verse from Psalm 16:10 also is called to testify to the resurrection of the Messiah. God would not allow His body to decay.

36. For David, after he had served his own generation by the will of God, fell on sleep, and was laid unto his fathers, and saw corruption.

The promise of Psalm 16:10 could not possibly apply to David himself, for he died and was buried, and his body decayed.

37. But he, whom God raised again, saw no corruption.

In Jesus was the fulfillment and explanation of the promise. His body did not decay because God promptly restored it to life. Peter used this same line of teaching in Acts 2:25-32.

38. Be it known unto you therefore, men and brethren, that through this man is preached unto you the forgiveness of sins.

Paul was not offering anything on his own authority; he spoke for the one whom God had approved and had shown His approval by raising Him from the dead. In the name of this risen Saviour Paul offered *forgiveness of sins*.

39. And by him all that believe are justified from all things, from which ye could not be justified by the law of Moses.

The inadequacy of the old law is discussed at length in Hebrews, and Paul may have said more than is recorded on this point. He declared emphatically that complete justification is available through Christ.

40. Beware therefore, lest that come upon you, which is spoken of in the prophets.

To the shining promise to believers (v. 39), Paul added a solemn warning to unbelievers. Here again he did not give his own statement, but drew on the prophets known and honored by his hearers.

41. Behold, ye despisers, and wonder, and perish: for I work a work in your days, a work which ye shall in no wise believe, though a man declare it unto you.

The quotation is from Habakkuk 1:5. Many of Paul's hearers, no doubt, considered his report of a resurrection hard to believe. He reminded them that a work hard to believe was just what they ought to expect in the days of the Messiah. But there was no end but death for the unbelievers who persisted in despising the mighty works of God.

42. And when the Jews were gone out of the synagogue, the Gentiles besought that these words might be preached to them the next sabbath.

There is some difference in the manuscripts at this point. The American Standard Version reads, "And as they went out, they besought that these words might be spoken to them the next sabbath." This seems to fit well with the following verse. Whatever the original reading may have been, it is clear that Paul was invited to speak again the following sabbath, and he accepted the invitation.

43. Now when the congregation was broken up, many of the Jews and religious proselytes followed Paul and Barnabas: who, speaking to them, persuaded them to continue in the grace of God.

Many were not willing to wait a week to hear more. They followed Paul and Barnabas, perhaps to their place of lodging, and it may be that some returned every day throughout the week.

44. And the next sabbath day came almost the whole city together to hear the word of God.

The previous verses recount the sermon of Paul, in essential features very much like the sermon of Peter on the Day of Pentecost; declaring Jesus to be the fulfillment of prophecy, recounting His sacrificial death and resurrection, and proclaiming salvation in Him. An interested audience asked to hear more the next Sabbath. *Almost the whole city*. Gentiles as well as Jews, gathered. The sermon of the first Sabbath had been a central topic of conversation, and the missionaries themselves had not been idle during the intervening days. The crowd almost certainly overflowed the synagogue. The speaker, standing at the door, could be heard by those within and by a throng outside. *To hear the word of God*. Whether or not they knew the divine source of Paul's message, the populace was interested, and Paul spoke the word of God.

45. But when the Jews saw the multitudes, they were filled with envy, and spake against those things which were spoken by Paul, contradicting and blaspheming.

Paul's popularity aroused the resentment of the Jews, and the inclusion of Gentiles in his following gave them a religious reason to express it. *They were filled with jealousy*, "and contradicted the things which were spoken by Paul" (American Standard Version). Comments interrupting a synagogue sermon were not uncommon. On this occasion they turned the sermon into a debate, informal and heated. "And blasphemed" (American Standard Version). The American Standard Version footnote has "railed." The railing against Paul became blasphemous as it reviled the name of Jesus.

46. Then Paul and Barnabas waxed bold, and said, It was necessary that

the word of God should first have been spoken to you: but seeing ye put it from you, and judge yourselves unworthy of everlasting life, lo, we turn to the Gentiles.

The possibility for an orderly discourse by one speaker had passed. Insistently, and probably repeatedly, both Paul and Barnabas made clear God's plan and their intentions concerning it. *It was necessary that the word of God should first have been spoken to you*. Both in the flesh and in the gospel Jesus came first "unto his own, and his own received him not. But as many as received him, to them gave he power to become the sons of God" (John 1:11, 12). The order of approach was to the Jews first, and also to the Greek (Romans 1:16). "Ye thrust it from you, and judge yourselves unworthy of eternal life" (American Standard Version). Their attitude showed them to be unworthy of God's gift and fitted only for the condemnation spoken by Christ, "Cast . . . your pearls before swine" (Matthew 7:6). *Lo, we turn to the Gentiles*. Paul would not continue in the synagogue, violating the Jews' right to control their own worship. The transfer of attention was deliberate and announced (compare Acts 18:6; 28:28).

47. For so hath the Lord commanded us, saying, I have set thee to be a light of the Gentiles, that thou shouldest be for salvation unto the ends of the earth.

The command here quoted referred to the evangelizing of the Gentiles rather than the turning from the Jews. *I have set thee to be a light of the Gentiles*. The quotation is from Isaiah 49:6 in which God's servant is commissioned to go to the Gentiles

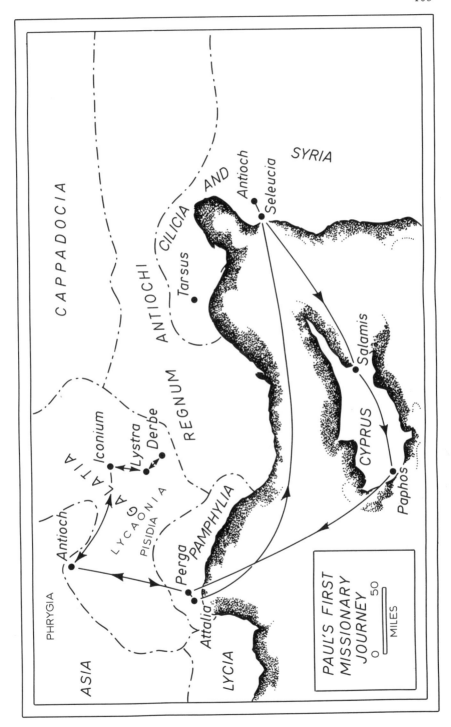

PAUL'S FIRST MISSIONARY JOURNEY

0   50
MILES

SYRIA

CAPPADOCIA

CILICIA AND

Antioch
Seleucia

ANTIOCHI

Tarsus

Salamis

CYPRUS

REGNUM

Iconium

Lystra Derbe

GALATIA

LYCAONIA

Paphos

Antioch

PISIDIA

PAMPHYLIA

Perga

PHRYGIA

Attalia

ASIA

LYCIA

as well as to the Jews. Luke 2: 32 applies the prophecy to Jesus. The apostles accepted the world-wide mission of Jesus as the God-given responsibility of the church. The salvation that Jesus provides is effective only as His gospel goes forth to the ends of the earth.

48. And when the Gentiles heard this, they were glad, and glorified the word of the Lord: and as many as were ordained to eternal life believed.

Earnest, high-minded Gentiles had long been impressed with the moral qualities of the Jewish religion, and many had either become proselytes or at least interested and sympathetic observers. Now to be accepted equally with the Jews into the salvation that had been spoken by the prophets was almost more than these Gentiles could believe. *Glorified the word of the Lord,* by their acceptance of it even more than by their words of admiration for it. "As many as were disposed for eternal life" (Living Oracles translation). The word translated "ordained" in the King James Version signifies "to place in rank or order." The usual interpretation views God as "ordaining" to eternal life, and this is acceptable if it is understood to allow the freedom of the human will. God has planned and provided for the salvation of all men (1 Timothy 2:4; 4:10), and has placed in the ranks of the saved the honest, sincere, and obedient ones who will accept His provision. In a very real sense, those who were "ordained to eternal life" were thus ordained by themselves through their own choice. Cook has, "as many as had marshalled themselves, placed themselves in the ranks of those who welcomed the offer of eternal life."

Believed. The word includes full and steadfast obedience.

49. And the word of the Lord was published throughout all the region.

This explains why Pisidian Antioch was chosen for special attention by the apostles. It was the kind of city from which the fame and influence of the gospel would radiate to a considerable territory.

50. But the Jews stirred up the devout and honourable women, and the chief men of the city, and raised persecution against Paul and Barnabas, and expelled them out of their coasts.

It seems that prominent *women* of the city had considerable influence and were persuaded to join the leading Jews in bringing pressure on *the chief men of the city.* We are not told what propaganda line was used. Possibly the accusers said Paul and Barnabas were troublemakers. They could point to the synagogue service that had become disorderly, and show that large crowds were gathering about the teachers. They may have planted the suspicion that Paul and Barnabas were inciting the people to riot and insurrection. It was easier for the rulers to banish these teachers than to investigate the case and establish justice. They were more interested in keeping the peace than in fair treatment for a pair of foreigners. They simply ordered Paul and Barnabas to get out of town.

51. But they shook off the dust of their feet against them, and came unto Iconium.

Shaking off the dust indicated that the departing messengers had nothing in common with those who drove them out—not even the bit of dust that might cling to their sandals. Specifically, it signified that Paul and Barnabas had no responsibility for those who rejected them. Since these people rejected God's message and drove out God's messengers, they alone were responsible for their own condemnation. Note Matthew 10:14, 15. Of course, this condemnation did not fall on those in Antioch who had obeyed the gospel. A thriving young church remained when Paul and Barnabas went on to *Iconium*.

52. And the disciples were filled with joy, and with the Holy Ghost.

Though sorry to lose their teachers, the new Christians were happy in their salvation and in the guidance of the Holy Spirit.

CHAPTER 14

1. And it came to pass in Iconium, that they went both together into the synagogue of the Jews, and so spake, that a great multitude both of the Jews and also of the Greeks believed.

It was God's plan to offer the gospel to the Jews first (Acts 13: 46; Romans 1:16), and so the preachers went to the synagogue in *Iconium* as they had done in Antioch. Here too interest was immediate and strong. Here too there were Gentiles as well as Jews, and many of both accepted the gospel. *Greeks* is used to mean Gentiles: Iconium of course was not in Greece, but since the conquests of Alexander the Great three hundred years earlier, Greek language and culture had prevailed so strongly in all the Mediterranean countries that all who were not Jews were loosely called Greeks.

2. But the unbelieving Jews stirred up the Gentiles, and made their minds evil affected against the brethren.

As in Antioch, some were bitterly jealous of the popular new teachers. As in Antioch, they went to work with accusation and misinformation to arouse the city against Paul and Barnabas.

3. Long time therefore abode they speaking boldly in the Lord, which gave testimony unto the word of his grace, and granted signs and wonders to be done by their hands.

It took a long time to stir up enough hostility to drive the missionaries out. One reason was that *the Lord* himself *gave testimony unto the word of his grace*—that is, showed His approval of the gospel message—by doing miracles, *signs and wonders*, through Paul and Barnabas.

4. But the multitude of the city was divided: and part held with the Jews, and part with the apostles.

As always, there were those who rejected the gospel. People who were unwilling to give up their life of pleasure and sin were easily induced to join the jealous Jews in opposition to Paul and Barnabas.

5. And when there was an assault made both of the Gentiles, and also of the Jews with their rulers, to use them despitefully, and to stone them.

The enemies of the gospel found that persuasion and argument were not enough for their purpose. The influence of the gospel continued to grow. The enemies therefore decided to resort to mob violence to get rid of the missionaries.

6. They were ware of it, and fled unto Lystra and Derbe, cities of

Lycaonia, and unto the region that lieth round about.

A large mob can hardly be assembled in complete secrecy. Probably some of the Christians heard of the plot and reported it to Paul and Barnabas. The problem of when to flee and when to stay has been a difficult one for many missionaries, ancient and modern. It must have perplexed Paul and Barnabas, unless the Holy Spirit gave them special guidance in this matter. In this case they judged it better to flee. To stay would not only endanger their lives and their future work, but also might bring persecution on the other Christians in Iconium.

7. And there they preached the gospel.

Wherever they went there were people needing the gospel, and Paul had Barnabas were eager to give it to them.

8. And there sat a certain man at Lystra, impotent in his feet, being a cripple from his mother's womb, who never had walked.

Impotent means powerless, without strength. Since the man's feet had been paralyzed from birth, they must have been withered also. The muscles would not have developed properly without exercise.

9. The same heard Paul speak: who stedfastly beholding him, and perceiving that he had faith to be healed.

We are not told whether or not Paul had already done some miracles in Lystra. Neither are we told just what he said as he preached the gospel (v. 7). No doubt he told of some of Jesus' miracles. But whatever Paul said or did, it was enough to make this man believe he could be healed. Paul could have perceived

this through inspiration of the Holy Spirit, but perhaps the man's faith was evident in his eager face and the straining of his crippled body toward the preacher.

10. Said with a loud voice, Stand upright on thy feet. And he leaped and walked.

Paul spoke in *a loud voice* so that everyone in the crowd would know the crippled man was healed at his command. Thus the miracle served a twofold purpose. Besides healing the helpless man, it gave evidence that divine power was working through Paul, and so it made the people more ready to believe that Paul's message was from God.

11. And when the people saw what Paul had done, they lifted up their voices, saying in the speech of Lycaonia, The gods are come down to us in the likeness of men.

Perhaps most of the people in Lystra knew nothing of the true God, or knew only vaguely that He was the deity of the Jews who lived among them. Seeing the working of divine power, they naturally attributed it to some of the mythical gods of which they had been taught. Excitedly they announced their belief in their native dialect. Paul probably had been speaking in Greek, which most of the people used readily as a second language.

12. And they called Barnabas, Jupiter; and Paul, Mercurius, because he was the chief speaker.

In Roman mythology, *Mercurius*, or Mercury, was the messenger of the gods. Therefore the *chief speaker* was thought to be this messenger. *Jupiter* seems to have been the patron of Lystra (v. 13), and so the people supposed that he would be the god most likely to visit them. Jupiter was also thought to be the chief of the gods. Barnabas may have been larger and more impressive in appearance than Paul. The Greek language has the name Zeus instead of Jupiter and Hermes instead of Mercurius, but our translators used the Roman names because they were better known to English readers of the time.

13. Then the priest of Jupiter, which was before their city, brought oxen and garlands unto the gates, and would have done sacrifice with the people.

Jupiter, which was before their city may indicate that a statue of Jupiter was kept in a shrine or temple outside the city gates, serving as a worship center for the people of Lystra. *The priest,* perhaps with a group of assistants, led the worship and offered sacrifices for the people. Apparently he had *oxen* ready and could bring them without delay, with *garlands* of flowers or leaves to decorate them. Various commentators suppose that *the gates* mentioned were the gates of Jupiter's temple, or of the city, or of the house where Paul and Barnabas were staying. The picture is not detailed enough to enable us to be sure which gates are meant. In any case, the intent is clear. The priest, *with* the people, was about to offer a *sacrifice* to the supposed gods, Paul and Barnabas.

14. Which when the apostles, Barnabas and Paul, heard of, they rent their clothes, and ran in among the people, crying out.

Tearing the clothing was a customary sign of intense grief and shock. The usual method was to grasp the outer garment at the neck with both hands and tear it downward. Apparently Paul and Barnabas did not realize what was going on until the oxen were brought for sacrifice, else they would have protested sooner. The cry recorded in verse 11 evidently did not reach them, either because they did not understand the language of Lycaonia or because it was confused by many people speaking at once and in the back of the crowd rather than close to the supposed gods.

15. And saying, Sirs, why do ye these things? We also are men of like passions with you, and preach unto you that ye should turn from these vanities unto the living God, which made heaven, and earth, and the sea, and all things that are therein.

Paul and Barnabas gave two reasons why the proposed sacrifices should not be offered to them. First, they were not gods, but men like the would-be worshipers. Second, they had come for the very purpose of turning men away from the worship of Jupiter and Mercury; of leading them to worship the only real God, the living Creator. *Vanities* is a good name for the imaginary gods and all the things and ceremonies involved in worshiping them. The word means things that are empty or useless: without truth or power or result.

16. Who in times past suffered all nations to walk in their own ways.

The gospel with its call to turn to the true God was now coming to Lystra for the first time. For ages God had allowed the nations to go in *their own ways* without any such special message to guide them.

17. Nevertheless he left not himself without witness, in that he did good, and gave us rain from heaven, and fruitful seasons, filling our hearts with food and gladness.

Even without any special revelation such as the gospel, people of all nations ought to know something of God. The falling rain, the growing crops, the harvests that provided *food and gladness*—all these gave their testimony to a Creator wise and powerful and good.

18. And with these sayings scarce restrained they the people, that they had not done sacrifice unto them.

With some difficulty Paul and Barnabas persuaded the eager people not to offer the proposed sacrifice.

19. And there came thither certain Jews from Antioch and Iconium, who persuaded the people, and, having stoned Paul, drew him out of the city, supposing he had been dead.

This evidently took place some days after the attempt to worship Paul and Barnabas. News of that event had apparently reached Iconium and Antioch, forty and one hundred thirty miles away respectively. *There came thither certain Jews from Antioch and Iconium.* Those who had driven Paul and Barnabas from Antioch (13:50) joined forces with those who had plotted against their lives at Iconium (v. 5) to pursue them even here. "Having persuaded the multitudes" (American Standard Version). Speaking with the prestige of popular leaders, bringing (perhaps with seeming reluctance) an evil report of their fellow Jews, they apparently had no trouble in swaying the fickle Lycaonians. (Compare Galatians 1:6; 3:1; 4:15). "They stoned Paul" (American Standard Version). The visiting Jews did the stoning, with the consent of the Lystrians. Stoning was the Jewish punishment prescribed for

blasphemy, which charge they could fabricate from Paul's alleged disregard for the law of Moses and the temple (compare 21:28). Barnabas' characteristic exhortations had 'not roused their anger as had the reasonings and doctrines of Paul. The fact that Paul had "advanced in the Jews' religion beyond many of mine own age among my countrymen" (Galatians 1:14, American Standard Version) may account for some of the bitterness of the Jews against him now. "Dragged him out of the city" (American Standard Version). Since Lystra was not a Jewish city, the Jews seem to have had no conscience against doing the actual stoning within its walls (compare 7:58), but they would not leave the body there. *Supposing he had been dead.* No one, including Paul himself (see 2 Corinthians 12:2-4), seems to know just how close to death's door, or on which side of it, he actually was. He alluded to this event in 2 Corinthians 11:25—"Once was I stoned"seeing in it the climax of the "persecutions, afflictions, which came unto me at Antioch, at Iconium, at Lystra" (2 Timothy 3:11).

20. Howbeit, as the disciples stood round about him, he rose up, and came into the city: and the next day he departed with Barnabas to Derbe.

As the disciples stood round about him. The Jews apparently departed as soon as they had completed their mission, leaving the battered body of Paul to his friends. This verse is the first indication of evangelistic success in Lystra. The group of sorrowing disciples almost certainly included Timothy (16:1), and this event seems to be reflected in Paul's later reference to Timothy's tears on his behalf (2 Timothy 1:4). The disciples apparently concurred in the notion that Paul was dead, or they would have been nursing his wounds, rather than standing about. *He rose up, and came into the city.* Paul's swift recovery from apparent death required something more than the recuperative powers of a clean and energetic body dominated by a courageous spirit. Some sort of miracle is indicated, though not named. One may suppose that Paul was cared for in the home of Timothy's family during the ensuing hours. *The next day he departed with Barnabas to Derbe.* Strange method of ridding himself of the bruises and soreness of his stoning! Derbe was thirty-five to forty miles southeastward in the edge of the Lycaonian plain, and was one of the least advanced of the cities visited by Paul. Gaius of Derbe was one who accompanied Paul to Jerusalem with the gifts from the Gentile churches (20:4).

21. And when they had preached the gospel to that city, and had taught many, they returned again to Lystra, and to Iconium, and Antioch.

Preached the gospel to that city. The events of a considerable time are compressed into a very few words. The preaching at Derbe seems to have been attended with no special difficulties, and no details are given. "And had made many disciples" (American Standard Version). The winning of converts to Christ is a teaching process, as indicated also in Matthew 28:18-20. A great deal of moral, doctrinal, and practical teaching is necessary also after the convert is won. The work at Derbe was successful. *They returned again to Lystra.* For the sake of the converts there,

the apostles went back, as soon as it was safe, to the more difficult and dangerous places. The work they had begun must be continued.

22. Confirming the souls of the disciples, and exhorting them to continue in the faith, and that we must through much tribulation enter into the kingdom of God.

Confirming the souls of the disciples. These Christians needed strengthening in the faith. There is no evidence of the apostles' engaging in aggressive evangelistic activity on these visits. Such work would still be dangerous both to the evangelists and to the disciples. *Exhorting them to continue in the faith.* The exhortation to steadfastness was needed, especially among the fickle Lycaonians, and more especially if they were under persecution. *That we must through much tribulation enter into the kingdom of God.* This part of the exhortation is apparently a direct quotation of an oft-repeated warning. It is in harmony with the teaching of Jesus (Matthew 10:21-23; John 15:18; 16:1, 33) and later writing of the apostles (Romans 5:3; 2 Corinthians 4:17; Hebrews 12:5-11). The "kingdom of God" may signify either the church, which is actually entered through symbolic sharing in the death, burial, and resurrection of Christ, or it may be the heavenly realm which is prepared for those who have suffered with Christ in order that they may also reign with Him (2 Timothy 2:11, 12; compare 3:12).

23. And when they had ordained them elders in every church, and had prayed with fasting, they commended them to the Lord, on whom they believed.

The American Standard Version
has "appointed for them elders." The
word here translated "ordain" means
literally "stretch out the hand"; from
that it later signified "appoint by a
show of hands"; and finally "to appoint or elect by any means." The
method of selection was probably
very similar to what is described in
Acts 6:6 for the choosing of the
seven in Jerusalem. Similar language
is used. There the people chose their
leaders at the apostles' suggestion,
and the apostles set them apart to
their work. *Elders in every church.*
These leaders were otherwise called
presbyters and overseers, or bishops
(Acts 11:30; Philippians 1:1). The
rule of one man in any place was
carefully avoided. The elders were
men qualified by age, experience, and
piety to oversee the church. While
comparatively new to the church,
having been converted not much over
a year before, many of the Christians
were "in character and knowledge,
the ripest fruits of the Jewish synagogue" (Walker). *And had prayed
with fasting.* The language would
make it appear that the fasting and
prayer came after the appointment or
ordination rather than as a part of it.
It was in any case the usual accompaniment to such a solemn dedication
(Acts 6:6; 13:3). Although this
verse does not mention the laying on
of hands, that also was probably included. *They commended them to
the Lord, on whom they believed.* In
parting from them and leaving the
infant churches, with their manifold
problems, to the care of these men,
the apostles prayed for them the sustaining presence of Christ (see Matthew 28:20), whom they had come
to accept as Lord and Saviour.

**24. And after they had passed
throughout Pisidia, they came to Pamphylia.**

Retracing the route by which they
had come (13:14), they made their
way toward the seacoast. Pisidia is
the region in which they had begun
their preaching in Asia Minor. *They
came to Pamphylia,* the coastal dis-
trict.

**25. And when they had preached
the word in Perga, they went down into
Attalia.**

Preached the word in Perga, the
chief city of Pamphylia, on the
Cestrus River approximately sixteen
miles from the coast. For reasons not
yet explained, they had not lingered
here on their journey inland. No
special emphasis seems to have been
given to it even now, but the apostles would make the best possible use
of their time while awaiting shipping
to Antioch of Syria. *They went down
into Attalia,* a smaller town on the
seacoast, where ship landings were
more frequent.

**26. And thence sailed to Antioch,
from whence they had been recommended to the grace of God for the
work which they fulfilled.**

The sea voyage to Seleucia, the
port which served Antioch of Syria,
was evidently direct. "From whence
they had been committed to the grace
of God" (American Standard Version). Judging from the known interval between the visits to Jerusalem
recorded in Acts 11:29 and 15:2, the
apostles' absence from Antioch was
probably three to four years. They
now returned to give an accounting
of their stewardship in the task that
had been given to them (13:2, 3).
As the Holy Spirit had commanded

the work, so the power of God had accomplished it through their hands.

27. And when they were come, and had gathered the church together, they rehearsed all that God had done with them, and how he had opened the door of faith unto the Gentiles.

This "missionary meeting" involved the whole congregation, and perhaps more than one congregation in the city of Antioch. They had an investment and a vital concern in the work that had been done. *They rehearsed all that God had done with them.* This seems to have been the first report to the church at Antioch since the time of Paul and Barnabas's commissioning. The report included the account of miracles and other evidences of divine intervention in the accomplishments of the journey.

The conversion and salvation of men is the work of God, whatever and whoever the human agents may be. *He had opened the door of faith.* This expression is characteristic of Paul, who elsewhere spoke of opportunities as open doors (1 Corinthians 16:9; 2 Corinthians 2:12; Colossians 4:3).

28. And there they abode long time with the disciples.

They tarried probably at least a year before going to Jerusalem to confer with the apostles and elders there about the matter of circumcision of Gentile converts. The time could be spent profitably in sharing with others what they had learned in their labors, helping and teaching the church, and recuperating from the strenuous labors of the intervening years.

CHAPTER 15

1. And certain men which came down from Judaea taught the brethren, and said, Except ye be circumcised after the manner of Moses, ye cannot be saved.

These certain men probably were believers from among the Pharisees (verse 5). Coming from Jerusalem, they falsely claimed to have authority as representatives of the apostles that were there (Acts 15:24). *Taught the brethren.* They contradicted the apostles' teaching in the church, and taught privately as they were able to gain a hearing. Their teaching was directed to the converts from among the Gentiles. *Except ye be circumcised.* This was made the key to the whole controversy, both by the Judaizers and by Paul, who insisted that the Christian in his baptism had already received the blessings which

circumcision was supposed to confer (Colossians 2:11), and that the person who depends on circumcision thereby rejects Christ and makes His sacrifice of no effect (Galatians 5:2). *After the manner of Moses.* Circumcision "after the custom of Moses" (American Standard Version) implied the authority of the whole ritual law (Galatians 5:3). *Ye cannot be saved.* Thus the Gentiles were told that they must follow the whole system of Jewish ritual observance, centering in circumcision, if their Christianity were to be valid.

2. When therefore Paul and Barnabas had no small dissension and disputation with them, they determined that Paul and Barnabas, and certain other of them, should go up to Jerusalem unto the apostles and elders about this question.

The controversy involved both assertions and questions addressed to each party by the other, as the claims of each were challenged and confuted. "The brethren appointed that Paul and Barnabas, and certain other of them, should go up to Jerusalem" (American Standard Version). Paul himself said that he "went up by revelation" (Galatians 2:1, 2), even more to teach the church at Jerusalem concerning the status of the Gentiles than to inquire of anyone there what it ought to be. The apostles, all equally inspired, were in complete agreement on the matter. *Unto the apostles and elders about this question.* Paul approached the church in Jerusalem, not as making a plea to the court of highest authority, but for the purpose of joining with them in a clear expression of the revealed truth about the troublesome question at hand. That was the only way to prevent continued and recurrent controversy.

3. And being brought on their way by the church, they passed through Phenice and Samaria, declaring the conversion of the Gentiles: and they caused great joy unto all the brethren.

The Greek word for *being brought on their way* can mean that the brethren at Antioch accompanied the messengers on the first part of the trip as in Acts 20:38 or that the church helped the messengers on the way by paying their traveling expenses as in Titus 3:13. In the case now before us, the brethren may have done either of these, or very probably may have done both. *Phenice,* or Phoenicia, was a coastal area along the way; *Samaria* was the area just north of Judea. Paul and Barnabas stopped with Christians at various places in these areas and told of *the conversion of the Gentiles* in Antioch and the other places they had preached the gospel. The news brought *great joy:* the Christians were delighted that lost souls were being saved and the church was being strengthened by the addition of many who had been heathen.

4. And when they were come to Jerusalem, they were received of the church, and of the apostles and elders, and they declared all things that God had done with them.

Barnabas had been a popular and trusted leader in Jerusalem (Acts 4:36, 37; 9:27; 11:22). We can imagine the joy of his old friends as they welcomed him back from his strenuous and effective missionary work. Some of *the apostles,* possibly all of them, were in Jerusalem at the time; and an unspecified number of *elders* shared the leadership of the church, as noted in Acts 11:30. It seems that there was a great mass meeting of Jerusalem Christians to welcome Paul and Barnabas and to listen eagerly as *they declared all things that God had done with them.* They told that God had sent them from Antioch through Cyprus and Asia Minor. He had used them to win many Gentiles as well as Jews to faith in Christ.

5. But there rose up certain of the sect of the Pharisees which believed, saying, That it was needful to circumcise them, and to command them to keep the law of Moses.

The Pharisees are perhaps best known as angry and envious opponents of Jesus, though a few of them did regard Him with cautious favor before His death (John 3:1, 2; Matthew 22:34-40; Mark 12:32-34).

After His resurrection many Pharisees *believed* He was the Messiah. They became Christians without losing any of their almost fanatical devotion to the law of Moses. This posed no problem in Jerusalem, where all the Christians were Jews and continued to keep the law and observe the ancient Jewish ceremonies of worship. But when Gentiles began to be won to Christ, the Christian Pharisees were shocked. Probably they took the lead in criticizing Peter for his approach to Cornelius (Acts 11). At that time the overwhelming evidence apparently compelled them to agree that Gentiles might become Christians, but they still insisted that they must become Jews also, else they could not be saved. This Paul and Barnabas denied.

6. And the apostles and elders came together for to consider of this matter.

The outstanding leaders of the Jerusalem church now got together to talk over the question. We are not told whether they did this in a private place or in the presence of the whole congregation, but the mention of the multitude in verse 12 seems to suggest that the whole large group was allowed to listen to the discussion by the apostles and elders.

7. And when there had been much disputing, Peter rose up, and said unto them, Men and brethren, ye know how that a good while ago God made choice among us, that the Gentiles by my mouth should hear the word of the gospel, and believe.

Disputing seems to suggest an acrimonious argument, which the Greek word does not necessarily mean. "Questioning" or "discussion" might be a better translation, but it

seems that even the apostles and elders did not all have the question settled in their minds. Peter, however, had no doubts. He stood up and reminded the others that he, by God's own appointment, had been the first one to take the gospel to Gentiles and lead them to Christ. What he called to mind was the episode recorded in Acts 10.

8. And God, which knoweth the hearts, bare them witness, giving them the Holy Ghost, even as he did unto us.

When God gave the Holy Spirit to Cornelius and others as fully as to the apostles themselves, it would be absurd for men to say those Gentiles were not acceptable to God.

9. And put no difference between us and them, purifying their hearts by faith.

Jews and Gentiles both were guilty of sin. The Jews had not been able to cleanse their hearts and lives by obeying the law of Moses. God had purified their hearts, taken their sins away, when they came to Him in faith, trusting the salvation He offered through Jesus. In the same way God had purified the hearts of Cornelius and other Gentiles.

10. Now therefore why tempt ye God, to put a yoke upon the neck of the disciples, which neither our fathers nor we were able to bear?

As Peter saw it, the Pharisees' argument was not with Paul and Barnabas, but with God. It was God who had cleansed the hearts of Gentiles by faith; how could anyone say they must be consecrated by circumcision and other ceremonies? The law was *a yoke* too heavy for anyone to bear. Through the centuries the Jews had failed to find salvation by it. It was doubly absurd, then, to bind it upon the Gentiles whom God had chosen to save without it.

11. But we believe that through the grace of the Lord Jesus Christ we shall be saved, even as they.

After all their futile efforts to keep the law, the Jews must rely on the grace of Jesus for their salvation, just as must the Gentiles who had never tried to keep the law.

12. Then all the multitude kept silence, and gave audience to Barnabas and Paul, declaring what miracles and wonders God had wrought among the Gentiles by them.

Quieted by the words of Peter, the people were now ready to listen without further interruptions to what Paul and Barnabas had to say. "And they hearkened unto Barnabas and Paul" (American Standard Version). Barnabas spoke first, as the one who was more favorably known in Jerusalem (Acts 4:36, 37; 9:26, 27), and therefore less likely to cause offense. Paul also was heard with interest.

13. And after they had held their peace, James answered, saying, Men and brethren, hearken unto me.

The missionaries were permitted to give a full report without interruption. Then, *James answered.* This was the brother of Jesus. He was not a believer in Jesus during most of His earthly ministry (John 7:5), but received word of the resurrection immediately (John 20:17) and was an eyewitness of the risen Lord (1 Corinthians 15:7). He became a respected leader in the church at Jerusalem. In his "answer" James took notice of the questions and objections raised by the Pharisaic brethren. *Hearken unto me.* There is nothing in the record, except that James's statement was the final one, to set it

apart from the earlier addresses of Peter and the others.

14. Simeon hath declared how God at the first did visit the Gentiles, to take out of them a people for his name.

James's familiar use of the Hebrew form of Peter's name, Simeon, was consistent with the character of both men and well designed to allay any fears that Jewish tradition would be flouted. *God at the first did visit the Gentiles.* James recognized the event at the house of Cornelius as of divine influence. *To take out of them a people for his name.* Christians are a new race of people, "taken out" of every nation, and belong to God rather than men.

15. And to this agree the words of the prophets; as it is written.

Having heard reasonings from Peter and the testimony of experience from Barnabas and Paul, the Jews looked for one more evidence more convincing than either of these —the word of the prophets. James quoted from only one, Amos, but rightly indicated that the words of other prophets were in harmony with Amos' prediction.

16. After this I will return, and will build again the tabernacle of David, which is fallen down; and I will build again the ruins thereof, and I will set it up.

In this verse and the next, James makes a free quotation of Amos 9:11, 12. "After these things I will return" (American Standard Version). After the desolation that was to come because of Israel's sin, God would restore the remnant. *Will build again the tabernacle of David, which is fallen down.* The kingly family of

David was compared to a fallen tent. *I will build again the ruins thereof, and I will set it up.* The Messiah was to be of the line of David, and His reign would be God's way of fulfilling His promises to David. Through the acceptance of Christ, the Jewish people would be restored to a right relationship with God.

17. That the residue of men might seek after the Lord, and all the Gentiles, upon whom my name is called, saith the Lord, who doeth all these things.

The salvation of the penitent remnant was a theme much emphasized by Amos. "Even all the heathen upon whom my name is called" (Living Oracles translation). The remnant to be saved through Messiah was not limited to the Jewish people but included all those Gentiles who would respond to the authority represented in the name of God. This declaration that the Gentiles were included in God's plan was the heart of the message as James used it. *Saith the Lord, who doeth all these things.* The promise was of God, and Amos quoted it in the words of God. He who had spoken was He who also fulfilled the promise.

18. Known unto God are all his works from the beginning of the world.

James reminded his hearers that the events of their day had been known and indicated by God from ancient times. The American Standard Version ties this verse more closely to the former one: "Saith the Lord, who maketh these things known from of old."

19. Wherefore my sentence is, that we trouble not them, which from among the Gentiles are turned to God.

James's judgment was in harmony with the leading of the Holy Spirit as the others also had received it (compare verse 28). The Gentiles had received and accepted the message of Christ. They had been obedient to His commands. Any insistence on further requirements would be an occasion of disturbance, unsettling the faith of new Christians who had been taught that the sacrifice of Christ was sufficient for their salvation.

20. But that we write unto them, that they abstain from pollutions of idols, and from fornication, and from things strangled, and from blood.

The apostles used the method of communication most sure to be understood and to make for a permanent settlement of the issue. The four prohibitions that follow are excellently designed to sustain the Gentiles in basic Christian morality and to minimize the conflicts that might arise in familiar fellowship between Jewish and Gentile believers. *They abstain from pollutions of idols.* The worship of idols was ingrained in Gentile thought and habit, but the prohibition of it was not limited to the law of Moses. Idolatry was recognized as wrong by the patriarchs before Moses, and it was specifically forbidden to Christians. If the believing Gentiles would abstain from meats sacrificed to idols it would remove one of the principal objections of the Jews to eating with their Gentile brethren (Galatians 2:12). *And from fornication.* The heathen world, ancient and modern, has regarded fornication, not as sin, but as the harmless gratification of a natural appetite. Warning against impurity could not be too often given nor

too firmly insisted upon. *And from
things strangled.* From the days of
Noah (Genesis 9:4) the people of
God had been forbidden to eat blood.
Because an animal that had been
slain by strangling could not have
the blood well drained out of it, the
eating of such animals was prohib-
ited (Leviticus 17:13, 14; Deuteronomy 12:16, 23). Many Gentiles, on
the other hand, were particularly
fond of bloody meat. Hence a Jew
could not in good conscience eat at
a Gentile table. *And from blood.*
Probably a reinforcement of the fore-
going prohibition. Some have considered it as a prohibition of the shed-
ding of blood through pride, anger,
or revenge.

**21. For Moses of old time hath in
every city them that preach him, being
read in the synagogues every sabbath
day.**

James gives here the reason for di-
recting these prohibitions to the Gentiles. "The Jews, who heard the law
in their synagogues every sabbath,
did not need instruction." It could be
taken for granted that they would
continue to abstain from these things
as their fathers before them had done.

**22. Then pleased it the apostles
and elders, with the whole church,
to send chosen men of their own
company to Antioch with Paul and
Barnabas; namely, Judas surnamed
Barsabas, and Silas, chief men among
the brethren.**

The conference at Jerusalem was
drawing to a close. It was neither an
ecclesiastical court nor a general
council of the church. It was rather
a meeting of the whole church at
Jerusalem, under the leadership of
the apostles, with representatives
from the church at Antioch. Judaism

was the problem. Must a person observe the rules and regulations of the
old law in order to be a Christian?
Paul and Barnabas said "No." There
were some men from Judea, however, who had come to Antioch and
insisted that the Gentiles must keep
the law of Moses as well as obey
Christ. To settle the dispute Antioch
had sent men directly to Jerusalem.
There it was agreed that Paul and
Barnabas were correct in their stand,
but the task still remained to inform
the brethren. A letter was written.
This is the earliest notice we have
concerning a written document is-
sued by the apostles and elders and
the church. With these written
teachings, the Jerusalem brethren
sent *chosen men* to circulate and explain them. The term used here for
chosen is commonly used for voting
or passing a measure in the assembly.
It is interesting that even in the presence of the apostles and the elders,
it was with the consent of the whole
congregation that men were selected
to go to Antioch. *Judas surnamed
Barsabas* was perhaps a brother of
the Joseph called Barsabas mentioned
in Acts 1:23. He and Silas were already considered *chief men among
the brethren.* It is impossible to say
from this description the type of
leadership these men showed in Jerusalem. Some think that the title
was given especially to teachers.
From the information that follows,
we do know they were prophets (v.
32).

**23. And they wrote letters by them
after this manner; The apostles and
elders and brethren send greeting unto
the brethren which are of the Gentiles
in Antioch and Syria and Cilicia.**

Antioch was the city that had

sent messengers to talk with the apostles and elders as related in the opening verses of this chapter. *Syria* was the area around that city. We have no information about the other churches in it, but it seems evident that there were several of them. *Cilicia* was the adjoining territory that lay north of the east end of the Mediterranean. Tarsus was one of its chief cities, and we wonder if Paul established churches in that area before he went to Antioch (Acts 9:30; 11:25, 26). The teachers who had started the trouble in Antioch probably had gone on to other churches, and so the message was sent to all the brethren in these areas.

24. Forasmuch as we have heard, that certain which went out from us have troubled you with words, subverting your souls, saying, Ye must be circumcised, and keep the law: to whom we gave no such commandment.

The teachers causing the trouble perhaps had claimed to represent the true teaching that was given in Jerusalem. The letter made it clear that this claim was not true. These men had gone out from Jerusalem, but they had not been sent. They did not represent the church, the elders, the apostles, or the Lord. They spoke for themselves only.

25. It seemed good to us, being assembled with one accord, to send chosen men unto you with our beloved Barnabas and Paul.

If Barnabas and Paul had come back alone, their adversaries in Antioch might have accused them of misrepresenting the apostles and elders, or even of altering the letter. Men from Jerusalem were sent to protect them against any such accusations.

26. Men that have hazarded their lives for the name of our Lord Jesus Christ.

To guarantee the faithfulness of the messengers, the letter mentioned that they had risked their lives in enduring the bitter persecution brought against the disciples in Jerusalem.

27. We have sent therefore Judas and Silas, who shall also tell you the same things by mouth.

The faithful messengers would testify that the letter really came from "the apostles and elders and brethren" (v. 23) in Jerusalem and stated the stand that they had taken publicly.

28. For it seemed good to the Holy Ghost, and to us, to lay upon you no greater burden than these necessary things.

Not only "the apostles and elders and brethren," but also *the Holy Ghost* concurred in the message: in other words, this was an inspired message and not just a ruling of the church or its leaders. The few prohibitions given were *necessary* in order to live righteously and promote good fellowship, not because they were established in the Jewish law.

29. That ye abstain from meats offered to, idols, and from blood, and from things strangled, and from fornication: from which if ye keep yourselves, ye shall do well. Fare ye well.

This of course does not mean that other sins are permissable. Stealing and lying, for example, are also forbidden (Ephesians 4:25, 28). Perhaps the special warning of our text was directed against sins so common among the heathen that they were not even recognized as wrong until Christian teaching denounced them

30. So when they were dismissed, they came to Antioch: and when they had gathered the multitude together, they delivered the epistle.

They were dismissed in the sense that they were sent on their way by the Jerusalem church. This group included Paul, Barnabas, Titus (Galatians 2:1), and certain others, with Judas and Silas from Jerusalem. Having gathered together the whole congregation of Christians in Antioch, they fulfilled their mission by delivering the conclusions of the conference.

31. Which when they had read, they rejoiced for the consolation.

The relief of the Antiochians is evident. This decision was significant not only for them, but also for all generations of Christians to follow. The law had been nailed to the cross. It helps our understanding of the new covenant, but we are not required to keep the rules and regulations of the old covenant. This was a comfort to the Gentiles in Antioch, and the Jewish Christians seem to have joined with them in the rejoicing. No word of the false teachers is given here. Their teachings had been silenced for the time being.

32. And Judas and Silas, being prophets also themselves, exhorted the brethren with many words, and confirmed them.

Judas and Silas now supplied the added assurance of those who had come from the Jerusalem church itself. They had the advantage of being prophets. This classification is given second only to the apostles as it is listed in Ephesians 4:11 and 1 Corinthians 12:28. "But he that prophesieth speaketh unto men to edification, and exhortation, and

comfort" (1 Corinthians 14:3). Besides prediction of certain future events, the prophets were at times commissioned to make an authoritative announcement of the divine will. All of this made it particularly appropriate that these prophets from the church at Jerusalem, Judas and Silas, would present the conclusion concerning the problem at hand. The church at Antioch also had prophets (Acts 13:1), but the words of these outstanding men from Jerusalem were particularly appreciated.

33. And after they had tarried there a space, they were let go in peace from the brethren unto the apostles.

Any church is enriched when good and capable men come to help in the work of teaching, and Judas and Silas stayed for *a space* of time to help the church in Antioch. No doubt the brethren there were reluctant to see such teachers leave. Nevertheless they did not try to keep them, but let them go *in peace*. These messengers had been sent by the whole church; but the apostles held a place of preeminence by Jesus' own appointment, and so it is appropriate to say the messengers were let go *unto the apostles*.

34. Notwithstanding it pleased Silas to abide there still.

For reasons not explained, Silas chose to stay in Antioch when Judas went back home. Apparently he liked Antioch and had no compelling reason to return to Jerusalem.

35. Paul also and Barnabas continued in Antioch, teaching and preaching the word of the Lord, with many others also.

Acts 13:1 names several prophets and teachers in Antioch, and probably others were added while Paul and Barnabas were away. It was fitting for a church so blessed with good teachers to send some of them to people who had none.

36. And some days after Paul said unto Barnabas, Let us go again and visit our brethren in every city where we have preached the word of the Lord, and see how they do.

When John Mark left them, Paul and Barnabas continued without him. It was probably three years later that they returned to their starting point, Antioch, to remain for several months or perhaps a year. This stay was broken by the visit to Jerusalem that is recorded in Acts 15. It was *some days after* their return from that visit that Paul suggested another trip. The brethren referred to were the Christians in Cyprus, Antioch of Pisidia, Iconium, Lystra, and Derbe, where Paul and Barnabas had preached on their first trip, recorded in chapters 13 and 14. Paul's proposal resulted in the two evangelists' second missionary tour; but the following verses show that they did not go together this time.

37. And Barnabas determined to take with them John, whose surname was Mark.

The verb "determined" in the King James Version is translated "was minded" in the American Standard Version. Barnabas, who was noted for his generosity and helpfulness, wanted to give his young relative another opportunity. Paul did not evidence such a charitable attitude.

38. But Paul thought not good to take him with them, who departed from them from Pamphylia, and went not with them to the work.

Paul recalled that John Mark *departed from them from Pamphylia.* He had withdrawn from the very field to which they were now preparing to return. Why give him a second opportunity? Paul objected because the youth *went not with them to the work.*

39. And the contention was so sharp between them, that they departed asunder one from the other: and so Barnabas took Mark, and sailed unto Cyprus.

And the contention was so sharp between them, that they departed asunder one from the other. As is true in many disagreements, we can not say definitely that one man was completely right and the other was entirely wrong. The important thing to remember is that the disagreement was not over doctrinal matters, but simply over who should be included in the missionary party. While the two men disagreed, they remained Christian. The disagreement was so sharp that they parted, but there is no evidence that either of them ever said an unkind word about the other afterward. However, so far as we know, Paul and Barnabas never worked together again as missionaries. They continued to serve their Lord in different areas. *And so Barnabas took Mark, and sailed unto Cyprus.* We wait in vain for a report of this venture. Luke, the author of the book of Acts, was associated with Paul and his work. Hence his writing is concerned more with Paul's missionary activities than with Barnabas' work. Paul took Silas with him and visited part of the churches founded on his first tour (15:40—16:5). Barnabas and Mark doubtless did the same with the churches on the island of Cyprus. Their additional work is not recorded.

40. And Paul chose Silas, and departed, being recommended by the brethren unto the grace of God.

The choice of Silas seems especially appropriate. Both Paul and Silas had Jewish backgrounds, but showed an interest in preaching salvation to the Gentiles. Silas had been among the leaders in Jerusalem and was a prophet, as Paul had been in the church at Antioch (Acts 13: 1). *Recommended by the brethren unto the grace of God* probably alludes to a service of the congregation

similar to the one described in Acts 13:3, including fasting, prayers, and the laying on of hands.

41. And he went through Syria and Cilicia, confirming the churches.

While Barnabas went to his former home, Cyprus, Paul went in the direction of his home, Tarsus of Cilicia. Although no mention is made of the locations of individual churches in these areas of Syria and Cilicia, except the one at Antioch, such passages as Acts 15:23 and Galatians 1:21 imply that missionary activity had already made headway here.

CHAPTER 16

1. Then came he to Derbe and Lystra: and, behold, a certain disciple was there, named Timotheus, the son of a certain woman, which was a Jewess, and believed; but his father was a Greek.

Paul had begun his second missionary journey. Silas was now his companion instead of Barnabas; and there was no young man to take the place of John Mark, who had been with him at the beginning of the first journey. Paul had already passed among churches of Syria and Cilicia when he came to two of the cities where he had established churches during his first missionary journey. Since Lystra is last mentioned, it appears that Timothy's home was there. His mother's name was Eunice (2 Timothy 1:5). It is possible that his father, a Gentile, was already dead. Both mother and son were Christian believers.

2. Which was well reported of by the brethren that were at Lystra and Iconium.

Although Timothy was probably a young man in his early twenties, he was already witnessing for the Lord in such an active way that his reputation had spread to the neighboring town of Iconium.

3. Him would Paul have to go forth with him; and took and circumcised him because of the Jews which were in those quarters: for they knew all that his father was a Greek.

Here was a young man whom Paul found to be promising. He could give the apostle encouragement and fellowship, and also be an added witness to the truths of God. Paul asked that Timothy be circumcised, not to make him more of a Christian, but in order that he might be received freely in the synagogues of the Jews and would not have his influence weakened because of his mixed parentage.

4. And as they went through the cities, they delivered them the decrees for to keep, that were ordained of the apostles and elders which were at Jerusalem.

121

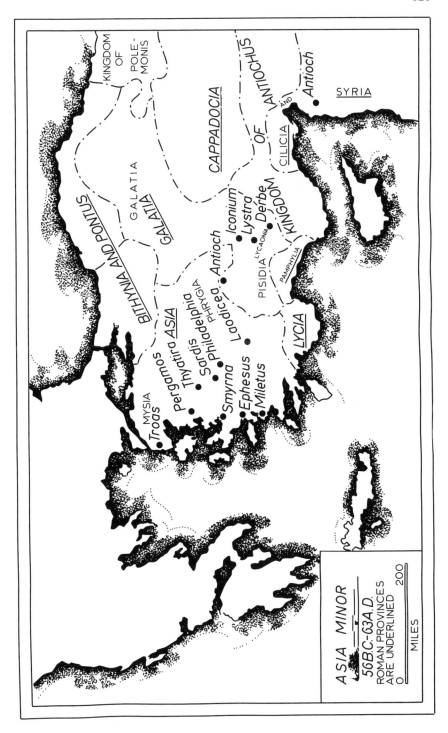

ASIA MINOR
56 B.C.-63 A.D.
ROMAN PROVINCES
ARE UNDERLINED
0   200
MILES

The letter from Jerusalem was addressed to Gentile Christians in Antioch and Syria and Cilicia (Acts 15:23), but it was equally appropriate for Gentile Christians in other places. Paul and Silas probably continued to deliver it even after they left Cilicia.

5. And so were the churches established in the faith, and increased in number daily.

This strengthening in the faith and increase in numbers no doubt was due to all of Paul's teaching and the work of others besides, not merely to the decision brought from Jerusalem. However, the same problem that had disturbed Antioch (Acts 15:1, 2) probably had been raised elsewhere. The definite teaching that Gentile Christians need not become Jews helped to end dissension, exalt the Christian faith, and make Christianity more attractive to the Gentiles.

6. Now when they had gone through Phrygia and the region of Galatia, and were forbidden of the Holy Ghost to preach the word in Asia.

Paul and his party were proceeding to the northwest through Asia Minor. *Asia* here is not the huge continent now called by that name, but the Roman province at the west end of Asia Minor, bordering on the Aegean Sea. For some reason not given, the Holy Spirit forbade Paul to preach there at this time, but later he spent more than two years in one of Asia's principal cities, Ephesus (Acts 19).

7. After they were come to Mysia, they assayed to go into Bithynia: but the Spirit suffered them not.

Mysia was an area that the Romans had included in their province of Asia. Coming to it, Paul and his companions would have gone north *into Bithynia,* a province along the Black Sea, but again the Holy Spirit forbade.

8. And they passing by Mysia came down to Troas.

No doubt wondering why the Spirit restrained them from preaching in Asia or Bithynia, Paul and his companions went on to the northwest till they came to the sea. *Troas* was a port in Asia Minor.

9. And a vision appeared to Paul in the night; There stood a man of Macedonia, and prayed him, saying, Come over into Macedonia, and help us.

Macedonia lay still farther to the northwest. It was on the European continent across the Aegean Sea from Troas.

10. And after he had seen the vision, immediately we endeavoured to go into Macedonia, assuredly gathering that the Lord had called us for to preach the gospel unto them.

Now the missionaries could see why they had been prevented from preaching in Asia and Bithynia. For reasons unknown to them, but known to God, the time was right to plant the gospel in Macedonia, and so God led them on to that area. Note that the historian, Luke, now uses *we* and *us* in referring to the missionary party. Apparently he joined the group at Troas. We wonder if there is here an additional reason for bringing the others to Troas without delay. If they had stopped to preach in Asia and Bithynia, would Luke have been gone before they reached Troas? Would the inspired record of their travels have been written by someone else, or not written at all?

11. Therefore loosing from Troas, we came with a straight course to Samothracia, and the next day to Neapolis.

Loosing from Troas. They took a ship to sail from Troas across the sea to Macedonia, where they were to begin a new ministry. *Straight course.* Since they were traveling by sailing vessel, the description indicates that they had a very favorable wind. They made the trip in two days or less. The distance was nearly 150 miles. The same voyage in the opposite direction at a later time took five days (Acts 20:6). *Samothracia.* This is an island about halfway between Troas and the Macedonian coast. Its mountains rise over five thousand feet above the level of the sea. *Neapolis.* A seaport about ten miles from Philippi.

12. And from thence to Philippi, which is the chief city of that part of Macedonia, and a colony: and we were in that city abiding certain days.

Philippi. This was a Roman city with a large Greek population. It was originally an insignificant town, but was fortified by Philip of Macedon in the fourth century B.C. and was named for him. It was enlarged and taken over by the Romans in about 42 B.C. It was given the status of a "colony" by Augustus. This meant that its citizens were given special privileges as Roman citizens. The city had self-government and was free from the special tax of the emperor that was levied on all conquered towns. *The chief city.* Or the first city. This title is given to Philippi, not because it was the capital of the province, but either because of its importance in general or because it was the first Macedonian

city reached by the traveling evangelists. *We.* Use of this pronoun indicates that the author, Luke, was now with Paul. The first use of the "we" appears in Acts 16:10. Luke apparently joined Paul and his group at Troas and went with them to Macedonia. It seems that he remained at Philippi when Paul moved on (Acts 17:1), and rejoined him when he passed through Philippi several years later, when Paul's next journey was nearing its close (Acts 20:6). Some therefore have concluded that Philippi was Luke's home. When he left that city as recorded in Acts 20:6, he accompanied Paul to Jerusalem, and later to Rome.

13. And on the sabbath we went out of the city by a river side, where prayer was wont to be made; and we sat down, and spake unto the women which resorted thither.

On the sabbath. Paul made it a custom to worship with the Jews on the Sabbath Day when he went into a new place. He was usually invited to preach to them because he was recognized as a visiting teacher. *Out of the city.* In Philippi there was no synagogue for the regular worship of God. This would indicate that there were very few Jews in Philippi, since it was customary to have a synagogue in any town where there were as many as ten heads of families. There probably were not ten families of Jews in the place. *By a river side.* This was a quiet place to which the Jews could go and worship undisturbed. *Where prayer was wont to be made.* We today would say, "Where it was customary to worship." *Sat down.* Even in formal worship services it was customary for the speaker to sit, though he would stand up to read the Scripture. This is seen in Jesus' appearance in the synagogue at Nazareth (Luke 4:16-21). Paul took the customary position as he began to teach. Notice the use of "we," which may indicate that Luke also spoke to the women as a teacher. If he was a resident of Philippi, he may have introduced Paul to the group of women. *The women.* The group of worshipers consisted only of women. There seem to have been no Jewish men to lead the services or even to participate. The courage of these women in carrying on their religious activities under such circumstances is very commendable. *Which resorted thither.* In everyday English, we would say, "Who came there."

14. And a certain woman named Lydia, a seller of purple, of the city of Thyatira, which worshipped God, heard us: whose heart the Lord opened, that she attended unto the things which were spoken of Paul.

Lydia. This was a popular name for women of the time. The name may be a personal name or it may mean "the Lydian," since she was from a city of the province of Lydia. It is of great interest that Lydia was Paul's first convert on the continent of Europe. *A seller of purple.* "Purple" was either a costly dye that was used in coloring very expensive garments or the material colored by that dye. There is no way of knowing which of these Lydia sold. She may have dealt in both. The fact that she dealt in such expensive merchandise indicates that she probably was a woman of some means. This is confirmed by the fact that she had a home in which she could entertain several guests over a period of time,

and that the church appears to have met in her home (Acts 16:40). *Which worshipped God.* This phrase probably means that Lydia was a Gentile who had accepted the Jewish religion. *Whose heart the Lord opened.* This has caused commentators a great deal of difficulty. Some have concluded that one cannot believe unless the Holy Spirit miraculously acts upon his heart and makes it possible for him to believe. Such a conclusion does not do justice to the power of the gospel and God's means of salvation through the preaching of the gospel. The statement probably means that through all the circumstances involved, such as the presence of Paul and his company, the message of Christ that they brought, and the sincerity of their lives dominated by the Spirit of Christ, Lydia's heart was made ready to receive the gospel and accept Christ as her Saviour. The Lord works through all of the means that He has provided for our salvation. Whatever is accomplished by sincere preachers of the gospel is properly considered the work of the Lord (Acts 14:27; 15: 12). *Attended unto the things which were spoken.* Lydia listened carefully to the message that Paul brought, and she accepted the message as true. She believed that Jesus was indeed the Christ, and she wanted to surrender her life to Him.

15. And when she was baptized, and her household, she besought us, saying, If ye have judged me to be faithful to the Lord, come into my house, and abide there. And she constrained us.

When she was baptized. Baptism is assumed as the act by which one publicly accepts Jesus as Saviour and Lord. This procedure was followed in other conversions recorded in the book of Acts. See Acts 2:36-41; 8:12, 35-38 etc. *And her household.* The baptism of Lydia's household can hardly be taken to have any bearing on the question of infant baptism, for there is no way of knowing who composed her household. It may have consisted of the women who worked with her. It is likely that they also worshiped with her, and this supposition is in harmony with verse 13. If they did, they shared her opportunity to hear the gospel and accept it. This same chapter tells of the conversion of a jailer and his household in Philippi. In that case, it is stated that all the household believed in God along with the jailer (v. 34). This is in harmony with the rest of the book of Acts, where there is no record of the baptism of any except those who believed in Christ and repented of their sins. *If ye have judged me to be faithful.* The idea seems to be, "If I am worthy, if you will accept the hospitality I offer." Hospitality is pictured as a Christian virtue throughout the New Testament. See Hebrews 13:2; Matthew 25:35; 1 Timothy 3:2.

16. And it came to pass, as we went to prayer, a certain damsel possessed with a spirit of divination met us, which brought her masters much gain by soothsaying.

The Gospels tell of several people who were possessed by evil spirits. It seems that in some cases, at least, such spirits had more than human knowledge. They recognized Jesus as the Son of God and feared Him (Luke 8:28). The spirit who possessed this girl at Philippi was able to perceive and declare things hidden from ordinary humans, or else to give a convincing pretense. People were willing to pay for such revelations, but the profit went to the girl's *masters.* Apparently she was a slave owned by two or more men in partnership.

17. The same followed Paul and us, and cried, saying, These men are the servants of the most high God, which shew unto us the way of salvation.

It is hard to understand just why the spirit in possession of the girl impelled her to make this announcement. Presumably he was an evil spirit not interested in helping the proclamation of the gospel. Possibly he was maliciously trying to stir up opposition to Paul among the heathen of the town, who might resent the claim that these strangers could show them a better way than their own. But such suggestions have little value; we simply have no information on the spirit's motive or purpose.

18. And this she did many days. But Paul, being grieved, turned and said to the spirit, I command thee in the name of Jesus Christ to come out of her. And he came out the same hour.

Was Paul *grieved* because the unfortunate girl was being mistreated by the demon, or because he did not wish to have an evil spirit's support for himself and his work? In either case, why did he tolerate the grievous situation *many days* before driving the demon out? Did he wait until a riot was about to develop, or did he merely wait till a crowd was present to see him demonstrate the power of Jesus? Or did he anticipate the trouble that would follow, and therefore wait until he was ready to leave before he took action against the demon? We have no answers: here again Luke records the facts and leaves us to guess the reasons.

19. And when her masters saw that the hope of their gains was gone, they caught Paul and Silas, and drew them into the marketplace unto the rulers.

The masters of this slave girl had been using her soothsaying powers to collect gain for themselves. When they realized their source of income had been cut off they wanted to take revenge on Paul and Silas. They stirred up a movement that resulted in the seizure of Paul and Silas. These two were dragged into the agora, or open square, which ordinarily marked the central part of an ancient town.

20. And brought them to the magistrates, saying, These men, being Jews, do exceedingly trouble our city.

It may be that the rulers referred to in the last verse were men of lower rank, and that these men brought Paul and Silas to the chief magistrates of this Roman colony. The accusations made against these two Christian leaders were quite different from the real reasons why the girl's owners attacked them. The charges were well calculated to arouse the ire of both the Roman rulers and the people. There was a charge of causing trouble in the town, which was counter to Rome's insistence upon peace and order. Then there was the statement that they were Jews, which was enough to incite the mob, because the Jews were an unpopular and suspected people.

21. And teach customs, which are not lawful for us to receive, neither to observe, being Romans.

In the third place, the evangelists were spreading customs that were wrong; and in the fourth place, these Philippians were good Romans and could not practice such customs. So argued the accusers of Paul and Silas. There is no explanation as to what the wrong customs were. In fact, the trial may have been so hurried that no one bothered to specify what unlawful practices were meant.

22. And the multitude rose up together against them: and the magistrates rent off their clothes, and commanded to beat them.

There is no indication that Paul and Silas were given an opportunity to defend themselves. As in the case of Jesus, the cries of the mob made their impression on the Roman magistrates. With no further ado, the word was given to the lictors to ply their rods on the bare backs of Paul and Silas. This public punishment no doubt appeased the demonstrators.

23, 24. And when they had laid many stripes upon them, they cast them into prison, charging the jailor to keep them safely: who, having received such a charge, thrust them into the inner prison, and made their feet fast in the stocks.

Following the example of the mob and the rulers, the jailer added his own extra forms of punishment. When commissioned with the safe-keeping of these two, he not only put them in the prison, but in the inner prison. Still this was not enough. He fastened their feet in stocks. This meant they could neither stand up nor sit down without pain, nor could they change their position with freedom.

25. And at midnight Paul and Silas prayed, and sang praises unto God: and the prisoners heard them.

This is a stirring scene. The faith, courage, and loyalty of these Christian leaders were being tried to the utmost. With bleeding backs, legs fastened in stocks, the despair of darkness, the uncertainty of the morrow, and the injustice of the whole situation—still by midnight both Paul and Silas had regained their senses sufficiently to apply the best remedies for their trials. They prayed and sang hymns to God.

The prisoners heard them. Rather, the prisoners "were listening" to them. They must have been somewhat amazed at what they heard from these men, for such reaction to imprisonment was unusual. Is it any wonder that the prisoners listened closely to this witness of dedicated lives? We too would gather to listen to the plaintive strains of Christian hymns coming from a Philippian prison, bearing witness to the lives of Christian leaders.

26. And suddenly there was a great earthquake, so that the foundations of the prison were shaken: and immediately all the doors were opened, and every one's bands were loosed.

The singing and praying of Paul and Silas was interrupted by an earthquake of such force that the prison doors were opened and the prisoners' bands loosed by the force of the earthquake. We can readily see how the doors could have been shaken open, but it is difficult to see how the prisoners' bands could have been loosed by the earthquake. While Luke does not expressly say so, may we assume that what happened in other situations when prison doors were opened for God's messengers also happened here? For example, when the apostles were thrown into prison in Jerusalem, "the angel of the Lord by night opened the prison doors, and brought them forth" (Acts 5:19). There is also the case of Peter, whom Herod had thrown into prison, who was delivered by an angel, who released him from his chains and before whom "the iron gate that leadeth unto the city . . . opened to them of his own accord" (Acts 12:10).

27. And the keeper of the prison awaking out of his sleep, and seeing the prison doors open, he drew out his sword, and would have killed himself, supposing that the prisoners had been fled.

Evidently the jailer had not heard the singing of Paul and Silas. But the earthquake was of such force that it wakened him. Seeing the doors of the prison open and supposing that all the prisoners had taken advantage of the situation and escaped, he was ready to kill himself. He was responsible for his prisoners, having been expressly charged to "keep them safely." If they had escaped, his own life would be taken. According to the Roman code it was better to commit suicide than to suffer death at the hands of an enemy or an executioner. "Suicide to a Roman of that day was very much a matter of indifference. Brutus and Cassius, models of Roman virtue, had committed it at or near Philippi. . . . Christianity first taught men to estimate life and death rightly" (Cook, *Bible Commentary*).

28. But Paul cried with a loud voice, saying, Do thyself no harm: for we are all here.

Luke leaves us to draw our own conclusion as to how Paul knew that the jailer was about to commit suicide. Some think that his purpose was indicated to the apostle by some outcry; others think that it was by divine revelation. At any rate, Paul knew that the man who had treated them so cruelly was about to kill himself. Quickly the prisoner called to him to refrain from his contemplated act of self-destruction.

We are all here. Paul knew, also, that not one of the prisoners had taken advantage of the opportunity to escape. Again we are led to wonder why. Were they overcome by the strangeness of what had happened? Was there some divine restraint in their case? Luke does not tell us, perhaps, because these details are not essential to the narrative that he is writing.

29. Then he called for a light, and sprang in, and came trembling, and fell down before Paul and Silas.

The jailer called for lights so that an examination of the prison could be made. He found that Paul's word concerning the prisoners was true: not one had escaped. Impressed by the night's happenings, and connecting these strange occurrences with Paul and Silas, he came to fall down before them in an attitude of reverence and worship.

30. And brought them out, and said, Sirs, what must I do to be saved?

He did not leave Paul and Silas in their cell, but brought them out into another part of the prison.

What must I do to be saved? It would seem that the jailer had some previous knowledge of the mission and character of these two prisoners. While they had been cast into prison

on the grounds that they were perverting the religious customs of the Romans, it is entirely possible that the jailer had heard the story of the maiden who had followed them and the words she kept repeating: "These men are the servants of the most high God, which shew unto us the way of salvation" (verse 17). At any rate, he turned to them for an answer to his question.

31. And they said, Believe on the Lord Jesus Christ, and thou shalt be saved, and thy house.

Believe on the Lord Jesus Christ. This was the starting point for the jailer, as for all other men, for faith in Christ is essential to salvation. Without faith in Christ no man can be saved, for salvation centers in Him. Without this faith, what incentive would there be for one to become a Christian? It would be strange indeed to begin following a person in whom one has no faith!

And thy house. The jailer's "house" would receive salvation upon the same basis as the jailer himself. They would not be directly affected and become saved persons because of the jailer's actions. If they desired salvation, then they too must believe on Jesus as the Christ and Saviour.

32. And they spake unto him the word of the Lord, and to all that were in his house.

If Paul and Silas taught the word "to all that were in his house," then all must have been capable of hearing and believing. From these men they learned about Jesus: His birth, life, death, burial, resurrection. They were also told of the steps they must take in order to comply with Jesus' will—what they must do in order to be reconciled to God through Christ.

33. And he took them the same hour of the night, and washed their stripes; and was baptized, he and all his, straightway.

Washed their stripes. The word used here for "wash" refers to the bathing of the entire body, rather than just the cleansing of the wounds caused by the beating. The blood that had accumulated on the prisoners' bodies was washed away, and their wounds were treated.

And was baptized. Evidently the place of baptism in the program of Christ had been indicated by Paul and Silas. Baptism was deemed of such importance that these were baptized immediately.

34. And when he had brought them into his house, he set meat before them, and rejoiced, believing in God with all his house.

Instead of despised prisoners, these men were now Christian brothers. While the jailer had been responsible for thrusting them into prison, they had been responsible for freeing him from the bondage of sin. At one time he might have been happy to see them die, but they were greatly concerned about seeing him live. He was twice saved through their instrumentality: physically and spiritually. He rejoiced greatly because of the salvation that had come to his house that night.

35. And when it was day, the magistrates sent the serjeants, saying, Let those men go.

When it was day. The following events took place the morning after. *The serjeants.* The police. They were directed by the magistrates who had ordered Paul and Silas to prison to release them.

36. And the keeper of the prison told this saying to Paul, The magistrates have sent to let you go: now therefore depart, and go in peace.

The messengers from the magistrates naturally carried the order to the jailer to whom the prisoners had been delivered the night before. The jailer quickly went to release Paul and Silas, explaining that the magistrates had ordered it.

37. But Paul said unto them, They have beaten us openly uncondemned, being Romans, and have cast us into prison; and now do they thrust us out privily? nay verily; but let them come themselves and fetch us out.

Being Romans. Under the rule of the Roman Empire, Jews or others who were not Romans by birth might be naturalized as citizens of Rome, even though they did not live in Rome itself. Sometimes this citizenship was granted in recognition of service to the empire; sometimes it was given in return for a large sum of money (Acts 22:28). Paul's father probably had become a Roman citizen in some such way, so that Paul was born a citizen. Romans had certain rights not enjoyed by the conquered people of the empire. For one thing, they could not legally be punished till they were tried and found guilty. The officials of Philippi had violated this right in their hasty beating and imprisonment of Paul and Silas. *Privily.* In private. The beatings had been public, marking Paul and Silas as criminals. Paul demanded that the release also be public, making it clear to all that the punishment was undeserved. His demand probably was not motivated by personal pride, but was for the sake of the new church, which would be helped by clearing Paul and Silas.

38. And the serjeants told these words unto the magistrates: and they feared, when they heard that they were Romans.

The magistrates evidently had ordered the beating and imprisonment hastily, perhaps to appease the crowd that seemed to be angered and might riot (v. 22). They had not known the prisoners were Romans, and had not given them any opportunity to say that they were.

39. And they came and besought them, and brought them out, and desired them to depart out of the city.

They came. This refers to the magistrates. They were afraid because they had committed a serious violation of Roman law, for which they might be punished severely. *Besought them.* Probably they begged Paul and Silas not to report them to higher authorities. *Desired them.* Requested them.

40. They went out of the prison, and entered into the house of Lydia: and when they had seen the brethren, they comforted them, and departed.

The house of Lydia. Paul and Silas had been staying there. They returned to get their luggage and take courteous leave of their hostess and the other Christians. *Seen the brethren.* It is possible that many had been gathered in Lydia's home for prayer in behalf of Paul and Silas, as disciples in Jerusalem had once gathered in the home of Mary for prayer in behalf of Peter. See Acts 12:4-17. *Comforted them.* The brethren were comforted by the release of Paul and Silas, who now encouraged them to be steadfast through all the trials that might come to them from the heathen population of the city. *Departed.* They had organized a church in Philippi that could care for itself. They now went on to other fields of evangelism.

CHAPTER 17

1. Now when they had passed through Amphipolis and Apollonia, they came to Thessalonica, where was a synagogue of the Jews.

The group moved westward to another important city, *Thessalonica.* Now Luke's record says *they* instead of "we," indicating that the author remained at Philippi when Paul and Silas left. Timothy is next mentioned at Berea (v. 14), so we may suppose he either went with Paul and Silas or followed them a little later.

2. And Paul, as his manner was, went in unto them, and three sabbath days reasoned with them out of the scriptures.

Went in unto them means Paul went in to the Jews as they met in their synagogue (v. 1). This was *his*

manner or custom in every town where he found a synagogue. He may have talked with either Jews or Gentiles between the weekly meetings, but he came back to reason with the Jews in their meetings on three *sabbaths,* using *the scriptures* that told of the Messiah to show that the Messiah had come.

3. Opening and alleging, that Christ must needs have suffered, and risen again from the dead; and that this Jesus, whom I preach unto you, is Christ.

Paul showed that the Old Testament Scriptures foretold the death and resurrection of the coming Messiah or Christ, and then declared that Jesus was proved to be the Christ by His fulfillment of those

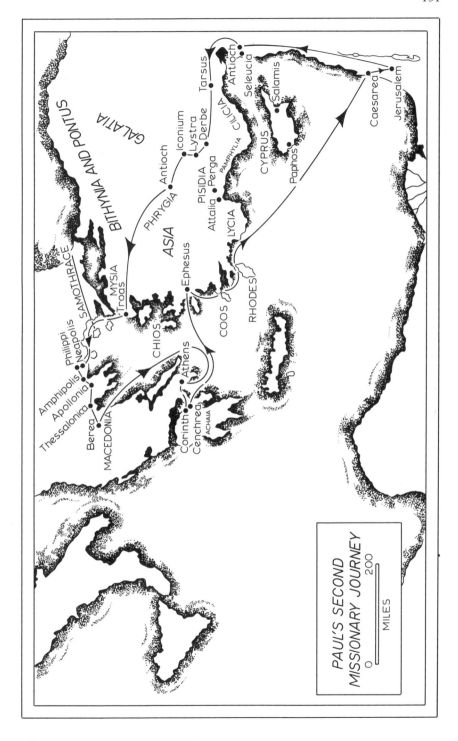

PAUL'S SECOND
MISSIONARY JOURNEY

0   200

MILES

Scriptures. Jesus himself had taught this line of reasoning to some of His disciples (Luke 24:44-48), and Peter had used it (Acts 2:22-36; 3:13-18).

4. And some of them believed, and consorted with Paul and Silas; and of the devout Greeks a great multitude, and of the chief women not a few.

Some of the Jews were convinced that Jesus was the long-awaited Messiah, and even more of the *devout Greeks* who had already accepted the true God now accepted His Son. A considerable number of prominent and influential women were among those who became Christians.

5. But the Jews which believed not, moved with envy, took unto them certain lewd fellows of the baser sort, and gathered a company, and set all the city on an uproar, and assaulted the house of Jason, and sought to bring them out to the people.

As in other places, some of the Jews not only rejected the message but also persecuted the messengers. In this case they enlisted the help of worthless riffraff, probably by paying for it. *Lewd fellows* represents a Greek word meaning such men as loaf about the marketplace or public square. The ones chosen were not merely lazy, however. They were *of the baser sort*: bad, troublesome characters, perhaps including thugs, pickpockets, and sneak thieves. These easily *gathered a company* of their own kind and started a riot. They *assaulted the house of Jason,* probably because they had learned it was the lodging place of Paul and Silas, intending to *bring them out to the people.* We can only guess what would have happened if this mob had caught the missionaries.

6. And when they found them not, they drew Jason and certain brethren unto the rulers of the city, crying, These that have turned the world upside down are come hither also.

Perhaps the missionaries just happened to be away from the home; perhaps they had been warned to go to another place. Whatever the reason, the mob failed to find them, but did find Jason and some of the Thessalonian Christians and dragged them to the rulers. Their first charge was that the missionaries were known troublemakers—they had *turned the world upside down.* The Jewish leaders doubtless had heard of the trouble that had centered about these men in Philippi; possibly they had received word of earlier and more distant troubles in Antioch, Iconium, and Lystra.

7. Whom Jason hath received: and these all do contrary to the decrees of Caesar, saying that there is another king, one Jesus.

The first charge against Jason was that he had received these troublemakers, given them aid and comfort. It is not clear whether *these all* means Jason and those with him or the missionaries. Perhaps it means both, plus all the other Christians. The final charge was that these all were rebels who would enthrone Jesus in place of Caesar. The Jews must have known this was false— Paul doubtless had told them Jesus had ascended to heaven after His resurrection—but they knew also that it would disturb the rulers who were responsible to higher officials in Caesar's empire.

8. And they troubled the people and the rulers of the city, when they heard these things.

Already there had been a small riot. If it grew into open rebellion, the rulers might lose their jobs and the people might be punished with heavier taxes. Rome insisted that the peace be kept!

9. And when they had taken security of Jason, and of the other, they let them go.

This *security* may have been in the nature of a bond to keep the peace: that is, the men may have been required to deposit a sum of money that would be forfeited if they were responsible for further disturbances. Of course the Jews and not the disciples were responsible for the disturbance; but the departure of Paul and Silas (v. 10) would placate them and permit peace to prevail for the time being.

10. And the brethren immediately sent away Paul and Silas by night unto Berea: who coming thither went into the synagogue of the Jews.

Berea may have been chosen as a quiet town where Paul might find rest after the pressures of the recent weeks. "Who when they were come thither went into the synagogue of the Jews" (American Standard Version). After their many afflictions at the hands of the Jews, Paul and Silas might be expected to seek other circles in which to serve, but they were looking for opportunities rather than safety, and the synagogues offered the best opportunities for evangelizing.

11. These were more noble than those in Thessalonica, in that they received the word with all readiness of mind, and searched the scriptures daily, whether those things were so.

"These were of a more noble disposition than those of Thessalonica" (Living Oracles translation). With less of importance and station to boast in their humbler synagogue, the Jews of Berea were more open-minded than the synagogue worshipers in Thessalonica. No comparison is made here with the Thessalonian believers, who became examples to all the Christians in Macedonia and Achaia (1 Thessalonians 1:7). *They received the word with all readiness of mind.* They heard respectfully, and they examined carefully the one body of material in which they had unbounded confidence. Both the substance of Paul's preaching and their own conviction led them to the Scriptures.

12. Therefore many of them believed; also of honourable women which were Greeks, and of men, not a few.

Belief, the complete, active response that set the Christians apart from the unbelieving world, came naturally as a result of the Bereans' investigation of the truth. In Thessalonica "some" in the synagogue had believed, but the larger number of converts had come from among the devout Greeks. Here the order was reversed.

13. But when the Jews of Thessalonica had knowledge that the word of God was preached of Paul at Berea, they came thither also, and stirred up the people.

Again we are reminded of two things that have been made evident earlier in the book of Acts. First, there was frequent communication between synagogues in different cities: soon *the Jews of Thessalonica had knowledge* of what was being done in Berea. Second, the Jews opposing the gospel were vigorous and determined: *they came thither also, and stirred up the people.* Perhaps they began with the same methods they had used in Thessalonica, finding a group of unprincipled men to help them (v. 5).

14. And then immediately the brethren sent away Paul to go as it were to the sea: but Silas and Timotheus abode there still.

Knowing what had happened in Thessalonica, the Christians in Berea did not wait for the disturbance to become a riot, but sent Paul away *immediately.* The malice of the Jews was chiefly directed against him because he was the principal speaker in the synagogues. His departure quieted the opposition enough so that *Silas and Timotheus* (Timothy) could stay and give further teaching to the new Christians in Berea.

15. And they that conducted Paul brought him unto Athens: and receiving a commandment unto Silas and Timotheus for to come to him with all speed, they departed.

Some of the Berean Christians went with Paul, not only to signify their friendship and good will, but probably also to protect him against possible attack by thugs sent by the unbelieving Jews. At *Athens,* some two hundred miles away, they judged that danger was past. As they went back to Berea, Paul sent word to *Silas and Timotheus* to join him as soon as they could. However, it seems that the Bereans wanted them to stay in Berea as long as necessary to establish the church firmly, for they did not join him in Athens, but later in Corinth (Acts 18:5).

16. Now while Paul waited for them at Athens, his spirit was stirred

in him, when he saw the city wholly given to idolatry.

American Standard Version has "full of idols" instead of *wholly given to idolatry.* Often quoted is the comment of Petronius, a Roman satirist, that it was easier to find a god than a man in Athens. Statues and shrines to imaginary gods were everywhere—in the homes, in the public square, in the street. Knowing all these deities were false, Paul was *stirred* to oppose them and point their worshipers to the true God.

17. Therefore disputed he in the synagogue with the Jews, and with the devout persons, and in the market daily with them that met with him.

As in other towns, Paul went to the *synagogue* on the Sabbath and reasoned *with the Jews, and with the devout persons,* the Gentiles who believed in the true God and worshiped Him along with the Jews. But this time emphasis is given to his work between Sabbaths. He went to the *market,* a public square that served as a forum for discussions, a meeting place for friends, and a haven for loafers as well as a market. There he reasoned with any who would listen. Most of them *that met with him* there were heathen.

18. Then certain philosophers of the Epicureans, and of the Stoicks, encountered him. And some said, What will this babbler say? other some, He seemeth to be a setter forth of strange gods: because he preached unto them Jesus, and the resurrection.

The *Epicureans* accepted the system of philosophy taught by Epicurus some three hundred years earlier. Epicureans made pleasure the greatest good in life. By the beginning of the Chrisian era this philosophy had often degenerated into an "eat, drink, and be merry" approach to life. The *Stoicks* accepted rather the philosophy of Zeno, who had taught in a *stoa* or porch of the very market where Paul was now teaching. The Stoics taught that duty was the highest good. In their dedication to duty they were to accept without emotion whatever life happened to bring, whether pain or pleasure. These philosophers spent much time in the public square, debating their views and taking delight in hearing and criticizing any new ideas that might be presented. *Babbler* is literally "seed picker." The Greek word was used of seed-eating birds, and perhaps in the market it was often used of idlers, who would pick up bits of merchandise without paying. The philosophers may have used it of anyone who frequented the market to pick up bits of information. If that is the meaning, the word could be used of any of them. *A setter forth of strange gods.* The conversation about Paul seems to have been carried on by people on the fringe of the crowd, people who had not heard his teaching distinctly. They heard him speak of Jesus, who they gathered was a *strange* or foreign god, one unknown to them. The word *resurrection* probably was not often used in Athens; some who heard but little may have thought Paul mentioned a second god named resurrection.

19. And they took him, and brought him unto Areopagus, saying, May we know what this new doctrine, whereof thou speakest, is?

The philosophers were interested enough to lead Paul to a quieter place, away from the crowded market. The place chosen was the meeting place of the court of Athens, but there is no indication that the court was in session or that Paul was on trial. Perhaps the place was open to the public for meetings such as this. It was a leveled place on a hill not far from the market. The name *Areopagus,* meaning Ares' hill, reflected the tradition that the god Ares (called Mars by the Romans) had once been tried there.

20. For thou bringest certain strange things to our ears: we would know therefore what these things mean.

The philosophers were saying, in effect, "You have been talking about things that are new to us. We want to hear more about them."

21. (For all the Athenians and strangers which were there spent their time in nothing else, but either to tell, or to hear some new thing.)

This explains why these people were so eager to hear more of Paul's teaching: it was their occupation, their chief interest, to hear and tell something new. *All the Athenians* of course means the philosophers and students who had leisure and interest for this exchange of ideas. Athens had also its merchants and artisans and slaves who were busy in other occupations. The *strangers* were philosophers from other places who were staying in Athens for a time. They came in great numbers because Athens was known as the best place in the world to tell or hear something new.

22. Then Paul stood in the midst of Mars' hill, and said, Ye men of Athens, I perceive that in all things ye are too superstitious.

Mars' hill. Or the Areopagus (verse 19). This was the meeting place of the famed Athenian court. It was here that Socrates was tried and convicted as a perverter of the accepted religion. The name Mars' Hill was applied to it because of the legend that Mars, the god of war, was tried here for murdering the son of Poseidon (Neptune), the sea-god, in one of the many squabbles among the gods. While the Areopagus was associated with court proceedings, and some have thought that the statement in verse 19—"they took him, and brought him unto Areopagus"— indicates some kind of a trial, there seems to be little to indicate that the apostle was actually on trial. The explanation seems to lie in another direction. Paul had brought a strange, new doctrine to Athens, and these philosophers and others desired to hear him more fully concerning it. See verses 19-21. The Areopagus was the natural place for such a meeting.

Too superstitious. Literally, "demon-fearing." The practice of worshiping demons was very prevalent. "Demons" seems to have been a general term for spiritual beings of all kinds, real or imaginary. It is doubtful that Paul would have begun his message by accusing the Athenians of being "too superstitious." But to call them "very demon-fearing" would be equivalent to saying they were "very religious," which is the translation given in the American Standard Version.

23. For as I passed by, and beheld your devotions, I found an altar with this inscription, TO THE UNKNOWN GOD. Whom therefore ye ignorantly worship, him declare I unto you.

As I passed by. Passing through the streets of Athens.

Beheld your devotions. Paul's reference is probably to the objects and evidences of their devotions, rather than to the worship itself. He had observed with interest the temples, statues, and idols which were associated with their worship or devotions.

TO THE UNKNOWN GOD. Rather, "to an unknown God." Why had the Athenians erected an altar having this particular inscription? Many conjectures have been made to account for it: (1) An older altar which had fallen into decay had been repaired, and, the original inscription having been lost, the altar was dedicated to the god whose name they no longer knew; (2) It had been erected to some unknown god by whom they felt they had been especially blessed; (3) They feared lest, in honoring the gods, one had been inadvertently omitted, and so they erected the altar to appease this god. Paul seized upon this altar and its inscription as a good introduction for his message on the living God.

Whom therefore ye ignorantly worship. "Ignorantly" is not used in a bad sense, but in the sense of "not knowing." Their worship of an unknown god was evidence of their religious nature and devotion.

Declare I unto you. This unknown deity, whom they worshiped unknowingly, Paul was prepared to make known to them. They would then be able to worship Him knowingly.

24. God that made the world and all things therein, seeing that he is Lord of heaven and earth, dwelleth not in temples made with hands.

God that made the world. Not just a god among the many gods of the Athenians, but *the* God. This

God whom Paul was prepared to declare unto them was Creator of the world and all that is within it.

He is the Lord of heaven and earth. As the Creator, He is the Lord of *all* His creation, not just a certain portion of it. He not only made the world, He also sustains and rules it.

Dwelleth not in temples made with hands. It is impossible to confine this God to a building made by the hands of men, even such magnificent temples as those built by the Greeks.

25. Neither is worshipped with men's hands, as though he needed any thing, seeing he giveth to all life, and breath, and all things.

Worshipped. Rather, "served." The Creator is not dependent upon the creature. The living God is not like lifeless idols: helpless, incapable of movement, unable to speak, confined to a temple.

He giveth to all life, and breath, and all things. God is both the giver and the sustainer of life. All life comes from Him. He has made provision for every need of man, both physical and spiritual.

26. And hath made of one blood all nations of men for to dwell on all the face of the earth, and hath determined the times before appointed, and the bounds of their habitation.

Made of one blood all 'nations. Rather, "made of one"—Adam. All men are kin; all are the creation of God; all come under His love; all partake of the provisions He has made for food and raiment. If this God made all nations, then He should be worshiped by all nations. He is not a tribal God, or the God

of one nation, but the God of every nation, including the Greeks.

Hath determined the times before appointed. "Having determined their appointed seasons, and the bounds of their habitation" (American Standard Version). According to Daniel, God "changeth the times and the seasons: he removeth kings, and setteth up kings" (2:21).

The bounds of their habitation. God may have determined the boundary lines of the nations, even as in the settlement of Canaan by the Israelites, but this is not to say that men have always respected the boundary lines which God has drawn.

27. That they should seek the Lord, if haply they might feel after him, and find him, though he be not far from every one of us.

"Finally he shows them that the purpose of God in all these things was to induce men to obtain the very knowledge of himself which Paul was now trying to impart to his hearers. What nobler pursuit of knowledge than to seek such a God, even though we have to 'feel after him' like blind men. But such obscure seeking, he lets them know in the same breath, is not needful, seeing that he is not far away, but round about us at all times and in all places" (McGarvey, *Commentary on Acts*).

28. For in him we live, and move, and have our being; as certain also of your own poets have said, For we are also his offspring.

God is the source of all life, the sustainer of life. Without Him life could neither begin nor continue.

Certain also of your own poets. Particularly Aratus and Cleanthes.

We are also his offspring. This statement of the Greek poets Paul uses to express the relation of men to the living God, or to their unknown god. However, the Greeks did not approach the concept of God's creation of man as revealed in Genesis (1:26; 2:7).

29. Forasmuch then as we are the offspring of God, we ought not to think that the Godhead is like unto gold, or silver, or stone, graven by art and man's device.

In the previous verses are Paul's declarations concerning God as the maker and provider of all things, and therefore not to be limited to man-made temples nor served as though He had material need. Verse 28 applies to God the words of the poet Epimenedes of Crete, "For in him we live, and move, and have our being," and of Aratus of Cilicia, "For we are also his offspring." *Forasmuch then as we are the offspring of God.* Paul proceeded to logical deductions from the words of Aratus. *We ought not to think that the Godhead is like unto gold . . . graven by art and man's device.* Idolatry, the worship of that which was made by the worshiper and is therefore lower than himself, is an insult to mankind. The Greeks had a high view of the human body, mind, and spirit. How could the Maker of these things be, or be represented by, a lifeless image?

Godhead. Literally, "that which is divine."

30. And the times of this ignorance God winked at; but now commandeth all men every where to repent.

"The times of ignorance therefore God overlooked" (American Standard Version) Without approving idolatry even in times when men did not know better, God refrained from bringing them into judgment for it until such time as He could give them a fuller revelation of himself. "But now he commandeth men that they should all everywhere repent" (American Standard Version). The former things had left man ignorant of God and far from His presence. They had to be changed. The repentance indicated here is very different from mere remorse for sins committed. It is the change of one's mind that issues in a changed life.

31. Because he hath appointed a day, in the which he will judge the world in righteousness by that man whom he hath ordained; whereof he hath given assurance unto all men, in that he hath raised him from the dead.

The thought that each of them would one day stand in judgment before a just and righteous God, must have come as a tremendous shock to the Greeks, who had no such idea in their religion—a religion built on offering sacrifices to deities who were thought to share every human sin and foible in magnified proportion. *By that man whom he hath ordained.* All that was said to this point was introductory to it. Here Christ was introduced, not as the promised Messiah, but rather as the Man through whom God would execute judgment; not in the beginning of His ministry, but in the climax and conclusion of it. Compare John 5:22-29. *Whereof he hath given assurance . . . in that he hath raised him from the dead.* The resurrection established the deity of Christ, guaranteed His return, and assured the judgment of which Paul spoke. Without it, there would be no gospel.

32. And when they heard of the resurrection of the dead, some mocked: and others said, We will hear thee again of this matter.

The Greek philosophers disdained the idea that any kind of body might rise from the dead. Supremely sure of their intellectual superiority, some could scoff at the credulity of the superstitious Jew. "But others said, we will hear thee concerning this yet again" (American Standard Version). The resurrection bombshell had broken up the meeting.

33. So Paul departed from among them.

Having lost his audience for this occasion, he left them to discuss his sermon among themselves.

34. Howbeit certain men clave unto him, and believed: among the which was Dionysius the Areopagite, and a woman named Damaris, and others with them.

"Nevertheless, some men adhered to him, and believed" (Living Oracles translation). Vitally interested, certain ones followed Paul to learn and accept the gospel plan of salvation. The word "believed" signifies the total life commitment that distinguished the Christians from the non-Christian world. *Dionysius the Areopagite.* A member of the council of the Areopagus. Later tradition speaks of him as a bishop of Athens, and attaches his name to a spurious bit of post-apostolic writing. *A woman named Damaris.* Nothing more is known of her. The presence of a woman among the philosophers on the Areopagus indicates the independent status achieved by Greek women. *Others with them.* Paul's evangelistic effort at Athens was not the failure that some have labeled it. The description would indicate at least a half dozen converts, including a member of the council.

CHAPTER 18

1. After these things Paul departed from Athens, and came to Corinth.

After these things. After the apostle Paul's experiences in Athens. *Athens.* Athens was the intellectual center of the ancient Greek world, the university center to which ambitious young scholars hoped to go. Nothing further is written of the church that came into being at Athens with the conversion of Dionysius, Damaris, and the others. Paul's stay with them was apparently short. *Corinth.* Corinth was a commercial city, a crossroads of commerce between the provinces and the city of Rome. This great seaport had all the

problems of mixed populations, displaced people, and pleasure seekers who would pay any price. Corinth was considered to be one of the most corrupt cities of the world. The word *Corinthianize* was coined from its name and meant to indulge in lust, immorality, and vice. It was to this great center that Paul now came.

2. And found a certain Jew named Aquila, born in Pontus, lately come from Italy, with his wife Priscilla; (because that Claudius had commanded all Jews to depart from Rome:) and came unto them.

Aquila. He and his wife became lasting friends of Paul and later accompanied him to Ephesus. When

Paul wrote 1 Corinthians from Ephesus, he could send greetings from Aquila and Priscilla and the church that met in their house (1 Corinthians 16:19). Later, Aquila and Priscilla were back in Rome, and Paul sent his greetings to them there (Romans 16:3). Finally, in the last days of his life, Paul wrote to Timothy from Rome and sent his greetings to Aquila and Priscilla, who had returned to Ephesus (2 Timothy 4:19). The travels of these two help us to realize how mobile the population of the Roman Empire was. Commerce and social circumstances caused many to move frequently from place to place. *Born in Pontus.* There were many Jews in the region of Pontus. (See Acts 2:9; 1 Peter 1:1). Aquila's trade had probably caused him to leave his home. *Priscilla.* In view of the subordinate place usually held by women, the prominence given to Priscilla seems strange. In Romans 16:3 and 2 Timothy 4:19 she is named before her husband. She must have been a very talented person. *Claudius.* Claudius was the emperor of Rome. He dealt harshly with any who would disturb the peace of the empire. The Roman historian Suetonius wrote that he expelled the Jews from Rome because of tumults "raised at the instigation of Chrestus." Though no clear identification can be made, it has been supposed that the term "Chrestus" referred to Jesus Christ and that the tumults revolve around the Jewish Christians in Rome. This must remain in the realm of speculation. Since there is no indication that Aquila and Prsicilla were baptized after they came into contact with Paul, it is sometimes supposed that they were already Christians when they left Rome for Corinth. This is entirely possible. The church in Rome was famous when Paul wrote to it perhaps six years after his first coming to Corinth (Romans 1:18). It may have been planted by some of those who were driven out of Jerusalem after the death of Stephen early in the history of the church (Acts 8:1-4; 11:19).

3. And because he was of the same craft, he abode with them, and wrought: for by their occupation they were tentmakers.

Because he was of the same craft. Every Jewish boy was taught a trade by which he would be able to sustain himself. Paul took some pride in the fact that he did not depend for his living on the generosity of his converts (Acts 20:34; 1 Thessalonians 2:9; 2 Thessalonians 3:8; 1 Corinthians 4:12). *By their occupation they were tentmakers.* Tentmaking was not an unusual craft in Paul's native Cilicia, where numerous goats furnished the long hair that was woven into tent cloth. The work was hard, especially with the limited equipment that would be available in a private home. Aquila and Priscilla and Paul were tentmakers by trade. People of different trades were, in the ancient world, organized into guilds very much like our modern labor unions, or even like lodges or clubs. Even in the synagogue the Jews sometimes sat together according to trades. *Abode with them.* Paul lived in their house. Apparently it was large enough for their shop as well as for living quarters. We read elsewhere of the church in the house of Aquila and Priscilla. The church may have met in the large room that was used during the week as a shop. *Wrought.* Paul worked at his trade.

He did not then receive support from the churches for his missionary work, so he was forced to work for his living. He preached to people while he worked or after hours. He seems to have felt no great difficulty in this. In fact, when he was speaking to the elders of the church at Ephesus, he made the point that he worked with his own hands for his support while he was at Ephesus, and he cited this as an example for every Christian to follow (Acts 20: 33-35).

4. And he reasoned in the synagogue every sabbath, and persuaded the Jews and the Greeks.

Daily toil limited his opportunities for teaching. His "reasoning" seems to have been preparatory to the bold declaration of Jesus' messiahship mentioned in the next verse. *Persuaded the Jews and the Greeks.* Devout Greeks as well as Jews attended the synagogue services. In Corinth especially there was every reason that high-minded citizens would turn away from the native expressions of religion.

5. And when Silas and Timotheus were come from Macedonia, Paul was pressed in the spirit, and testified to the Jews that Jesus was Christ.

Silas and Timothy had been left at Berea, with instruction to come to Paul in Athens (17:15, 16). Timothy did so, but was sent back to Thessalonica to assist the Christians there (1 Thessalonians 3:1, 2). The two now completed their errands, bringing financial gifts from the brethren in Macedonia to sustain Paul in his work (2 Corinthians 11:9). "Paul was constrained by the word" (American Standard Version). The encouragement that came with the presence of his co-workers and the easing of his material needs was accompanied by a compelling urgency to a bolder and more constant ministry. *Testified to the Jews that Jesus was Christ.* He boldly declared the central fact to which his former discussions had been leading.

6. And when they opposed themselves, and blasphemed, he shook his raiment, and said unto them, Your blood be upon your own heads; I am clean: from henceforth I will go unto the Gentiles.

The Jews who rejected the gospel in Corinth followed the pattern that Paul had come to expect since the beginning of his missionary efforts. *Blasphemed.* Spoke evil of Jesus, calling Him accursed, or anathema (1 Corinthians 12:3). *He shook his raiment.* He rid himself of the contamination of the very dust of their synagogue, as Jesus had instructed His disciples to do (Luke 10:11; Matthew 10:14; compare Acts 13:51). *Your blood be upon your own heads; I am clean.* The responsibility for their ultimate condemnation rested with themselves and not with him, since he had not shunned to declare to them all the counsel of God (20:26, 27; compare Ezekiel 3:18). *From henceforth I will go unto the Gentiles.* For a second time Paul made a clear and announced transfer of mission, according to the Lord's command (Acts 13:46; 22:21).

7. And he departed thence, and entered into a certain man's house, named Justus, one that worshipped God, whose house joined hard to the synagogue.

Paul accepted the invitation of one, Justus, to use his home as a place of meeting and teaching. *One that worshipped God.* This phrase is used regularly of devout Gentiles, sometimes called "proselytes of the gate," consorting with the worshipers of the true God, but not being full-fleged proselytes to Judaism. "Whose house was adjoining the synagogue" (Living Oracles translation). The location next door gave Paul an excellent opportunity still to influence many of the Jews.

8. And Crispus, the chief ruler of the synagogue, believed on the Lord with all his house; and many of the Corinthians hearing believed, and were baptized.

Crispus was one of the few converts in Corinth whom Paul baptized with his own hands (1 Corinthians 1:14), the others probably being baptized by Silas and Timothy, and later by leaders among the Corinthian Christians. *Believed on the Lord with all his house.* As in the cases of Lydia and the Philippian jailer, the family and the domestic servants were both convinced and converted at the same time. *Many of the Corinthians hearing believed, and were baptized.* This outlines the New Testament pattern of conversion crisply. "Faith cometh by hearing, and hearing by the word of God" (Romans 10:17). The believing hearers were baptized into Christ (Romans 6:3, 4; Galatians 3:27).

9. Then spake the Lord to Paul in the night by a vision, Be not afraid, but speak, and hold not thy peace.

On the Damascus road, Jesus had said that He would appear to Paul yet other times (Acts 26:16). *Be not afraid.* Paul knew that the opposition of the Jews would become more bitter with the growing success of the gospel (see 17:13), and especially

with the conversion of the ruler of their synagogue. "Speak, and do not keep silence" (Living Oracles translation). It would require some courage to open his mouth boldly, "to make known the mystery of the gospel" (Ephesians 6:19) in the face of the known opposition.

10. For I am with thee, and no man shall set on thee to hurt thee: for I have much people in this city.

The continued presence of the Lord was a great comfort to Paul on many occasions (Acts 17:23, 24), and occasionally it was the only real comradeship he had (2 Timothy 4:16, 17). The opposition at Corinth was limited to legal procedure rather than mob violence, and even that attempt was frustrated (vv. 12-17). *I have much people in this city.* Besides those already believing in Christ, many others were weary of the wickedness in Corinth, religious as well as secular, and would respond to the gospel.

11. And he continued there a year and six months, teaching the word of God among them.

"He dwelt there a year and six months" (American Standard Version). During this time he wrote the two epistles to the Thessalonians. *Teaching the word of God among them.* Besides continuing evangelism, Paul engaged in "teaching them to observe all things whatsoever I have commanded you" (Matthew 28:20). In a city like Corinth this was especially important.

12. And when Gallio was the deputy of Achaia, the Jews made insurrection with one accord against Paul, and brought him to the judgment seat.

Paul probably worked in Corinth

for some time before *Gallio* arrived there as *deputy* or proconsul, of the province *Achaia,* of which Corinth was the capital. *The Jews who were* opposed to the gospel perhaps hoped the new proconsul would be eager to establish friendly relations and therefore could be swayed by a protest made by a large number of people. *With one accord,* therefore, they took action *against Paul.* The American Standard Version expresses the meaning well for modern English readers by saying, "rose up" instead of *made insurrection.* In some way not described, these Jews brought Paul to the judgment seat where Gallio sat to hear complaints and settle disputes.

13. Saying, This fellow persuadeth men to worship God contrary to the law.

The unbelieving Jews thought that Paul's gospel led people away from the treasured law of Moses. Since the Jewish religion was recognized as legitimate by the Roman government, the Jews may have argued that in trying to overthrow it Paul was opposing the Roman decree. No details of their accusation are recorded, however, so we can only guess how they tried to support their charge.

14. And when Paul was now about to open his mouth, Gallio said unto the Jews, If it were a matter of wrong or wicked lewdness, O ye Jews, reason would that I should bear with you.

Paul was ready to answer, probably intending to preach the gospel to Gallio rather than to defend himself, but Gallio decided the charge was so weak that no defense was necessary. The charge was not *a matter of wrong or wicked lewdness:*

that is, of injustice or evil villainy of any kind. If it had been, Gallio would have been willing to hear the case.

15. But if it be a question of words and names, and of your law, look ye to it; for I will be no judge of such matters.

Gallio readily recognized that the case before him did not involve any criminal acts, but only a dispute about the Jewish *law* and such *words and names,* probably, as salvation, law, prophets, Moses, Christ, Jesus. Jews were noted for continual arguments among themselves, and the proconsul had no intention of becoming involved in *such matters.*

16. And he drave them from the judgment seat.

Gallio simply threw the case out of court.

17. Then all the Greeks took Sosthenes, the chief ruler of the synagogue, and beat him before the judgment seat. And Gallio cared for none of those things.

This seems to indicate that *the Greeks* of Corinth were more favorable to Paul than to the Jews, and probably they were. However, some of the best manuscripts omit *the Greeks* and read "they all took Sosthenes." This reading indicates that the *Jews* beat their own *chief ruler.* Possibly they were angered because he had led them to make a protest and then failed to win the case before Gallio. This disturbance evidently was too small to appear dangerous to the peace of the city, so Gallio merely ignored it.

18. And Paul after this tarried there yet a good while, and then took his leave of the brethren, and sailed

thence unto Syria, and with him Priscilla and Aquila; having shorn his head in Cenchrea: for he had a vow.

Probably Paul wanted to report back to his home church at Antioch in Syria as well as to attend a Jewish feast at Jerusalem (v. 21). He had been in Corinth eighteen months or more (v. 11). *Shorn his head.* Just what the occasion was, we do not know. Religious vows of the Jews often involved letting the hair grow for a time. Paul may have cut his hair because his vow had been fulfilled, or he may have cut it for the last time before the period involved in His vow. The final completion of this ceremony may be part of what is recorded in Acts 21:26. *Cenchrea.* The port near Corinth from which he sailed to return to Syria.

19. And he came to Ephesus, and left them there: but he himself entered into the synagogue, and reasoned with the Jews.

Ephesus. This was a strategic city on the great trade routes. It would make an excellent center from which the gospel might spread into Asia Minor. *Left them there.* Aquila and Priscilla had accompanied him this far. They were to remain in Ephesus while he went on. Their task would be to lay a foundation for the evangelistic work that Paul would take up when he returned. *Reasoned with the Jews.* Paul did not leave, however, without opening up the field in which Aquila and Priscilla were to work.

20. When they desired him to tarry longer time with them, he consented not.

The Ephesians were much interested in Paul's message and wanted

to hear more, but he postponed further work in this city until a later time.

21. But bade them farewell, saying, I must by all means keep this feast that cometh in Jerusalem: but I will return again unto you, if God will. And he sailed from Ephesus.

Keep this feast. Paul was often accused of opposing the religion of his fathers. He did not ask Christians who were Jews to give up their ancestral religious customs. He even continued such customs himself. But he did not require Gentiles to accept Jewish practices. He insisted that people are saved by faith in Christ and not by keeping the Jewish law. Though he himself observed certain Jewish practices, he did not consider them to be essential to salvation and he did not demand that others join him in keeping them. To allow liberty in such matters is a true mark of Christian toleration. It may be noted, however, that some ancient manuscripts omit the mention of the feast and Jerusalem at this point. Some students therefore doubt that Paul had any intention of visiting Jerusalem at this time.

22. And when he had landed at Caesarea, and gone up, and saluted the church, he went down to Antioch.

There is no mention of Jerusalem here. Some take this as confirmation of the opinion that Paul did not go to Jerusalem on this trip. Others, however, think the language indicates that Paul went up to Jerusalem, *saluted the church* there, and then *went down to Antioch.* This ended what is commonly called Paul's second missionaary tour or journey.

23. And after he had spent some time there, he departed, and went over all the country to Galatia and Phrygia in order, strengthening all the disciples.

After staying *some time* in Antioch, Paul set out on his third missionary journey. He began by revisiting and strengthening churches previously established, just as he had done at the start of his second tour (Acts 15:41—16:5).

24. And a certain Jew named Apollos, born at Alexandria, an eloquent man, and mighty in the scriptures, came to Ephesus.

Apollos. This man made an excellent impression at Ephesus and later at Corinth. In fact, so impressed were the Corinthian Christians that some of them grouped themselves together as followers of Apollos in opposition to others who were loyal to Paul. Neither of the two men approved of this. Paul condemned it severely. (See 1 Corinthians 1:12-15; 3:4-7). *Alexandria.* This was the great city of north Africa. There was a large Jewish population, and the city was an intellectual center where Jewish and Greek thought came into contact. Rhetoric, or speech, was one of the important studies in the Alexandrian schools. It was here, apparently, that Apollos had secured his education; and he had become a very capable young man. *Mighty in the scriptures.* He had specialized in the study of the Old Testament Scriptures, probably in the Greek language.

25. This man was instructed in the way of the Lord; and being fervent in the spirit, he spake and taught diligently the things of the Lord, knowing only the baptism of John.

The way of the Lord. The term "Lord" here may refer to God as Apollos had learned of Him from the Old Testament. *Fervent in the spirit.* He was a very enthusiastic man. *Taught diligently.* He may have established a school where he taught pupils who came to him for instruction. He also taught as a rabbi in the synagogue (v. 26). *Knowing only the baptism of John.* Apollos had heard of the preaching of John the Baptist and of his prediction of the coming Christ. He had received baptism, perhaps not from John himself but from disciples of John. There were followers of John who continued to teach and baptize. (See Matthew 9:14; Mark 2:18; Acts 19:1-7.) If Apollos had heard that Jesus was the Christ, his teaching was obviously very incomplete.

26. And he began to speak boldly in the synagogue: whom when Aquila and Priscilla had heard, they took him unto them, and expounded unto him the way of God more perfectly.

The synagogue. Aquila and Priscilla continued to worship on the Sabbath in the synagogue as they had always done as Jews. No doubt they also carried on their Christian worship; probably in their home, on the Lord's Day. *Took him unto them.* They probably took Apollos to their home. They seem to have been ready to extend hospitality freely wherever they lived. *The way of God more perfectly.* They probably began with the preaching of John the Baptist and taught about the Christ who had been introduced by John. The story of the life, death, and resurrection of Christ transformed Apollos' preaching.

27. And when he was disposed to

pass into Achaia, the brethren wrote, exhorting the disciples to receive him: who, when he was come, helped them much which had believed through grace.

Achaia. This was Greece, the region where Corinth was located. *The brethren wrote.* This was a true church letter, a letter from one group of Christians to another introducing and recommending one of their members. *Helped them much.* This help is described in verse 28.

28. For he mightily convinced the Jews, and that publickly, shewing by the Scriptures that Jesus was Christ.

Paul had met strenuous opposition from the Jews of Corinth, but their chief leader and many others had accepted the gospel. Apparently Apollos found many others receptive to his preaching.

CHAPTER 19

1. And it came to pass, that, while Apollos was at Corinth, Paul having passed through the upper coasts came to Ephesus: and finding certain disciples.

Coasts might better be translated "parts." It does not refer to the seacoast, but to the hill country, the higher parts of Asia Minor through which Paul passed on his way to *Ephesus.* Presumably Aquila and Priscilla were still in Ephesus with the brethren mentioned in Acts 18: 26, 27. They were there when Paul wrote to the Corinthians some two years later (1 Corinthians 16:19). It seems, however, that the *certain disciples* mentioned in this verse were not of that group—at least, they had not received the teaching that Aquila and Priscilla gave to Apollos (Acts 18:26). In a large city like Ephesus, it would be quite possible for two groups of disciples to exist for a time without knowing about each other.

2. He said unto them, Have ye received the Holy Ghost since ye believed? And they said unto him, We have not so much as heard whether there be any Holy Ghost.

Comparing this with verse 6, we conclude that Paul was asking whether the Holy Spirit had brought these disciples any special gifts such as the ability to speak in tongues and to prophecy. Such abilities were given to some in many churches so that the churches would have inspired guidance even when the apostles could not be with them. *Whether there be any Holy Ghost* is literally "if the Holy Spirit is." The American Standard Version translates it "whether the Holy Spirit was given." If these disciples had been taught by followers of John the Baptist, they probably had heard of the Holy Spirit (Matthew 3:11); but if they had not been told of the events recorded in Acts 2, they naturally supposed that the giving of the Spirit was still in the future. If the King James Version has the correct meaning, then these certain disciples must have received only an incomplete report of John's teaching. Furthermore, they must have been Gentiles, for the Jews knew something of the Holy Spirit from the Old Testament

3. And he said unto them, Unto

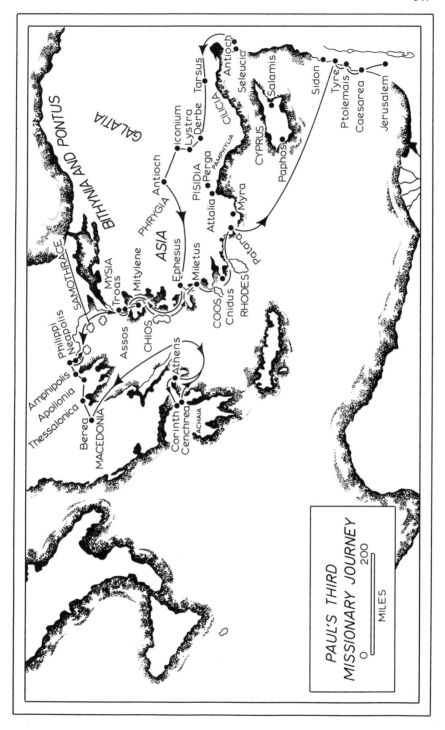

PAUL'S THIRD
MISSIONARY JOURNEY

0   200

MILES

what then were ye baptized? And
they said, Unto John's baptism.

If the disciples had not heard that
there was a Holy Ghost, Paul could
be sure they had not been baptized
"in the name of the Father, and of
the Son, and of the Holy Ghost"
(Matthew 28:19). If they had not
heard that the Holy Ghost was given,
he well might doubt that they had
been told, "Repent, and be baptized
. . . and ye shall receive the gift of
the Holy Ghost." Paul inquired about
their baptism to learn about their understanding of the Christian way.
They had been baptized *unto John's
baptism*: that is, in the way practiced
by John the Baptist. This leads us to
suspect that they had been taught
by Apollos before Apollos had been
taught by Aquila and Priscilla (Acts
18:24-26). This is not necessarily
true, however. They may have been
taught by some other disciples of
John, or even by John himself. We
have no information about where
they had traveled or how long they
had been in Ephesus.

4. Then said Paul, John verily baptized with the baptism of repentance,
saying unto the people, that they
should believe on him which should
come after him, that is, on Christ
Jesus.

Repentance had been very prominent in John's teaching, and so had
the announcement of a greater one
to come. Probably these disciples
knew both of these. They may have
known also that the greater one was
Jesus; but if so, their knowledge of
Him certainly was far from complete.
Paul probably talked with them at
length about Jesus and His way, but
Luke records only this brief summary
of the crucial point.

5. When they heard this, they were
baptized in the name of the Lord
Jesus.

Obviously Paul's teaching included
an explanation of Christian baptism.

6. And when Paul had laid his
hands upon them, the Holy Ghost
came upon them; and they spake with
tongues, and prophesied.

Presumably all Christians receive
"the gift of the Holy Ghost" as an in-
dwelling presence (Acts 2:38, 1 Corinthians 6:19), but when the apostle
laid his hands on these men, the Holy
Ghost empowered them to speak in
different languages and to give inspired messages.

7. And all the men were about
twelve.

It seems probable that these men
now were associated with the other
disciples in Ephesus and did their
part in the work of the church.

8. And he went into the synagogue,
and spake boldly for the space of
three months, disputing and persuading the things concerning the kingdom
of God.

Paul had taught in this synagogue,
apparently with favorable response,
on his brief former visit to Ephesus
(18:19). *Spake boldly for the space
of three months.* The opposition of
the Jewish leaders was much less
quickly stirred here than in places
like Iconium (14:1, 2) and Thessalonica (17:2-5). It may have been
because the converts were fewer.
"Reasoning and persuading as to the
things concerning the kingdom of
God" (American Standard Version).
Pointing out in the Old Testament
Scriptures the evidence that leads to
faith in Jesus of Nazareth as the
Messiah, and meeting the objections

and doubts that might be raised to that evidence.

9. But when divers were hardened, and believed not, but spake evil of that way before the multitude, he departed from them, and separated the disciples, disputing daily in the school of one Tyrannus.

"But when some were hardened and disobedient" (American Standard Version). The opposition among the Jews in Ephesus came not from leaders swaying the whole company against Paul, but it grew gradually among individuals who refused to accept the implications of the gospel claims. *Spake evil of that way before the multitude.* This, rather than their resistance within the synagogue meetings, was the reason for the separation. Because of them the name of Christ was misrepresented among the Gentiles (see Romans 2:24), and Paul could not let it continue. "The Way" (American Standard Version). A designation used frequently and most appropriately to describe the Christian system as a way of life eternal, provided by Him who declared that He himself was the way (John 14:6). *He departed from them, and separated the disciples.* Paul withdrew from the synagogue, taking with him the believing Jews. The separation was between Christians and non-Christians. "Reasoning daily in the school of Tyrannus" (American Standard Version). Of this Tyrannus nothing more is told. He evidently owned a lecture hall where he conducted philosophic, or perhaps rabbinic, instruction.

10. And this continued by the space of two years; so that all they that dwelt in Asia heard the word of the Lord Jesus, both Jews and Greeks.

"This continued for the space of two years" (American Standard Version). Added to the three months of Paul's teaching in the synagogue and perhaps a brief time at the close of Paul's stay at Ephesus, when he was no longer in this school, it constitutes nearly the round three years mentioned in Acts 20:31. It is the longest time on record that Paul ever served in one place. *That all they which dwelt in Asia heard the word of the Lord.* The Roman province of Asia, comprising the western part of Asia Minor, centered around Ephesus and largely influenced by it. Either Paul or his converts preached in the hinterlands. (Compare verse 26.)

11. And God wrought special miracles by the hands of Paul.

Special means extraordinary, not common. All miracles are extrordinary of course, but some of those at Ephesus were unusual even among miracles.

12. So that from his body were brought unto the sick handkerchiefs or aprons, and the diseases departed from them, and the evil spirits went out of them.

Diseases were ended and demons were driven out by the mere touch of a bit of cloth Paul had touched. Possibly this unusual way of working miracles was used here to help Christians who were carrying the gospel from Ephesus to the other cities of Asia (v. 10).

13. Then certain of the vagabond Jews, exorcists, took upon them to call over them which had evil spirits the name of the Lord Jesus, saying, We adjure you by Jesus whom Paul preacheth.

Exorcists were men who made a profession of driving out or seeming to drive out the evil spirits that had taken possession of people. Many exorcists claimed to do this by means of magic words or names. Naturally such practitioners were often *vagabond*, which means traveling or wandering, because their failures would soon compel them to move to new fields. Seeing the success of Paul, some of these professionals assumed that the name he used was better than any of their magic words. Consequently they promptly tried to copy it.

14. And there were seven sons of one Sceva, a Jew, and chief of the priests, which did so.

The Gospels speak often of "the chief priests" (Matthew 2:4; Mark 15:1; Luke 24:20; John 19:15). They were leaders among the priests, perhaps "kindred of the high priest" (Acts 4:6) who might be eligible for the office of high priest. We are not told whether Sceva himself was in Ephesus or not, but his seven sons were there. This shows that some of the high-priestly family, like some of other families of Israel, had scattered far from the homeland. These had also departed far from the proper work of the priesthood.

15. And the evil spirit answered and said, Jesus I know, and Paul I know; but who are ye?

To make this reply the spirit doubtless used the voice of the man he possessed. No doubt this spirit, like others, would have been compelled to yield to the power of Jesus if the order had been given by Paul, an authorized apostle of Jesus. But there was no magic in a name taken in vain.

16. And the man in whom the evil spirit was leaped on them, and over-came them, and prevailed against them, so that they fled out of that house naked and wounded.**

Demons sometimes were able to give extraordinary physical strength to the men they possessed. See Mark 5:2-4. Driven by the evil spirit within him, this man of Ephesus overwhelmed the would-be exorcists, beating them severely and tearing off their clothes. Some manuscripts have "overcame both of them," suggesting that only two' of the seven were involved in this particular case. Whether two or seven, they were no no match for the fury of the demon.

17. And this was known to all the Jews and Greeks also dwelling at Ephesus; and fear fell on them all, and the name of the Lord Jesus was magnified.

The incident helped people to see that the real miracles of Paul were done by divine power and will, not by the mere use of a magic name. Consequently the people gave greater honor to Jesus.

18. And many that believed came, and confessed, and shewed their deeds.

Seeing that divine power was working through Paul, increasing numbers believed that his message also was divine. In response to that message they openly confessed their sins and turned away from them.

19. Many of them also which used curious arts brought their books together, and burned them before all men: and they counted the price of them, and found it fifty thousand pieces of silver.

Curious arts perhaps included all the many crafts of magic, fortune-telling, and exorcism. There must have been many books filled with recipes for magic potions of various kinds, directions for sleight of hand and ventriloquism, incantations, blessings, cursings, and other magic formulae, plus minute instructions for reading the future in the entrails of a chicken or telling fortunes by the liver of a sheep. People who used these arts could see that the power working through Paul was totally different from their trickery. Becoming followers of Christ, they abandoned their crafts and burned their books. *Fifty thousand pieces of silver* would be about eight thousand dollars, but probably the purchasing power of that amount was many times greater than it is now.

20. So mightily grew the word of God and prevailed.

The influence of the gospel was strengthened and broadened by all these events.

21. After these things were ended, Paul purposed in the spirit, when he had passed through Macedonia and Achaia, to go to Jerusalem, saying, After I have been there, I must also see Rome.

Some take *in the spirit* to mean directed or inspired by the Holy Spirit. Such seems to be the meaning of "in spirit" in Matthew 22:43. Others are loath to give the expression that meaning here, partly because Paul later changed some of his plans (Acts 20:3), and partly because he seemed to have some fear that the plan would be frustrated (Romans 15:30-32). It would be possible, of course, for the Spirit to direct the overall plan and leave details for Paul's own arragement; and the direction of the Spirit does not necessarily free one from all misgivings and fears. Whether the plan was the Holy Spir-

it's or Paul's own, the statement of it here is a splendid summary of what is recorded in the rest of the book of Acts, and it is notable that Paul adhered to the plan tenaciously in the face of grave danger (Acts 20:22-24; 21:10-14).

22. So he went into Macedonia two of them that ministered unto him, Timotheus and Erastus; but he himself stayed in Asia for a season.

Timotheus, or Timothy, had been Paul's helper on much of his second tour; *Erastus* now appears in the story for the first time. He may be the same one who was mentioned not much later as the "chamberlain" (treasurer or perhaps city manager) of Corinth (Romans 16:23). Paul sent these two into *Macedonia*, perhaps to arrange the collection of funds for the impoverished Christians in Jerusalem—a collection that turned out to be very generous (2 Corinthians 8:1-5).

23. And the same time there arose no small stir about that way.

This *stir*, or tumult, was not the only difficulty attending Paul's ministry in Ephesus. See 1 Corinthians 16:9; 15:30, 31; Romans 16:3.

24. For a certain man named Demetrius, a silversmith, which made silver shrines for Diana, brought no small gain unto the craftsmen.

Demetrius was evidently a substantial and influential businessman, employing many in the making of silver objects to be used in connection with the worship of Diana. "Brought no little business unto the craftsmen" (American Standard Version), both the ones employed by him and the ones who supplied him with materials and tools.

25. Whom he called together with the workmen of like occupation, and said, Sirs, ye know that by this craft we have our wealth.

Workmen of like occupation. The makers of marble and terrá cotta shrines were affected also, as were the workmen in related trades supplying them. "Men, you know that our maintenance arises from this manufacture" (Living Oracles translation). Hurtful though he was to the cause of Christ, Demetrius is to be respected for his forthright candor. He spoke truly in every detail, choosing his words with consummate skill to appeal to the greed, the superstition, and pride of his audience. Paul's preaching had hit them where it hurt—in the pocketbook.

26. Moreover ye see and hear, that not alone at Ephesus, but almost throughout all Asia, this Paul hath persuaded and turned away much people, saying that they be no gods, which are made with hands.

These men supplied much more than a local trade. Pilgrims from near and far had been buying their shrines, and now many were turning from buying them as they were influenced by the gospel. *This Paul.* A skillfully unfriendly reference. Either by direct labor or spreading influence, the apostle had reached the people of the province. Writing from Asia to the emperor Trajan forty years later, Pliny said that Christianity had caused the temples of the gods to be deserted. "Telling them that gods made by human hands are not gods at all" (Goodspeed). Demetrius and his co-workers were in the best possible position to know that Paul was right. They did not deny it, but they did not want it told. Begin-

ning probably as souvenirs and reminders of their deity, the little shrines had come to be idols, and the craftsmen were willing to have it so.

27. So that not only this our craft is in danger to be set at nought; but also that the temple of the great goddess Diana should be despised, and her magnificence should be destroyed, whom all Asia and the world worshippeth.

"Not only is there danger that this our trade come into disrepute" (American Standard Version). This was the real objection, but it was so obviously selfish that a more "noble" motive must be found before the tradesmen would be able to arouse the city against Paul. "But also that the temple of the great goddess Diana be made of no account" (American Standard Version). The appeal here is to patriotism. The temple was the pride of Ephesus, and a wonder of the world. "And that she should even be deposed from her magnificence" (American Standard Version). The appeal was to religion. Their deity was in danger. *Whom all Asia and the world worshippeth.* The whole province had contributed to the building of the present temple after a former one was burned in 356 B.C. Under various names in various lands the mother goddess has been very widely worshiped.

28. And when they heard these sayings, they were full of wrath, and cried out, saying, Great is Diana of the Ephesians.

Demetrius was a successful orator and rabble rouser. *Full of wrath* which is much more easily aroused than good will. *And cried out.* The outcry of the mob arose from its being stirred, but the cry itself soon fired its passions to an uncontrollable fervor. *Great is Diana of the Ephesians.* Obviously a popular slogan in Ephesus, this could be either a declaration of devotion or an act of calling on the goddess herself to destroy her challengers.

29. And the whole city was filled with confusion: and having caught Gaius and Aristarchus, men of Macedonia, Paul's companions in travel, they rushed with one accord into the theatre.

Apparently the silversmiths left their meeting place and rushed through the streets, shouting their praise of Diana, and gathered others into their crowd as they went. Perhaps they sought Paul at his lodging place or the school of Tyrannus (v. 9), but did not find him. Knowing their movement would lose momentum if they spent time in searching, they seized *Gaius and Aristarchus* instead. These men perhaps were among Paul's helpers, as were Timothy and Erastus (v. 22). *Companions in travel* suggests that they may have come to Ephesus with Paul some years earlier. The fact that they were *men of Macedonia* suggests that they may have been planning to go with him to that area (v. 21). The *theatre* to which the crowd was led was a semicircular stadium with seats for nearly twenty-five thousand people.

30. And when Paul would have entered in unto the people, the disciples suffered him not.

Paul would have disregarded his own safety to present his message and reason with the crowd, but the other Christians restrained him. The mob was in no mood for reasoning, and very likely would have killed Paul if he had appeared.

31. And certain of the chief of Asia, which were his friends, sent unto him, desiring that he would not adventure himself into the theatre.

The American Standard Version adds a footnote defining the *chief of Asia* or "Asiarchs" as "officers having charge of festivals . . . in the Roman province of Asia." The record does not show whether any of these prominent citizens were Christians or not, but some of them were Paul's friends and did not want him to be killed by a mob. Doubtless they were concerned also about their city's good name and its standing with the Roman government, both of which might suffer if a riotous mob killed a man.

32. Some therefore cried one thing, and some another: for the assembly was confused; and the more part knew not wherefore they were come together.

Most of the people simply followed the crowd, not knowing who was leading it or why. Naturally all sorts of guesses were being made and unfounded rumors were being passed.

33. And they drew Alexander out of the multitude, the Jews putting him forward. And Alexander beckoned with the hand, and would have made his defence unto the people.

Why the Jews wanted Alexander to speak is not explained. Perhaps they had learned that the demonstration was directed against Paul, and they wanted to announce that the Jews were not responsible for his activities and had forced him to leave their synagogue (vv. 8, 9).

34. But when they knew that he was a Jew, all with one voice about the space of two hours cried out, Great is Diana of the Ephesians.

The people had no idea what Alexander wanted to say, but they knew a Jew would not say anything in favor of their Diana. Therefore they flaunted their praise of Diana before him and refused to let him say anything at all.

35. And when the townclerk had appeased the people, he said, Ye men of Ephesus, what man is there that knoweth not how that the city of the Ephesians is a worshipper of the great goddess Diana, and of the image which fell down from Jupiter?

The *townclerk,* the secretary or recorder of Ephesus, now appeared before the crowd. Perhaps his fellow officials selected him to do this because they knew he could meet the situation with effective tact and diplomacy. Since the people had now been shouting for two hours (v. 34), probably it was not very hard for one of their officials to quiet them. The clerk began by showing himself in complete agreement with the people. He too praised *the great goddess Diana*; he accepted their belief that the image of her *fell down from Jupiter*; he shared their pride in their city as the place of Diana's magnificent temple. *Worshipper* literally means "temple sweeper"; the American Standard Version translates it "temple-keeper.") At the same time the clerk subtly rebuked the two hours of shouting by asking if there was anyone who did not know these facts.

36. Seeing then that these things cannot be spoken against, ye ought to be quiet, and to do nothing rashly.

The rebuke now was perfectly plain, but very quiet and reasonable. It was nonsense to spend two hours shouting out what everyone knew and nobody contradicted.

37. For ye have brought hither these men, which are neither robbers of churches, not yet blasphemers of your goddess.

The clerk now called attention to Gaius and Aristarchus (v. 29), who had been brought to the stadium and perhaps handled roughly. This treatment was completely unjustified: they were not even accused of doing anything against Diana. *Robbers of churches* can be properly translated "temple robbers." The temple of Diana at Ephesus was the one in mind; these men had made no attempt to plunder it. They were not accused even of speaking against the goddess. Possibly such an accusation would have been made against Paul if he had been present, but Gaius and Aristarchus were not preachers.

38. Wherefore if Demetrius, and the craftsmen which are with him, have a matter against any man, the law is open, and there are deputies: let them implead one another.

Before taking the stage, this clerk evidently had done enough quiet investigating to know just what was going on. He now publicly pointed out the men who were responsible. This would cause them to think twice before continuing their riot. He reminded them and all the crowd that there were regular courts willing and able to consider any accusation worthy of consideration.

39. But if ye enquire any thing concerning other matters, it shall be determined in a lawful assembly.

If the silversmiths did not wish to make an accusation before the courts, but still had some matter that ought to be brought to the attention of the public, here was a legal town meeting at which it could be presented. This made the riot seem the more unnecessary.

40. For we are in danger to be called in question for this day's uproar, there being no cause whereby we may give an account of this concourse.

Rome insisted that her people keep the peace. A town where rioting occurred might be punished by heavier taxes or the loss of some of its liberty. The proconsuls might be replaced by men who would rule more sternly; more Roman troops might be quartered in the town. The clerk quietly warned of this danger.

41. And when he had thus spoken, he dismissed the assembly.

Already wearied by their senseless shouting, the people probably were so sobered and shamed by the clerk's plain and reasonable speech that they went quietly about their business.

CHAPTER 20

1. And after the uproar was ceased, Paul called unto him the disciples, and embraced them, and departed for to go unto Macedonia.

The mob was finally brought under control by the town clerk's skillful suggestions that the courts were prepared to handle any crime that had been done by Paul, and that the Roman authority would frown on such breaches of the peace as here demonstrated. "Paul having sent for the disciples and exhorted them, took leave of them (American Standard Version). His leaving was for their sakes, lest they come to greater danger because of him. Parting words of exhortation and blessing were in order (see 20:17-38). *Departed for to go into Macedonia.* This was according to plans made earlier, when he sent Timothy and Erastus on ahead (19: 21, 22; 1 Corinthians 16:5). Titus had gone to Corinth (after the writing of 1 Corinthians) to learn of the situation there.

2. And when he had gone over those parts, and had given them much exhortation, he came into Greece.

In Macedonia, probably somewhere among the brethren at Philippi, Thessalonica, or Berea, he met Titus, who brought comforting reports of the correction of evils in the church at Corinth; and he wrote 2 Corinthians. His journey took him also northwestward into Illyricum (Romans 15:19) for fruitful labors. *Had given them much exhortation,* including directions for the gathering of an offering for the relief of the poverty-stricken Jewish Christians in Jerusalem (1 Corinthians 16: 12; 2 Corinthians 8:1-15); *He came into Greece;* that is to Achaia, especially to Corinth.

3. And there abode three months. And when the Jews laid wait for him, as he was about to sail into Syria, he purposed to return through Macedonia.

"When he had spent three months there" (American Standard Version). He labored with the church at Corinth, and wrote the Epistle to the Romans. Although most of the opposition to his ministry had been corrected, fervent hatred lingered in the hearts of some. "A plot was laid against him by the Jews as he was about to set sail for Syria" (American Standard Version). No open attack was ever made on Paul in Corinth itself, but the unbelieving Jews learned of his plans to continue on to Jerusalem (19:21), and planned to waylay him either on the road to the port at Cenchrea or on shipboard as he traveled. "He determined to return through Macedonia" (American Standard Version).

4. And there accompanied him into Asia Sopater of Berea; and of the Thessalonians, Aristarchus and Secundus; and Gaius of Derbe, and Timotheus; and of Asia, Tychicus and Trophimus.

Perhaps several of these men had been chosen to take to Jerusalem the offerings made by the congregations of which they were members. See 1 Corinthians 16:1-4. Compare Romans 15:26, 27.

5. These going before tarried for us at Troas.

For some reason not recorded, the group separated to meet again at *Troas*. Note that Luke again uses the pronoun *us*, indicating that he now joined Paul and traveled with him from Macedonia. We suppose Paul had left him there a few years before, for he says "we" came to Philippi, but "they" left it (Acts 16:11, 12, 40).

6. And we sailed away from Philippi after the days of unleavened bread, and came unto them to Troas in five days; where we abode seven days.

The days of unleavened bread composed the Passover week, during which the Jews had no leaven in

their homes. This tells us the time was spring, probably April—a good time to begin a long journey. However, the wind must have been contrary at the outset, for it took five days to cross the Aegean Sea to *Troas*. Paul once had crossed in the opposite direction in only two days (Acts 16:11, 12). No reason is given for staying *seven days* at Troas. Perhaps the travelers waited to attend the regular weekly meeting of the church (v. 7); perhaps it was a week before they could get passage on a ship sailing toward Jerusalem.

7. And upon the first day of the week, when the disciples came together to break bread, Paul preached unto them, ready to depart on the morrow; and continued his speech until midnight.

This is one of the earliest indications that it was the custom of the church to meet *upon the first day of the week* for the Lord's Supper (*to break bread*). The word translated *preached* is sometimes given as "reasoned" (Acts 18:4) and sometimes as "disputed" (Acts 17:17). It is not likely that there was any disputing on this occasion, but Paul may have responded to questions and discussed various matters rather than simply continuing a sermon for several hours. Since he was *ready to depart on the morrow*, Paul perhaps thought this might be his last chance to talk with these Christians of Troas. (See Acts 20:25.) Both he and the others were so keenly interested that he *continued his speech until midnight*, and then after an interruption continued the rest of the night (v. 11).

8. And there were many lights in the upper chamber, where they were gathered together.

The *many lights* probably were oil lamps. Their open flames helped to exhaust the oxygen in the room, which may have been poorly ventilated at best. This detail perhaps is mentioned to explain why one person sought a window (v. 9).

9. And there sat in a window a certain young man named Eutychus, being fallen into a deep sleep: and as Paul was long preaching, he sunk down with sleep, and fell down from the third loft, and was taken up dead.

Perhaps this young man was not as interested as he should have been, but those of us who sometimes find ourselves nodding during the sermon can readily sympathize with him. We may note that he did not fall asleep during a half-hour sermon: it was midnight before he was overcome. We should remember, too, that Sunday was not a holiday in heathen Troas. Eutychus may have spent twelve hours in hard labor before he came to the meeting. In any case, the fresh air failed to keep him awake. He toppled from the third-story window and was killed by his fall.

10. And Paul went down, and fell on him, and embracing him said, Trouble not yourselves; for his life is in him.

God's power working through Paul restored life to the young man.

11. When he therefore was come up again, and had broken bread, and eaten, and talked a long while, even till break of day, so he departed.

Probably the whole congregation had rushed downstairs along with Paul. They now returned to their third-floor auditorium and observed the Lord's Supper. Afterward the talking was resumed. These brethren seldom had an opportunity to hear an apostle, and doubtless they had many questions to ask. Possibly some left before the night was over, feeling the need of rest before another day's work; but at least part of the group stayed *till break of day.* Then Paul *departed* to continue his journey.

12. And they brought the young man alive, and were not a little comforted.

If Paul told these people of the dangers that lay ahead (vv. 22-25), they were much in need of comfort; and they found it in the power of God made evident in the resurrection of Eutychus.

13. And we went before to ship, and sailed unto Assos, there intending to take in Paul: for so had he appointed, minding himself to go afoot.

Many preachers can understand the need for a time of solitude, fresh air, and exercise after a gripping all-night meeting. Paul wanted to go afoot to Assos, probably the next port where the boat would stop. It was a day's walk to the south. His companions went aboard at Troas, doubtless taking the luggage with them.

14. And when he met with us at Assos, we took him in, and came to Mitylene.

The plan described in verse 13 was carried out, and the following day's sailing took the party to *Mitylene,* an island off the coast of Asia.

15. And we sailed thence, and came the next day over against Chios;

and the next day we arrived at Samos, and tarried at Trogyllium; and the next day we came to Miletus.

Apparently this part of the trip was made in a small coastwise vessel that stopped at nearly every port. Another ship was taken later for the voyage across the open sea to Palestine (Acts 21:2).

16. For Paul had determined to sail by Ephesus, because he would not spend the time in Asia: for he hasted, if it were possible for him, to be in Jerusalem the day of Pentecost.

Paul had spent more than two years in Ephesus (Acts 19:10). The Christians there were very dear to him, and he to them. If he stopped there at all, it would be almost impossible to get away quickly; and he must get away quickly if he and his companions were to reach Jerusalem in time for the feast of Pentecost. The Jewish Christians were still Jews and would treasure the opportunity to join in the great festival of their people.

17. And from Miletus he sent to Ephesus, and called the elders of the church.

Though he decided not to stop at Ephesus, Paul was unwilling to pass without any contact with the church there. He asked the elders to meet him in Miletus, a long day's journey south of Ephesus. Perhaps the ship had to stay there a few days for repairs or loading.

18. And when they were come to him he said unto them, Ye know, from the first day that I came into Asia, after what manner I have been with you at all seasons.

These men were among the first fruits of the gospel in Ephesus, and had observed the ministry of Paul from its earliest days in the synagogue. "After what manner I was with you all the time" (American Standard Version). Paul offered his own ministry as an example of the steadfast attention to duty that he was about to urge upon them. He had been "instant in season, out of season" (2 Timothy 4:2).

19. Serving the Lord with all humility of mind, and with many tears, and temptations, which befell me by the lying in wait of the Jews.

Claiming no favors and seeking no exemptions because of his status as an apostle, Paul had labored diligently in obedience to Christ's command in the service of the Lord's people. In serving them, he had served the Lord (Matthew 25:40). *And with many tears* of urgency for the acceptance of the Word (compare Acts 20:31); and of sorrow for the rejection or the backsliding of the disobedient. "And with trials which befell me by the plots of the Jews" (American Standard Version). The earlier record of the Ephesian ministry mentioned only one plot of the Jews—that to set forward Alexander, apparently to testify against Paul before the mob in the theater (19:33, 34). That there were other attempts to destroy him and his influence is clear from the context. These plots by his own nation tried Paul's capacity for endurance.

20. And how I kept back nothing that was profitable unto you, but have shewed you, and have taught you publickly, and from house to house.

Under the impelling commission that was upon him, he went forward boldly to the fulfillment of his responsibility to each person, offering instruction, encouragement, correction, or rebuke, as the need of each person dictated. *Have taught you publickly.* Paul's public teaching had been given in the synagogue, in the school of Tyrannus, and in the meetings of the Christians. To it he had added a faithful ministry of teaching in the homes, instructing them in the doctrines he declared publicly.

21. Testifying both to the Jews, and also to the Greeks, repentance toward God, and faith toward our Lord Jesus Christ.

Testifying. Urgently declaring the need for the hearer's response to the gospel. *Both to the Jews, and also to the Greeks.* The same gospel was available to both and laid upon them the same requirements. *Repentance toward God.* This is infinitely better than mere repentance from sin. Repentance is the change of mind that grows out of godly sorrow (2 Corinthians 7:10) and issues in a change in the manner of life. Christian repentance is described in the command, "Let this mind be in you, which was also in Christ Jesus." Repentance depends upon hearing and acknowledging the truth that God is, "and that he is a rewarder of them that diligently seek him" (Hebrews 11:6). *Faith toward our Lord Jesus Christ.* This is the faith that marks the "believers" as a special company, separate from the world. It includes and involves the active commitment and obedience that distinguish living from dead faith (James 2:17).

22. And now, behold, I go bound in the spirit unto Jerusalem, not knowing the things that shall befall me there.

Bound in the spirit probably means that Paul felt within his own spirit an irresistible compulsion to *go unto Jerusalem.* Many of the Jews at Jerusalem were hostile to the gospel and particularly to Paul, but neither the gospel nor Paul was hostile to them. This would be shown in a wonderful way when Paul appeared with messengers from foreign Christians who had been won by the gospel and now were sending gifts for their poverty-stricken brethren in Jerusalem. This may have been the reason that Paul felt compelled to go. Some take the spirit in this verse to mean the Holy Spirit, who constrained Paul to go to Jerusalem. Whether we accept this interpretation or not makes little practical difference, for even if Paul meant that he was constrained in his own spirit he doubtless felt that the guidance of the Holy Spirit constrained him.

23. Save that the Holy Ghost witnesseth in every city, saying that bonds and afflictions abide me.

Over and over, *in every city,* the Holy Spirit warned Paul that *bonds and afflictions,* prison and trouble, were waiting for him in Jerusalem. Such warnings could be given to him either directly from the Spirit or through other prophets as recorded in Acts 21:10, 11. Apparently the warnings were not intended to keep Paul from going to Jerusalem, but to keep him from cherishing such high hopes of a favorable reception that he would be bitterly disappointed.

24. But none of these things move me, neither count I my life dear unto myself, so that I might finish my course with joy, and the ministry, which I have received of the Lord Jesus, to testify the gospel of the grace of God.

Warnings of danger could not *move* Paul to give up the trip; he was willing to give up his life in order to carry out the task the *Lord Jesus* had given him. He would *testify the gospel of the grace of God* in every way the Holy Spirit might lead and in the face of every danger that might appear.

25. And now, behold, I know that ye all, among whom I have gone preaching the kingdom of God, shall see my face no more.

A question arises about this verse because it is generally thought that Paul did return to Ephesus at a time later than that recorded in Acts (1 Timothy 1:3). Some think that Paul at this point was not speaking by inspiration, but merely giving his own opinion. They note that *I* is emphatic in the Greek text, and suppose that it is to be contrasted with "the Holy Ghost" in verse 23: that is, that Paul was saying, "The Holy Ghost testifies that bonds and afflictions await, but I myself know without His specific testimony that you will see my face no more." They note also that *know* can indicate a firm conviction rather than absolute knowledge, as in Acts 26:27 and Philippians 1:19. On the other hand, some hold that Paul's statement here is true, even though he did later return to Ephesus, because the men to whom he spoke had died or moved away before he came back.

26. Wherefore I take you to record this day, that I am pure from the blood of all men.

I take you to record, literally, "I testify to you," is a way of giving solemn emphasis to the statement that follows. Paul reminded the elders of his own faithfulness among

them in order to encourage them to be faithful.

27. For I have not shunned to declare unto you all the counsel of God.

Paul had proclaimed God's message fully, faithfully, and fearlessly. Anyone who rejected it or failed to follow it would be responsible for his own eternal condemnation, and so Paul was not guilty in his death (v. 26).

28. Take heed therefore unto yourselves, and to all the flock, over the which the Holy Ghost hath made you overseers, to feed the church of God, which he hath purchased with his own blood.

Take heed therefore unto yourselves. The faithful ministry of any elder must grow out of a faithful life. Hence the first care must be to establish one's own faith (see 1 Timothy 4:16). *And to all the flock.* The relationship of the elder to the church is that of the shepherd to the flock (1 Peter 5:1-5). No believer is above the need of an elder's ministry, and none is so unimportant as to be excluded from it. The Holy Spirit provided the pattern for the church, by which elders were chosen as shepherds. He had also provided the spiritual gifts which had qualified these men to the work. The word "bishop" represents, but does not translate literally, the Greek *episkopos*, "overseer." The elders in the New Testament church (see v. 17) were overseers, or bishops (Philippians 1:1). In later usage the word came to be "restricted . . . to the chief ruler of a church" (Dummelow). *To feed the church of God.* That is, to do the shepherd's work of providing sustenance, guiding, and guarding. *Which he hath purchased with his own blood.* Christ and the Father are one (John 14:7-11), and the blood which redeemed believers to constitute the church is His blood.

29. For I know this, that after my departing shall grievous wolves enter in among you, not sparing the flock.

The opposition of false teachers was already evident, but had been held in check by the apostle's presence. *Grievous wolves [shall] enter in among you, not sparing the flock.* Teachers of false and destructive doctrines, such as those of the Nicolaitanes (Revelation 2:6) at Ephesus, and the Gnostics, against whose errors John addressed much of his first epistle, are characterized as ravening beasts, scattering the church into divided fragments and bringing spiritual death to their victims.

30. Also of your own selves shall men arise, speaking perverse things, to draw away disciples after them.

"From among your own selves" (American Standard Version). False teachers might be expected to arise not only within the church at Ephesus, but perhaps from among the very group to whom Paul spoke. He hoped his warning would deter them. *To draw away disciples after them.* People love to follow human leaders (1 Corinthians 1:10-17), and some leaders love to be followed. It takes real Christian grace on the part of both preachers and people to prevent this sin.

31. Therefore watch, and remember, that by the space of three years I ceased not to warn every one night and day with tears.

Because of the danger, the shepherds must be alert to protect the flock. *By the space of three years I*

ceased not to warn. The watchman must give the warning. Paul offered his own diligence as an example of what he exhorted them to do. The three years of his ministry in Ephesus included three months in which he taught in the synagogue and a full two years of teaching in the school of Tyrannus. *Night and day with tears.* The urgency of the need left no room for rest or for relaxation. It was a matter of life and death.

32. And now, brethren, I commend you to God, and to the word of his grace, which is able to build you up, and to give you an inheritance among all them which are sanctified.

I commend you to God, for the help without which they would be unable to fulfill the responsibility Paul had laid upon them. *And to the word of his grace.* The inspired word, spoken by the apostles and later committed to writing in the New Testament, was a major channel through which God's help would be given. *Which is able to build you up.* The inspired Scripture is given that the man of God may, through its use, be furnished completely unto every good work (2 Timothy 3:16, 17). *An inheritance among all them which are sanctified.* Those that are sanctified—set apart and called saints —are simply Christians (1 Corinthians 1:2; 6:9-11). Their inheritance is eternal life. The Word of God is the gift which is able to provide all this.

33. I have coveted no man's silver, or gold, or apparel.

Again Paul offers his ministry as an example of the characteristics he would encourage in his hearers. The meagerness of his circumstances disturbed him not at all, even in the presence of the wealthy. A Christian attitude toward spiritual matters will naturally be accompanied by a Christian attitude toward material things. Self-interest and financial gain must never be the incentive for Christian service (1 Timothy 5:5-10).

34. Yea, ye yourselves know, that these hands have ministered unto my necessities, and to them that were with me.

Paul had come to Ephesus with Aquila and Priscilla, with whom he had worked at tentmaking in Corinth (18:3). He makes it clear, here and in 1 Corinthians 4:12, (although it is not told in Luke's account of his Ephesian ministry), that he had continued to earn his living at this or another trade. *And to them that were with me.* Sustaining his partners through some time of disability, and perhaps including some less fortunate converts.

35. I have shewed you all things, how that so labouring ye ought to support the weak, and to remember the words of the Lord Jesus, how he said, It is more blessed to give than to receive.

"In all things I gave you an example" (American Standard Version). Paul's moral teachings were conveyed more by demonstration than by word. "That so laboring ye ought to help the weak" (American Standard Version). The shepherd elders' spiritual ministry would be more effective if they first demonstrated their love through material generosity to the needy (see Ephesians 4:28). *It is more blessed to give than to receive.* These are the only known words of Jesus that are not recorded in any of the Gospels. They

describe most accurately, however, the blessedness of the Father (John 3:16), and they may well have served as a slogan for Jesus' own ministry. For elders in the Lord's church, they apply to the giving of instruction, encouragement, and understanding, as well as the giving of money.

36. And when he had thus spoken, he kneeled down, and prayed with them all.

Thus spoken does not necessarily mean that Luke reported Paul's address word for word; he may have summarized it. When it was finished, Paul and the elders prayed together, perhaps asking God to give all of them strength and wisdom for the work and trials that would face Paul in Jerusalem and the elders in Ephesus without his guidance.

37. And they all wept sore, and fell on Paul's neck, and kissed him.

Men of that time and area were usually more demonstrative in their grief than are British and American men of today, but certainly their grief was deep and sincere.

38. Sorrowing most of all for the words which he spake, that they should see his face no more. And they accompanied him unto the ship.

Paul's custom was to revisit the churches where he had worked. The prophecy that these Ephesians *should see his face no more . . .* doubtless was taken to mean that he would not live much longer. His sorrowing friends *accompanied him unto the ship,* staying with him as long as possible.

CHAPTER 21

1. And it came to pass, that after we were gotten from them, and had launched, we came with a straight course unto Coos, and the day following unto Rhodes, and from thence unto Patara.

Again, as in verse 15 in the preceding chapter, Luke seems to be recording the daily stages of the journey.

2. And finding a ship sailing over unto Phenicia, we went aboard, and set forth.

At Patara, Paul and his companions transferred from the coastwise boat to an ocean-going ship bound for *Phenicia.* For centuries this coastal area north of Palestine had been famous for its maritime commerce.

3. Now when we had discovered Cyprus, we left it on the left hand, and sailed into Syria, and landed at Tyre: for there the ship was to unlade her burden.

The ship did not stop at the island of *Cyprus,* but came in sight of it and passed near its south side, making an almost straight course to Tyre, one of the principal cities of Phoenicia. The cargo was to be unloaded there. *Syria* was a larger area of which Phoenicia was a part.

4. And finding disciples, we tarried there seven days: who said to Paul through the Spirit, that he should not go up to Jerusalem.

The disciples or Christians in Tyre probably gave lodging to Paul and the other traveling brethren. *Seven days* perhaps was the time required to unload the ship or to get passage on another ship for the next part of the journey. Some of the disciples at Tyre warned Paul not to *go up to Jerusalem,* and this they did *through the Spirit,* which probably means that the Holy Spirit inspired them. Considering this in the light of Acts 20:23 and 21:11, we take it to be not an order not to go to Jerusalem, but a warning that going would result in persecution.

5. And when we had accomplished those days, we departed and went our way; and they all brought us on our way, with wives and children, till we were out of the city: and we kneeled down on the shore, and prayed .

When the seven days at Tyre were completed, Paul and the other travelers *departed.* The Christians of Tyre, whole families together, went with them *out of the city* to the place where they would board the ship, and held a prayer meeting *on the shore.*

6. And when we had taken our leave one of another, we took ship; and they returned home again.

This reluctant parting must have been similar to the parting from the Ephesian elders (Acts 20:37, 38).

7. And when we had finished our course from Tyre, we came to Ptolemais, and saluted the brethren, and abode with them one day.

The ship sailed south along the coast to Ptolemais, the modern Acre, located about ten miles north of Mount Carmel. Here too the travelers were welcomed by *brethren.*

8. And the next day we that were of Paul's company departed, and came unto Caesarea: and we entered into the house of Philip the evangelist, which was one of the seven; and abode with him.

No ship is mentioned here, and *Paul's company* may have gone on foot to *Caesarea,* a coastal town south of Ptolemais. Here their host was *Philip the evangelist,* some of whose work is recorded in Acts 8. He was *one of the seven* chosen to care for the poor in Jerusalem at an earlier time (Acts 6:1-6).

9. And the same man had four daughters, virgins, which did prophesy.

Luke does not record any message from these inspired young ladies, but it seems likely that they repeated the same prophecy that was being given "in every city" (Acts 20:23).

10. And as we tarried there many days, there came down from Judaea a certain prophet, named Agabus.

The term *many days* is quite indefinite. The travelers were now close to Jerusalem and knew approximately how long it would take to get there. They .could remain in the peaceful fellowship at Caesarea and rest until near the time they wished to arrive in Jerusalem. *Agabus* no doubt was the same prophet who had foretold a famine some years earlier (Acts 11:27-30).

11. And when he was come unto us, he took Paul's girdle, and bound his own hands and feet, and said, Thus saith the Holy Ghost, So shall the Jews at Jerusalem bind the man that owneth this girdle, and shall deliver him into the hands of the Gentiles.

The *girdle* was perhaps a long band of cloth that was wound around the waist one or more times and tied to hold the loose outer garment snug about the body. Agabus wound it around his own hands and feet to dramatize the prophecy that had been made repeatedly before. This of course is not to be taken as meaning the Jews would literally tie Paul with a girdle, but only that they would seize him and bring him into the custody of the Romans.

12. And when we heard these things, both we, and they of that place, besought him not to go up to Jerusalem.

We means Luke and the other people who were traveling with Paul. They and the Christians of Caesarea urged Paul to give up his plan of going to Jerusalem.

13. Then Paul answered, What mean ye to weep and to break mine heart? for I am ready not to be bound only, but also to die at Jerusalem for the name of the Lord Jesus.

Paul was accustomed to God's direct leading, and obviously he was sure God was now leading him to Jerusalem in spite of the danger. His response to his friends may be paraphrased thus: "What do you mean by all this weeping? Your sorrow can only break my heart; it cannot keep me from going on. I understand the danger, and I am ready and willing to be put in prison or even put to death for Jesus' sake."

14. And when he would not be persuaded, we ceased, saying, The will of the Lord be done.

The friends of Paul finally gave up their useless pleading and made their prayer not that the prophecy would not be fulfilled but that God's will would prevail.

15. And after those days we took up our carriages, and went up to Jerusalem.

Carriages means what was carried by the travelers, their baggage.

16. There went with us also certain of the disciples of Caesarea, and brought with them one Mnason of Cyprus, an old disciple, with whom we should lodge.

Many of the disciples in Caesarea were Jews, and some of them went along with Paul and his companions to the national feast in Jerusalem. Mnason probably was a native of Cyprus who had moved to Jerusalem and had a home in which he would give lodging to Paul and his party. Perhaps he had gone to Caesarea to meet and welcome his guests.

17. And when we were come to Jerusalem, the brethren received us gladly.

Christian hospitality always welcomed brethren from afar, but in this case the welcome was especially warm because of the great work Paul had done and because of the large offerings his party brought from many churches (Acts 24:17; 1 Corinthians 16:1-4; 2 Corinthians 8:1-7; Romans 15:25-27).

18. And the day following Paul went in with us unto James; and all the elders were present.

The apostle James, brother of John, had been killed long before this time (Acts 12:1, 2), but James the brother of Jesus was an outstanding leader in the church at Jerusalem (Galatians 1:19; 2:9).

19. And when he had saluted them, he declared particularly what things God had wrought among the Gentiles by his ministry.

All the events of Paul's third missionary journey, at least, had occurred since he had visited Jerusalem before. He had many accomplishments to tell that God had accomplished through him.

20. And when they heard it, they glorified the Lord, and said unto him, Thou seest, brother, how many thousands of Jews there are which believe; and they are all zealous of the law.

These leaders among the Jewish Christians of Jerusalem first listened to Paul's account of the progress of the gospel among Gentiles, and praised God for it. They then remarked that *many thousands of Jews* also believed in Christ. These were all *zealous of the law*: that is, they conscientiously followed the Jewish law of the Old Testament.

21. And they are informed of thee, that thou teachest all the Jews which are among the Gentiles to forsake Moses, saying that they ought not to circumcise their children, neither to walk after the customs.

Paul worked much in Gentile lands, and it had been reported at Jerusalem that he taught Jews in those lands to abandon the Old Testament law. This was a false report, of course. Neither Paul nor the other apostles ever tried to get Jews to forsake the law, though they did insist that Gentiles need not accept the law in order. to be Christians.

22. What is it therefore? the multitude must needs come together: for they will hear that thou art come.

"So what can we do about this misunderstanding, this false report?" This was the question asked by the elders. The multitude of disciples in Jerusalem would be meeting. News of Paul's coming would reach all of them. His famous work would be much discussed, and the false report would be repeated again and again, no matter how many times it was denied.

23. Do therefore this that we say to thee: We have four men which have a vow on them.

The elders proposed a way by which Paul could show that he honored the law and customs of his fellow Jews. The proposal was that Paul should join with four Jewish Christians who had taken *a vow.* The exact nature of the vow is not important. One vow frequently taken bound a man to abstain from wine and not to cut ·his hair or beard for a specified time. Such a vow may have been taken by these four. Their vow also involved certain offerings (v. 26) as well as ceremonies.

24. Them take, and purify thyself with them, and be at charges with them, that they may shave their heads: and all may know that those things, whereof they were informed concerning thee, are nothing; but that thou thyself also walkest orderly, and keepest the law.

The four and their vow doubtless were well known among the Christians in Jerusalem. Paul's devotion to Jewish customs would be quite evident if he would join them, go through the ceremonies of purification, and share the *charges* for the sacrifices that were involved. This would complete the obligations of their vow, and they then

might *shave their heads.* Such a demonstration of Paul's regard for Jewish customs would be more convincing than any spoken declaration could be.

25. As touching the Gentiles which believe, we have written and concluded that they observe no such thing, save only that they keep themselves from things offered to idols, and from blood, and from strangled, and from fornication.

The suggestion was not designed to force the law on Gentiles who became Christians. Concerning them the elders reaffirmed the decision they had given years before (Acts 15).

26. Then Paul took the men, and the next day purifying himself with them entered into the temple, to signify the accomplishment of the days of purification, until that an offering should be offered for every one of them.

Paul accepted the suggestion and proceeded to carry it out, meticulously going through the familiar ceremonies and presenting the proper offerings.

27. And when the seven days were almost ended, the Jews which were of Asia, when they saw him in the temple, stirred up all the people, and laid hands on him.

The seven days of ceremonial purification for the four in whose sacrifices Paul was sharing. "Were almost completed" (American Standard Version). The plan proposed by James and the elders almost succeeded. *When they saw him in the temple.* Paul had been for three years in Ephesus and the Jews there knew him well. "Threw all the populace into confusion" (The Living Oracles translation). No clear-cut charge is ever necessary to stir up a mob. The more confused the issue, the higher the feelings often run. One wonders if these Ephesian Jews were deliberately imitating the methods they had seen used by Demetrius in stirring the mob against Paul in Ephesus (19:23-32). *And laid hands on him,* thus implying that he was a criminal deserving of punishment.

28. Crying out, Men of Israel, help: This is the man, that teacheth all men every where against the people, and the law, and this place: and further brought Greeks also into the temple, and hath polluted this holy place.

Crying out, Men of Israel, help. The anguished outcry of injured innocence pleading for help against the wicked invader was well calculated to stir the passions of the crowd and prevent any real investigation of the charges. *This is the man.* Paul's reputation, viciously twisted by the malignity of his enemies, had preceded him to Jerusalem. The slanders about him were known and accepted by many who had never seen his face. *Teacheth all men every where against the people.* "The people" were the Israelites, contrasted with "the nations," or the heathen Gentiles. Paul's refusal to require Gentile believers in Christ to follow the customs of the Jews was interpreted as an insult to the chosen nation. *And the law, and this place.* Three things were equally sacred to the Jews: their nation, their Scriptures, and their temple. To disregard all these was, to them, the ultimate blasphemy. A vast imagination to blatant dishonesty would be required to fashion these charges from

Paul's application to the Gentiles of the message that had been authorized by their own leaders in this very city (Acts 15:23-29). "And moreover he brought Greeks also into the temple, and hath defiled this holy place" (American Standard Version). Between the outer court of the temple, where Gentiles might come, and the sacred inner enclosure was a wall, over at least one of whose gates was an inscription: "Which forbade any foreigner to go in under pain of death."—Josephus, *Antiquities* 15:11:5.

29. (For they had seen before with him in the city Trophimus an Ephesian, whom they supposed that Paul had brought into the temple.)

Trophimus, a fellow townsman of these Jews, and thus well known by them to be a Gentile, had accompanied Paul to convey the gift of the Ephesian church to the Jewish Christians (20:4). He had been with Paul on the streets of Jerusalem, but the conclusion that he had accompanied him into the sacred precincts of the temple was false supposition.

30. And all the city was moved, and the people ran together: and they took Paul, and drew him out of the temple: and forthwith the doors were shut.

All the city was moved, and the people ran together. The mob scene in Ephesus was repeated (19:29), as excited citizens gathered from every direction to see what the disturbance was about. "And they laid hold on Paul, and dragged him out of the temple" (American Standard Version). Treating him as they would have treated an intruding Gentile, and not willing that the sacred pavement should be defiled with the blood of the murder they intended to commit, they hustled their victim out to the spacious court of the Gentiles. *Forthwith the doors were shut,* as if to seal the holy area against further pollution.

31. And as they went about to kill him, tidings came unto the chief captain of the band, that all Jerusalem was in an uproar.

"As they were seeking to kill him" (American Standard Version). The sudden, extreme, and unreasoning developments of mob violence are almost impossible to comprehend and terrible to contemplate. "Word was brought to the commander of the cohort" (Living Oracles translation). Accustomed to disturbances resulting from the tense political situation in Jerusalem and frequently flaring up amid the throngs in the temple, the Roman army kept a garrison in the castle of Antonia, adjoining the temple court at its northwest corner, and accessible to sit by stairways leading down into the temple area. Watchmen in the towers would be quick to notice and report the swift-spreading riot. A cohort of a thousand men—ten centuries with their centurion—was amid the throngs in the temple, the Roman army kept a garrison in the castle of Antonia, adjoining the temple court at its northwest corner, and accessible to sit by stairways leading down into the temple area. Watchmen in the towers would be quick to notice and report the swift-spreading riot. A cohort of a thousand men—ten centuries with their centurion—was commanded by a chiliarch. This is the officer to whom the news came.

32. Who immediately took soldiers and centurions, and ran down unto them: and when they saw the chief captains and the soldiers, they left beating of Paul.

Soldiers and centurions. Since each centurion was at the head of a hundred soldiers, the force included several hundred—enough to deal quickly and effectively with the riot. *Ran down* the stairways from the tower of Antonia "upon them" (American Standard Version). The sight of several hundred armed men bearing down on them at a run paralyzed the mob for the moment, and they "left off beating Paul" (American Standard Version).

33. Then the chief captain came near, and took him, and commanded him to be bound with two chains; and demanded who he was, and what he had done.

The man who had incited such violent action against himself might well be supposed a dangerous criminal. At least, the arrest of the central figure would be the quickest way to stop the uproar. Paul was accordingly manacled. "Inquired who he was, and what he had done" (American Standard Version). The question was addressed to the Jews who had been most active in assaulting Paul.

34. And some cried one thing, some another, among the multitude: and when he could not know the certainty for the tumult, he commanded him to be carried into the castle.

"Some shouted one thing, some another, among the crowd" (American Standard Version). No one person could give a clean answer, and the multitude gave confused, conflicting, and incoherent replies. "He could not know the certainty for the uproar" (American Standard Version). Any reasonable explanation would have been lost in the noise. *Carried into the castle*, which served as prison as well as army garrison. Perhaps because of injuries as well as because of the throng, Paul was for the moment unable to walk.

35. And when he came upon the stairs, so it was, that he was borne of the soldiers for the violence of the people.

Hoisting Paul to their shoulders and forming a protective screen about him, the soldiers prepared to carry him up into the tower of Antonia.

36. For the multitude of the people followed after, crying, Away with him.

The murderous intent of the mob had already been indicated. Their continued cry, so like that with which the Jews of this same city had bayed for the blood of Jesus thirty years before (Luke 23:18; John 19: 15), left no doubt as to what would happen if they got their hands on Paul again (compare Acts 22:22).

37. And as Paul was to be led into the castle, he said unto the chief captain, May I speak unto thee? Who said, Canst thou speak Greek?

Paul hoped to clear the matter, and perhaps even to win his freedom, before the closing of the castle door made him a prisoner indefinitely. "May I say something unto thee?" (American Standard Version). Any appeal had to be addressed first to the officer in charge. The modesty of the request, from a supposed brigand, must have astonished him as much as the language in which it was couched. "And he said, Dost thou know Greek?" (American Standard Version). The officer thought he knew who his prisoner was, but he was rather sure that man

was not literate enough to address him in the language of polite communication throughout the Empire.

38. Art not thou that Egyptian, which before these days madest an uproar, and leddest out into the wilderness four thousand men that were murderers?

This explains why the officer had come onto the scene with so large a company of soldiers. He suspected that his quarry was an important seditionist, perhaps supported by a band of followers. "Who . . . stirred up to sedition and led out into the wilderness the four thousand men of the Assassins" (American Standard Version). Josephus tells (Antiquities 20:8:6; Wars 2:13:5) of a certain Egyptian who shortly before this time mustered a force of thirty thousand violent zealots, promising to capture Jerusalem from the Romans. He led his followers to the Mount of Olives, whence he promised by miraculous power to destroy the walls of the city. He was attacked by Felix, and four hundred of his followers were slain and two hundred captured, while he himself escaped.

39. But Paul said, I am a man which am a Jew of Tarsus, a city in Cilicia, a citizen of no mean city: and, I beseech thee, suffer me to speak unto the people.

Not content with mere denial of the mistaken identity, Paul wasted no time in making his request, citing briefly the basis on which it might be respected. "I am a Jew, of Tarsus in Cilicia" (American Standard Version). Far from being an Egyptian intruder, he was of like nationality with the multitude about him. *A citizen of no mean city.* Tarsus had a proud heritage as an educational center, and the Jews there were respected. Citizenship in Tarsus was limited to a select few inhabitants, and so indicated a status of substance and honor. "Give me leave to speak unto the people" (American Standard Version). A man of such status, and already in custody, would hardly make a dangerous or seditious address. The officer expected Paul to speak of the charges against him. Paul sought to speak of his faith. The two subjects were very closely related.

40. And when he had given him license, Paul stood on the stairs, and beckoned with the hand unto the people. And when there was made a great silence, he spake unto them in the Hebrew tongue, saying.

It may have taken some time to quiet the crowd, but Paul waited with uplifted hand till there was *a great silence.* To the Roman captain he had spoken in Greek, the language common throughout the civilized world, but to the Jews he spoke in their own tongue.

CHAPTER 22

1. Men, brethren, and fathers, hear ye my defence which I make now unto you.

The "great silence" just mentioned was not yet complete, and Paul asked for a fair hearing. Though the people had been trying desperately to beat him to death, he spoke in a courteous and friendly way, calling to them as to his own people, *brethren and fathers.*

2. (And when they heard that he spake in the Hebrew tongue to them, they kept the more silence: and he saith.)

Most of the Jews could have understood if Paul had spoken Greek, but by speaking their own language he further identified himself with them and won their attention for a time.

3. I am verily a man which am a Jew, born in Tarsus, a city in Cilicia, yet brought up in this city at the feet of Gamaliel, and taught according to the perfect manner of the law of the fathers, and was zealous toward God, as ye all are this day.

Paul's ancestry and training were

such as to discredit the false charge that he taught against the Jews and the law and the temple (Acts 21: 28). Gamaliel was a teacher highly respected (Acts 5:34).

4. And I persecuted this way unto the death, binding and delivering into prisons both men and women.

This way is Christianity. Paul's vigorous persecution of it (Acts 8: 1-3) was evidence of his zeal for the Jewish way, just as the Jews' attack on him was evidence of their zeal.

5. As also the high priest doth bear me witness, and all the estate of the ·elders: from whom also I received letters unto the brethren, and went to Damascus, to bring them which were there bound unto Jerusalem, for to be punished.

Since Paul was speaking to an audience of Jews, most of whom were not Christians, *brethren* here means Jews, not Christians, and *the elders* are the elders of the Jews, nòt of the church. Many of those present could remember Paul's violent persecution of Christians; for the others Paul said their own high priest and elders could testify that he spoke the truth. Some of those officials were perhaps the very ones who had commissioned him to continue his persecution in Damascus (Acts 9:1, 2).

6. And it came to pass, that, as I made my journey, and was come nigh unto Damascus about noon, suddenly there shone from heaven a great light round about me.

Here Paul related the same events that are recorded in Acts 9, and most of the comments on that chapter are applicable. In this verse we have the added information that it was *about noon* when the *great light* appeared. This emphasized the brilliance of the light brighter than the sun (Acts 26:13).

7, 8. And I fell unto the ground, and heard a voice saying unto me, Saul, Saul, why persecutest thou me? And I answered, Who art thou, Lord? And he said unto me, I am Jesus of Nazareth, whom thou persecutest.

Thus Paul learned not only that Jesus was really alive from the dead as His followers had been saying, but also that the bitter persecution of those followers was persecution of the risen Lord himself.

9. And they that were with me saw indeed the light, and were afraid; but they heard not the voice of him that spake to me.

Acts 9:7 says Paul's companions heard a voice; the verse now before us says they *heard not the voice.* This is not a contradiction: the word *heard* is simply used with a different meaning as it often is in our speech today. The men with Paul heard the sound of the voice, but did not hear what words it said or could not understand the words.

10. And I said, What shall I do, Lord? And the Lord said unto me, Arise, and go into Damascus; and there it shall be told thee of all things which are appointed for thee to do.

Again it may be noted that the Lord has given to men the duty and privilege of preaching the gospel and telling people what to do to be saved. The same fact is evident in the record of Philip and the Ethiopian (Acts 8:26-40) and that of Peter and Cornelius (Acts 10). Jesus himself appeared to Paul, an angel appeared to Philip and Cornelius, and a special vision was given to Peter, but in each case it remained for a man to tell a man what to do to be rid of his sins.

11. And when I could not see for the glory of that light, being led by the hand of them that were with me, I came into Damascus.

Paul remained blind three days, fasting and no doubt praying for the information Jesus had promised (Acts 9:9).

12. And one Ananias, a devout man according to the law, having a good report of all the Jews which dwelt there.

To the Jews in Jerusalem Paul said that his instructions had come from a devout Jew of good reputation.

13. Came unto me, and stood, and said unto me, Brother Saul, receive thy sight. And the same hour I looked up upon him.

The miracle was evidence that the man through whom it was done was God's messenger. Paul recognized this, and so did other Jews who were not too much prejudiced (John 3:1, 2).

14, 15. And he said, The God of our fathers hath chosen thee, that thou shouldest know his will, and see that Just One, and shouldest hear the voice of his mouth. For thou shalt be his witness unto all men of what thou hast seen and heard.

Both Ananias and Jesus (Acts 26: 16-18) told Paul that he was called to be a witness of Jesus, to preach the gospel far and wide.

16. And now why tarriest thou? arise, and be baptized, and wash away thy sins, calling on the name of the Lord.

As already noted, Ananias and not Jesus told Paul what to do to be forgiven.

17. And it came to pass, that, when I was come again to Jerusalem, even while I prayed in the temple, I was in a trance.

This visit to Jerusalem probably was three years after Paul's conversion (Galatians 1:18). The Christians were afraid of him, and the Jews wanted to kill him (Acts 9:26-29). The Lord then came to him with a special revelation.

18. And saw him saying unto me, Make haste, and get thee quickly out of Jerusalem: for they will not receive thy testimony concerning me.

This revelation of the Lord's will was in line with instructions Jesus had given the other apostles (Matthew 10:23), and Paul obeyed it in many places (Acts 13:47; 14:6, 20; 17:10, 14).

19, 20. And I said, Lord, they know that I imprisoned and beat in every synagogue them that believed on thee: And when the blood of thy martyr Stephen was shed, I also was standing by, and consenting unto his death, and kept the raiment of them that slew him.

It seemed to Paul that his bitter persecution of Christians ought to make it evident to all the Jews that he was as devoted to the Jewish ways as they were. Therefore he thought they ought to listen to his story and be convinced as he had been convinced.

21. And he said unto me, Depart: for I will send thee far hence unto the Gentiles.

Knowing the depth and stubbornness of Jewish prejudice, the Lord knew Paul's testimony would be wasted in Jerusalem even if his life was not taken. But the Lord had work for this devoted follower in remote places.

22. And they gave him audience unto this word, and then lifted up their voices, and said, Away with such a fellow from the earth: for it is not fit that he should live.

This indicates that the bitterness of the Jewish multitude was not so much against Jesus as against Gentiles. They listened to Paul's testimony concerning Christ, but would not tolerate his' declaration that the Lord had sent him to offer to Gentiles the blessings of God's people. Those who bitterly opposed all the work of the church were the leaders rather than the common people.

23. And as they cried out, and cast off their clothes, and threw dust into the air.

At the mention of Gentiles the orderly audience suddenly became a riotous mob.

24. The chief captain commanded him to be brought into the castle, and bade that he should be examined by

scourging; that he might know wherefore they cried so against him.

It was not likely that Paul would be able to still the riot a second time, so the captain ordered him taken into the fort and beaten until he confessed what crimes had stirred up the people against him.

25. And as they bound him with thongs, Paul said unto the centurion that stood by, Is it lawful for you to scourge a man that is a Roman, and uncondemned?

A Jew or one of some other conquered nation might be tortured to obtain a confession, but Roman law forbade the beating of a Roman unless he had been tried and convicted. Paul's quiet question therefore brought the proceedings to a halt.

26. When the centurion heard that, he went and told the chief captain, saying, Take heed what thou doest: for this man is a Roman.

A centurion was in command of the scourging. The commander of the garrison was not in the torture room, but the centurion hurried to tell him what Paul had said.

27. Then the chief captain came, and said unto him, Tell me, art thou a Roman? He said, Yea.

The commander changed his attitude as swiftly as the centurion had. He came in person to talk with Paul.

28. And the chief captain answered, With a great sum obtained I this freedom. And Paul said, But I was free born.

Freedom is better translated "citizenship." The chief captain was not born a Roman, but had bought his citizenship. Paul, though a Jew, was born a Roman citizen because his father or grandfather had been granted citizenship, perhaps for money, or perhaps because of some service to the empire.

29. Then straightway they departed from him which should have examined him: and the chief captain was afraid, after he knew that he was a Roman, and because he had bound him.

The men ready to whip Paul were promptly dismissed, and even the commander was *afraid*. It was not illegal to fetter a Roman prisoner (Acts 26:29), but to tie him to the whipping post was at least perilously close to a violation. The commander tried to make amends by taking very good care of the prisoner thereafter (Acts 23:10, 23, 24).

30. On the morrow, because he would have known the certainty wherefore he was accused of the Jews, he loosed him from his bands, and commanded the chief priests and all their council to appear, and brought Paul down, and set him before them.

The Roman commander doubtless was often puzzled by the action of the Jews. He did not know why they were so incensed against Paul, but he hoped to find out by having him examined before the *council* or sanhedrin, the highest governing body among the Jews.

CHAPTER 23

1. And Paul, earnestly beholding the council, said, Men and brethren, I have lived in all good conscience before God until this day.

Paul once had been high in the favor of this council, and now he began with the same respectful and friendly tone he had used to the people the day before: *men and brethren.* He claimed to have lived as it seemed to him that God would have him live.

2. And the high priest Ananias commanded them that stood by him to smite him on the mouth.

Obviously the council already had condemned Paul, though he had not been tried or even accused before it. The mere claim of innocence was enough to call for a blow. *Them that stood by him* probably were Jewish guards or police.

3. Then said Paul unto him, God shall smite thee, thou whited wall: for sittest thou to judge me after the law, and commandest me to be smitten contrary to the law?

Paul vigorously answered that the judge who gave such an unfair order was not above God's judgment and punishment. *Whited wall* means a hypocrite, one like a tomb whitewashed outside but filled with corruption (Matthew 23:27). The priest earned that description by pretending to judge according to the law, but ordering Paul *to be smitten contrary to the law,* without being tried and convicted.

4. And they that stood by said, Revilest thou God's high priest?

The purpose of the gathering was to find some excuse for condemning Paul, and some were quick to call out that he had done wrong in speaking against the high priest.

5. Then said Paul, I wist not, brethren, that he was the high priest: for it is written, Thou shalt not speak evil of the ruler of thy people.

Paul readily agreed that it was against the law to *speak evil of the ruler,* and he quoted the law from Exodus 22:28. But he excused himself by saying, *I wist not,* that is, I did not know, *brethren, that he was the high priest.* Some students, supposing that the high priest must have been easily recognized, suggest that Paul may have spoken ironically, meaning, "When anyone gives such an illegal command it is hard to believe he is the high priest." It seems quite possible, however, that Paul's statement was literally true. Possibly the high priest was not distinguished from the rest by dress or position. Possibly Paul was looking in another direction and did not even see who gave the sudden order to strike him. There were about seventy men in the council. The police also were present and perhaps other spectators.

6. But when Paul perceived that the one part were Sadducees, and the other Pharisees, he cried out in the council, Men and brethren, I am a Pharisee, the son of a Pharisee: of the hope and resurrection of the dead I am called in question.

If the Sanhedrin should fail to bring a convincing charge against him, Paul had hope of going free. He made skillful use of his knowledge of the court to prevent their settling on an accusation against him.

One part were Sadducees, and the other Pharisees. Many of the Sanhedrin were known to Paul personally. The Sadducees controlled the priesthood; the Pharisees maintained their influence through the respect they commanded among the common people. *He cried out in the council.* His former effort at calm reasoning had been frustrated when the high priest commanded him to be smitten. It was obvious that justice by normal procedures would be impossible, and that an aggressive plea carried his only hope. *I am a Pharisee,* by birth, training, and basic convictions. "Touching the hope and resurrection of the dead I am called in question" (American Standard Version). This was the central Christian doctrine, differing from the convictions of the Pharisees before him only in that Paul preached the accomplishment through Christ of what was only an indefinite hope with them. It was this doctrine which had always especially offended the Sadducees (4:2).

7. And when he had so said, there arose a dissension between the Pharisees and the Sadducees: and the multitude was divided.

There arose a dissension. Paul's effort to win the sympathy of the Pharisees succeeded spectacularly. The council had been called together by the Roman officer to find Paul guilty of something that would convict him in a Roman court. This they knew they could not do. It seems that now the Pharisees saw a chance to slip out of the predicament and leave the whole burden of the charge to the Sadducees. Those worthies were quick to sense the scheme and to resent it. "The assembly was divided" (American Standard Version).

Concurrence in a criminal charge against the prisoner became immediately impossible.

8. For the Sadducees say that there is no resurrection, neither angel, nor spirit: but the Pharisees confess both.

The Sadducees had tried unsuccessfully to trap Jesus with a question about the resurrection (Matthew 22:23-33). *Neither angel, nor spirit.* These temple politicians were thoroughgoing materialists. *The Pharisees confess both,* the reality of the resurrection and of spirits, including angels.

9. And there arose a great cry: and the scribes that were of the Pharisees' part arose, and strove, saying, We find no evil in this man: but if a spirit or an angel hath spoken to him, let us not fight against God.

Feelings immediately became too fervent for quiet and orderly debate, so that the august Sanhedrin speedily came to resemble the recent mob in the temple court. *We find no evil in this man.* The spokesman was sure that he spoke for his party as well as for himself. This was the acquittal that, if it could have been concurred in, should have won Paul's freedom "And what if a spirit hath spoken to him, or an angel?" (American Standard Version). This was a direct and deliberate cut at the Sadducees, who denied the existence of any such beings.

10. And when there arose a great dissension, the chief captain, fearing lest Paul should have been pulled in pieces of them, commanded the soldiers to go down, and to take him by force from among them, and to bring him into the castle.

The conflict speedily came to include physical, as well as verbal violence. *The chief captain.* Claudius Lysias (v. 26), the chiliarch, saw that no good, and possibly great harm, could come from allowing the melee to continue. *Commanded the soldiers to go down.* The session had been held in an area of the temple court, rather than in the sacred precincts, where Lysias would not have been permitted to observe, nor the soldiers to enter. *The castle* of Antonia, housing both prison and army garrison, adjoined the temp'e court at its northwest corner.

11. And the night following the Lord stood by him, and said, Be of good cheer, Paul: for as thou hast testified of me in Jerusalem, so must thou bear witness also at Rome.

The appearances of the Lord to Paul, fulfilling the promise recorded in Acts 26:16, came at the times when they were most needed, when danger and cause of despondency were greatest and human companionship most wanting. *The Lord stood by him,* as at former times in Jerusalem (22:18-21) and Corinth (18:9), and was later to do on the way to Rome (27:23). *Be of good cheer, Paul.* There was little enough in Paul's surroundings to encourage optimism. Imprisonment had halted his ministry, and death at the hands of his countrymen awaited him if he should be released. This was one of the lessons by which he learned to "rejoice in the Lord" (Philippians 4: 4) and to be content in any circumstance (Philippians 4:4, 11). *As thou hast testified of me in Jerusalem.* Paul's address to the people (22:1-21) had been far more a presentation of Christ than a defense of himself.

So must thou bear witness also at Rome. His ministry may have been halted, but it was not ended. Henceforth Paul was confident that he would live to preach in the capital of the Roman Empire, and he laid his plans in that direction.

12, 13. And when it was day, certain of the Jews banded together, and bound themselves under a curse, saying that they would neither eat nor drink till they had killed Paul. And they were more than forty which had made this conspiracy.

This shows the intensity of the feeling against Paul. We can only wonder who these forty were. Police? Political hangers-on indebted to members of the council? Students? There is no answer.

14. And they came to the chief priests and elders, and said, We have bound ourselves under a great curse, that we will eat nothing until we have slain Paul.

The conspirators were so sure of the wishes of the chief priests that they did not hesitate to reveal their murderous plot.

15. Now therefore ye with the council signify to the chief captain that he bring him down unto you to morrow, as though ye would enquire something more perfectly concerning him: and we, or ever he come near, are ready to kill him.

Since Paul's first appearance before the council had ended in utter confusion, it would seem plausible to ask that he be returned for another hearing. The leaders probably would promise that the disorder of the former meeting would not be repeated. The commander could be expected to send only a small detachment of soldiers with him, and these could be overwhelmed by a surprise assault by the forty assassins.

16. And when Paul's sister's son heard of their lying in wait, he went and entered into the castle, and told Paul.

Paul's sister's son, otherwise not mentioned in Scripture, may have been a rabbinical student in Jerusalem as Paul himself had been a generation before (22:3). *He went and entered into the castle, and told Paul.* Not every prisoner would be visited so easily, but the officers in charge of the garrison were now keenly aware of Paul's rights as a citizen, and may have thought to gain some information about their prisoner from this visitor.

17. Then Paul called one of the centurions unto him, and said, Bring this young man unto the chief captain: for he hath a certain thing to tell him.

The soldiers evidently treated Paul with leniency and respect since they knew he was a Roman.

18. So he took him, and brought him to the chief captain, and said, Paul the prisoner called me unto him, and prayed me to bring this young man unto thee, who hath something to say unto thee.

The centurion referred to Paul by name with some respect, and made no apology for having obeyed the prisoner's summons and acceded to his request. *Who hath something to say unto thee.* Lysias had been eager for any information about this amazing prisoner.

19. Then the chief captain took him by the hand, and went with him aside privately, and asked him, What is that thou hast to tell me?

Took him by the hand. An understanding gesture designed to encourage a young and courageous, but thoroughly frightened, messenger. We admire Lysias for it. "And going aside asked him privately" (American Standard Version). The officer recognized the important and confidential nature of the message.

20. And he said, The Jews have agreed to desire thee that thou wouldest bring down Paul to morrow into the council, as though they would enquire somewhat of him more perfectly.

The Jews. Not all of the Jews, but their influential leaders. After what Lysias had seen in the temple court and in the council the term would be specific enough for him.

21. But do not thou yield unto them: for there lie in wait for him of them more than forty men, which have bound themselves with an oath, that they will neither eat nor drink till they have killed him: and now are they ready, looking for a promise from thee.

More than forty men. Perhaps hired assassins, but men of sufficient personal interest in the enterprise that they were willing to bind themselves with an oath to its accomplishment. *Bound themselves with an oath, that they will neither eat nor drink till they have killed him.* The nature of the vow—not its purpose —was fairly common in Jewry. The forty and more never fulfilled their rash vow. The Talmud says that those who took a vow were released from it, if it was impossible to carry it out.

22. So the chief captain then let the young man depart, and charged him, See thou tell no man that thou hast shewed these things to me.

The officer made no promises and revealed no plans that might possibly have gotten back to the plotters. "Tell no man that thou has signified these things to me" (American Standard Version). The young man's own safety, as well as the successful frustration of the plot, depended on the utmost secrecy.

23. And he called unto him two centurions, saying, Make ready two hundred soldiers to go to Caesarea, and horsemen threescore and ten, and spearmen two hundred, at the third hour of the night.

Lysias had three alternatives: to accede to the Jews' request and lose his citizen-prisoner; or to resist it, with resultant loss of favor with the Jewish authorities, and with probable bloodshed; or to avoid it by removing Paul before the request was made of him. He wisely chose the last course, sending a sufficient guard to discourage any attack the Jews might have desired to make on the way. A total force of 470 soldiers, with light and heavy arms, was assembled to depart at nine o'clock at night.

24. And provide them beasts, that they may set Paul on, and bring him safe unto Felix the governor.

Provide beasts. For added safety to Paul, as well as for his convenience. Lysias had developed a growing conviction that Paul was no criminal. *Felix the governor.* Felix, a freed slave of the imperial family, was made procurator of Judea in A.D. 52, probably through the influence of his brother Pallas, who was a favorite of Claudius Caesar. Cruel, greedy, and immoral, Felix was deposed two years later, and was subsequently assassinated.

25, 26. And he wrote a letter after this manner: Claudius Lysias unto the most excellent governor Felix sendeth greeting.

It probably was unusual to send a single prisoner to the governor with a large guard, and an explanation quite properly was sent at the same time.

27. This man was taken of the Jews, and should have been killed of them: then came I with an army, and rescued him, having understood that he was a Roman.

Should have been killed of course does not mean that Paul ought to have been killed, but merely that he would have been killed if he had not been rescued. With an eye to his own welfare, the commander said nothing of his order to beat Paul (Acts 22:24-26), but rather indicated that he knew all along that Paul was a Roman and therefore was the more careful to rescue him.

28, 29. And when I would have known the cause wherefore they accused him, I brought him forth into their council: Whom I perceived to be accused of questions of their law, but to have nothing laid to his charge worthy of death or of bonds.

The commander had learned little from the council, but it was apparent that Paul was not even accused of anything the Romans would regard as a crime. Probably neither he nor the governor knew much about the intricacies of Jewish law.

30. And when it was told me how that the Jews laid wait for the man, I sent straightway to thee, and gave

commandment to his accusers also to say before thee what they had against him. Farewell.

Thus the commander showed how promptly and shrewdly he had acted to avert a riot and keep the peace, as Rome expected her officers to do.

31. Then the soldiers, as it was commanded them, took Paul, and brought him by night to Antipatris.

The secret departure was designed to keep the assassins from knowing what was going on; but if they found out, the huge guard was designed to keep them from attacking. If they were rash enough to attack, the soldiers would be ready and could easily overwhelm them. Antipatris, built by Herod the Great, was about halfway between Jerusalem and Caesarea.

32. On the morrow they left the horsemen to go with him, and returned to the castle.

Apparently the movement had eluded the conspirators. It was very unlikely that there would be any attack during the last part of the jour-

ney, and even if there were, the seventy cavalrymen would be more than adequate to deal with a daylight assault.

33. Who, when they came to Caesarea, and delivered the epistle to the governor, presented Paul also before him.

As expected, the trip was completed without incident.

34, 35. And when the governor had read the letter, he asked of what province he was. And when he understood that he was of Cilicia; I will hear thee, said he, when thine accusers are also come. And he commanded him to be kept in Herod's judgment hall.

If Paul had belonged to a nearby province, possibly Felix would have considered getting in touch with a ruler far away, so he merely ordered Paul held till his accusers would come. The city of Caesarea had been built about seventy years earlier by Herod the great, and the *judgment hall,* or palace, still was known by his name.

CHAPTER 24

1. And after five days Ananias the high priest descended with the elders, and with a certain orator named Tertullus, who informed the governor against Paul.

Five days gave the Jewish rulers time to obtain the services of a skilled *orator* and to plan how to present their false charges most effectively. It is geographically accurate to say they *descended,* for Caesarea was on the seacoast and Jerusalem was near the top of the mountain ridge, about twenty-four hundred feet above sea level.

2, 3. And when he was called forth, Tertullus began to accuse him, saying, Seeing that by thee we enjoy great quietness, and that very worthy deeds are done unto this nation by thy providence, We accept it always, and in all places, most noble Felix, with all thankfulness.

Paul was *called forth* from prison to be in the courtroom and hear the charges made against him. The orator Tertullus began tactfully by giving high praise to the governor to whom he was speaking. Felix had been dealing with the Jewish leaders

for years, and probably knew how in-
sincere this praise was.

**4. Notwithstanding, that I be not
further tedious unto thee, I pray thee
that thou wouldest hear us of thy
clemency a few words.**

Like many another orator, Tertullus promised to be brief, not *tedious,*
and asked the governor to be kind
enough to listen.

**5. For we have found this man a
pestilent fellow, and a mover of sedition among all the Jews throughout
the world, and a ringleader of the
sect of the Nazarenes.**

These three accusations of a general nature were designed to prejudice the governor against Paul. First,
Tertullus said the prisoner was a
pest, a plague. Second, he charged
that Paul was accustomed to cause
sedition, uprisings, insurrections,
among the Jews wherever he went.
It was true that here had been riotous disorder in many places where
Paul had been (Acts 13:50; 14:5, 19;
17:5-9, 13; 18:12-16; 19:23-41). Felix, like other Roman authorities in
conquered provinces, was very anxious to prevent such disorder. Third,
the orator alleged that Paul was *a
ringleader of the sect of the Nazarenes.* This seems to have been the
Jews' contemptuous way of speaking
of the church. The name was derived from the fact that Jesus had
been reared in Nazareth. It was not
illegal to be a Christian, but Tertullus probably meant to imply that it
was despicable.

**6. Who also hath gone about to
profane the temple: whom we took,
and would have judged according to
our law.**

To profane the temple would not
in itself concern the governor, but to
start a riot by profaning the temple
would concern him. Tertullus now
made a specific charge, and of course
it was false (Acts 21:29). According
to our version, he added another
statement, equally false, to the effect
that Paul had been arrested in an orderly way and would have been given
a fair trial. The truth was that he
had been seized by a mob and would
have been beaten to death without
any trial. However, the latter part of
verse 6, all of verse 7, and the first
part of verse 8, are missing in some
of the best manuscripts and therefore
are left out of the American Standard
and Revised Standard Versions.

**7. But the chief captain Lysais came
upon us, and with great violence took
him away out of our hands.**

Accusations of "police brutality"
are not new. According to this verse,
Tertullus meant to imply that there
was no excuse for Lysias' action, but
this implication is contradicted by
the simple record in Acts 21:31, 32.

**8. Commanding his accusers to
come unto thee: by examining of
whom thyself mayest take knowledge
of all these things, whereof we accuse
him.**

According to Tertullus, Paul's
guilt was so inescapable that the
governor would find it proved by
Paul's own testimony.

**9. And the Jews also assented, say-
ing that these things were so.**

The high priest and the elders who
had come with him (v. 1) solemnly
declared that their "mouthpiece" had
spoken the truth.

**10. Then Paul, after that the gov-
ernor had beckoned unto him to speak,
answered, Forasmuch as I know that
thou hast been of many years a judge**

unto this nation, I do the more cheer-
fully answer for myself.

Without the exaggerated praise
Tertullus had used (vv. 2, 3), Paul
indicated that he was glad to be
heard by a judge who had experience
enough to be capable.

**11. Because that thou mayest un-
derstand, that there are yet but twelve
days since I went up to Jerusalem for
to worship.**

Paul had been in prison about half
of those twelve days. It would be
easy to investigate and find out what
he had done in the few days he had
been free in Jerusalem.

**12. And they neither found me in
the temple disputing with any man,
neither raising up the people, neither
in the synagogues, nor in the city.**

There was absolutely no evidence
that Paul had been "a pestilent fellow, and a mover of sedition" (v. 5)
during those days at Jerusalem.

**13. Neither can they prove the
things whereof they now accuse me.**

Paul appropriately pointed out
that an accusation is not evidence,
and there was no proof of what Tertullus said.

**14. But this I confess unto thee, that
after the way which they call heresy,
so worship I the God of my fathers,
believing all things which are written
in the law and in the prophets.**

One part of the accusation Paul
did not deny. He readily agreed that
he was a follower of Jesus. However,
he did not accept his accusers' estimate that the Christian way was a
heresy or sect. (The word for "heresy" here is translated "sect" in verse
5.) He still held to all that was
taught in the *law* and *prophets* of
the Old Testament, but he insisted ·

that now God had revealed a better
way of serving *the God of my fathers.*

**15. And have hope toward God,
which they themselves also allow, that
there shall be a resurrection of the
dead, both of the just and unjust.**

Paul was not a rebel or heretic.
He shared the highest hopes of his
own people, the Jews. Probably the
high priest was a Sadducee who held
no hope of a resurrection; but no
doubt some of the elders with him
were Pharisees who treasured such a
hope. The high priest would not
raise the question of resurrection and
risk a renewal of the strife recorded
in Acts 23:6-9.

**16. And herein do I exercise my-
self, to have always a conscience void
of offence toward God, and toward
men.**

Because he expected that both the
just and the unjust would be raised
from the dead to face God's judgment, Paul conscientiously tried to
do right in the sight of God and men.

**17. Now after many years I came
to bring alms to my nation, and offerings.**

After *many years* of absence, Paul
had returned to Jerusalem, not with
any subversive intent, but *to bring
alms.* He was one of several bearers
of money collected in Asia Minor
and Europe to relieve the poor of
Jerusalem and the vicinity (Romans
15:25-27; 1 Corinthians 16:1-4; 2
Corinthians 8:1-7).

**18. Whereupon certain Jews from
Asia found me purified in the temple,
neither with multitude, nor with tumult.**

The charges of stirring up trouble
and profaning the temple simply
were not true. Paul had cleansed

himself according to the strict Jewish custom before going into the temple, and he had gone quietly about his worship, doing nothing to assemble a *multitude* or start a *tumult*.

19. Who ought to have been here before thee, and object, if they had ought against me.

Paul made the very good point that his original accusers were not even present. They had quietly faded from the scene, knowing their wild charges would not stand in a court of law.

20. Or else let these same here say, if they have found any evil doing in me, while I stood before the council.

Paul now directly challenged the high priest and elders. He had been placed before them for judgment. Let them tell of what crimes they had convicted him. Naturally there was no response to the challenge. The high priest and elders wanted no talk about their council meeting that had degenerated into a riot (Acts 23: 1-10). To air this incident would be to bring upon them the condemnation of the governor.

21. Except it be for this one voice, that I cried standing among them, Touching the resurrection of the dead I am called in question by you this day.

By recalling this saying specifically, Paul subtly dared the high priest to take exception to it. Again there was no response. The Sadducees and Pharisees differed bitterly on the doctrine of the resurrection, but they were determined to maintain an appearance of unity before Felix, and therefore could not say what they thought.

22. And when Felix heard these things, having more perfect knowledge

of that way, he deferred them, and said, When Lysias the chief captain shall come down, I will know the uttermost of your matter.

Having been in Judea for several years while the church was active, Felix knew more about the Christian way than he learend from Tertullus and Paul. Possibly he already knew Christians were very generous in caring for the poor, and now he had learned that Paul came bringing alms from abroad. He must have surmised that a large sum of money was involved, and his greedy mind was alert to the possibility of getting some of it in return for Paul's freedom (v. 26). He made a plausible excuse to delay his judgment of the case. If he ever talked with Lysias about it, this is not recorded.

23. And he commanded a centurion to keep Paul, and to let him have liberty, and that he should forbid none of his acquaintance to minister or come unto him.

Liberty in this verse obviously does not mean that Paul was set free. He remained a prisoner, but was given as much indulgence or ease as possible for a prisoner. Christian friends could visit him as much as they wished, and could provide for his meals. Paul doubtless used much of his time in teaching those who came to him.

24. And after certain days, when Felix came with his wife Drusilla, which was a Jewess, he sent for Paul, and heard him concerning the faith in Christ.

As governor of Judea, Felix found it to his advantage to be informed about all movements among the Jews. With Paul in his charge, he had a remarkable opportunity to learn from an outstanding teacher of the new "way" or "sect." His Jewish wife no doubt helped him understand Jewish customs and ways of thinking.

25. And as he reasoned for righteousness, temperance, and judgment to come, Felix trembled, and answered, Go thy way for this time; when I have a convenient season, I will call for thee.

Apparently Paul did not merely explain Christianity on an intellectual plane, but became intensely practical and even personal. He talked about right and wrong, and inevitable judgment before a just God. This frightened Felix—not enough to make him turn from evil to righteousness, but enough to make him cut the interview short, promising to continue it some other time.

26. He hoped also that money should have been given him of Paul, that he might loose him: wherefore he sent for him the oftener, and communed with him.

Felix kept his promise to call Paul again—not once, but many times. We can only imagine what ways he found to drop hints that the machinery of justice might be speeded up by a bribe. We can imagine, too, that such a hint never brought him anything but another sermon on "righteousness, and temperance, and judgment to come."

27. But after two years Porcius Festus came into Felix' room: and Felix, willing to shew the Jews a pleasure, left Paul bound.

Felix was a merciless tyrant, and the Jews had good reason to be displeased with thim. When the emperor replaced him, Felix hoped to lessen their enmity by leaving Paul in prison. In spite of this, however, the Jews did send accusations against against him to the emperor. Felix was fortunate enough to have a brother who was influential in Rome, and probably only this saved him from punishment for his mismanagement in Judea.

CHAPTER 25

1. Now when Festus was come into the province, after three days he ascended from Caesarea to Jerusalem.

The Roman made his headquarters in Caesarea, but Jerusalem was the ancient capital where the high priest and other Jewish officials lived. The new governor went there to get acquainted and discuss affairs of state.

2. Then the high priest and the chief of the Jews informed him against Paul, and besought him.

Apparently two years had not dulled the hatred these men held for Paul. At their very first meeting with

the new governor they renewed their charges.

3. And desired favour against him, that he would send for him to Jerusalem, laying wait in the way to kill him.

The Jewish rulers revived the old plot to murder Paul (Acts 23:12-15). Perhaps saying the case had been too long deferred, they asked that Festus would do them the favor of sending immediately for Paul and judging the case while he was in Jerusalem. What they really intended, of course, was to prepare an ambush and kill Paul along the road.

4. But Festus answered, that Paul should be kept at Caesarea, and that he himself would depart shortly thither.

Festus was new in Judea, but he was not naive. He wisely refused to be hurried or to be managed by the people he was sent to govern.

5. Let them therefore, said he, which among you are able, go down with me, and accuse this man, if there be any wickedness in him.

Since Festus was to be the judge, he insisted that the Jews present their case in his courtroom, not theirs. *Able* describes men in power, men who would have authority to speak for the leaders of the Jews.

6. And when he had tarried among them more than ten days, he went down unto Caesarea; and the next day sitting on the judgment seat commanded Paul to be brought.

Felix had left the affairs of the province in a very unsatisfactory condition, and there was much for the new governor to discuss with the local leaders. Festus seems to have been a conscientious official, and he took more than ten days for this opening conference. Upon returning to Caesarea, he took up Paul's case without delay.

7. And when he was come, the Jews which came down from Jerusalem stood round about, and laid many and grievous complaints against Paul, which they could not prove.

Probably the accusations were basically the same that had been made two years earlier (Acts 24:5-9), though some additional specifications may have been fabricated. As before, however, they could present only accusations without proof.

8. While he answered for himself, Neither against the law of the Jews, neither against the temple, nor yet against Caesar, have I offended any thing at all.

Paul flatly denied every charge that was made. Probably his defense, like the charges, resembled that recorded in Acts 24.

9. But Festus, willing to do the Jews a pleasure, answered Paul, and said, Wilt thou go up to Jerusalem, and there be judged of these things before me?

As a newcomer unacquainted with Jewish ways, Festus must have found this case very puzzling. It was evident, however, that it concerned Jewish law and religion rather than Roman. The Jews probably urged strongly and repeatedly that such a case ought to be tried in Jerusalem. Festus did not wish to antagonize them, neither did he wish to allow injustice to be done. Seeking a compromise, he did not think of turning Paul over to the Jews for judgment, but of holding his own court in Jerusalem to please them. Cautiously feeling his way, he asked if Paul would consent to this.

10. Then said Paul, I stand at Caesar's judgment seat, where I ought to be judged: to the Jews I have done no wrong, as thou very well knowest.

Paul bluntly rejected the suggested compromise. He was a Roman citizen in a Roman court and no wrongdoing had been proved against him.

11. For if I be an offender, or have committed any thing worthy of death, I refuse not to die: but if there be none ot these things whereof these accuse me, no man may

deliver me unto them. I appeal unto Caesar.

Paul freely consented to legal procedure, even if it should involve his own death, but he refused to consent to his own murder. He knew, as Festus did not, that the proposed trip would not end in Jerusalem, but in violent death along the way. Already he had been held two years, and still justice was not in sight. But there was a way out of the present predicament. A Roman citizen dissatisfied with his treatment in provincial courts might appeal to Caesar. This meant he must be sent to Rome and judged by the emperor. Caesar had many other things on his mind, and a prisoner might wait long in Rome, but that was better than being murdered in Judea. Paul made his appeal.

12. Then Festus, when he had conferred with the council, answered, Hast thou appealed unto Caesar? unto Caesar shalt thou go.

To have his first case taken to Caesar might be considered a reflection on Festus' ability. Probably he was reluctant to see this happen. He took a few minutes to confer with his advisers. Among them probably were legal experts who told the governor he had no choice: the appeal must be respected. Festus then so informed Paul. The first part of his reply is better regarded as a statement, not a question: "You have appealed to Caesar; to Caesar you shall go."

13. And after certain days king Agrippa and Bernice came unto Caesarea to salute Festus.

There was no daily boat to Rome: the prisoner must wait till passage could be secured. In the meantime, a neighboring ruler arrived to pay his respects to the new governor.

Herod Agrippa II, the son of Herod Agrippa I (Acts 12), was king of territories to the north and east, which, like Judea, were part of the Roman Empire. Bernice was his sister.

14, 15. And when they had been there many days, Festus declared Paul's cause unto the king, saying, There is a certain man left in bonds by Felix: About whom, when I was at Jerusalem, the chief priests and the elders of the Jews informed me, desiring to have judgment against him.

In the many days they were together, Festus doubtless became aware of Agrippa's vast knowledge of Jewish ways. A discussion of Paul's case might help the new governor understand the puzzling people he must rule.

16. To whom I answered, It is not the manner of the Romans to deliver any man to die, before that he which is accused have the accusers face to face, and have license to answer for himself concerning the crime laid against him.

Festus thus stated one of the principles that made Roman justice famous. The accused was entitled to a fair trial. If we note that Roman rulers sometimes forgot or ignored this lofty principle, we must confess that our own courts too sometimes fall short of the ideal.

17. Therefore, when they were come hither, without any delay on the morrow I sat on the judgment seat, and commanded the man to be brought forth.

With pardonable pride Festus indicated that he intended to give justice promptly, in marked contrast with the dilatory methods of Felix, who had held Paul for two years without cause.

18, 19. Against whom when the accusers stood up, they brought none accusation of such things as I supposed: But had certain questions against him of their own superstition, and of one Jesus, which was dead, whom Paul affirmed to be alive.

Facing the extreme bitterness of the Jewish rulers, Festus naturally *supposed* Paul was charged with some such crime as insurrection or murder. To his surprise, the accusations concerned matters of the Jewish religion, about which Festus knew little or nothing. ("Religion" probably is a better translation than *superstition*.) The reference to *one Jesus* also indicates that the governor knew little of the affairs of Judea and perhaps had not heard of Jesus and Christianity until this case.

20. And because I doubted of such manner of questions, I asked him whether he would go to Jerusalem, and there be judged of these matters.

Feeling sure his fellow ruler would be sympathetic, Festus frankly admitted that he was puzzled by the kind of questions raised in Paul's case. This was an excuse for suggesting that the case be heard in Jerusalem.

21. But when Paul had appealed to be reserved unto the hearing of Augustus, I commanded him to be kept till I might send him to Caesar.

Augustus and *Caesar* were two titles frequently given to the reigning emperor, who at this time was Nero. *Augustus* means august or reverend; *Caesar* was originally the family name of the great Julius.

22. Then Agrippa said unto Festus, I would also hear the man myself. To morrow, said he, thou shalt hear him.

Paul was famous among both Jews and Christians, and Agrippa doubtless had heard of him. The king was careful to keep himself informed about activities among the Jews (Acts 26:3), and he welcomed an opportunity to hear what Paul himself might say.

23. And on the morrow, when Agrippa was come, and Bernice, with great pomp, and was entered into the place of hearing, with the chief captains, and principal men of the city, at Festus' commandment Paul was brought forth.

Paul's later appearance in Rome might lead some of the higher officials there to suspect that Festus had not dealt with his case fairly and capably. Perhaps it was to protect himself against such suspicion that Festus made a formal state occasion of this hearing in Caesarea. If any questions were raised later, there would be many reliable witnesses to testify that Paul had been heard openly, not oppressed or persecuted in a secret session.

24. And Festus said, King Agrippa, and all men which are here present with us, ye see this man, about whom all the multitude of the Jews have dealt with me, both at Jerusalem, and also here, crying that he ought not to live any longer.

The governor spoke primarily to his guest of honor, *King Agrippa*, but he included also *all men which are here present*. He might want some of them later to testify to his fair and open-minded attitude. He made it clear that the charges against

Paul were not brought by him or any of his officers, but were made vociferously by Jews.

25. But when I found that he had committed nothing worthy of death, and that he himself hath appealed to Augustus, I have determined to send him.

Note how carefully Festus continued to clear himself of blame. He had found nothing against Paul. It was the Jews who had brought the unfounded charges; it was Paul himself who had appealed to the emperor.

26, 27. Of whom I have no certain thing to write unto my lord. Wherefore I have brought him forth before thee, O king Agrippa, that, after examination had, I might have somewhat to write. For it seemeth to me unreasonable to send a prisoner, and not withal to signify the crimes laid against him.

We can readily appreciate the new governor's dilemma. He had to send a prisoner to Rome; but he could give no reason for sending him except that the prisoner had made an appeal, and he could give no valid reason at all for his being a prisoner. Only the charge of stirring up insurrection (Acts 24:5) could possibly concern the Roman government, and it was too vague and unfounded really to concern anyone. The charges of defiling the temple, teaching against Jewish customs, and preaching the resurrection were more confusing than enlightening to Festus. Perhaps they would be more meaningful to Agrippa, who was acquainted with Jewish thought. Festus appealed especially to the king, and incidently to the others who were present, to help him decide what to write to the emperor.

CHAPTER 26

1. Then Agrippa said unto Paul, Thou art permitted to speak for thy self. Then Paul stretched forth the hand, and answered for himself.

Agrippa said. This was Festus' court, but he had turned the investigation over to the visiting Jewish king, who now took charge. *Thou art permitted to speak for thyself.* The simplicity of his manner was in marked contrast to the grandiose introduction made by Festus (25:23-27).

2, 3. I think myself happy, king Agrippa, because I shall answer for myself this day before thee touching all the things whereof I am accused of the Jews: Especially because I

know thee to be expert in all customs and questions which are among the Jews: wherefore I beseech thee to hear me patiently.

This was not idle flattery; Agrippa really was expert in all customs and questions which are among the Jews. He was partly Jewish by birth, and for generations his family had been active in Jewish government. His father had killed the apostle James to please the Jews (Acts 12:1-3). His father's uncle had murdered John the Baptist (Mark 6:17-28). His great-grandfather had slaughtered the babes of Bethlehem shortly after Jesus' birth (Matthew 2:16). Of all the family, perhaps this king to whom Paul spoke was most sympathetic with the Jews and made the greatest effort to understand them and treat them justly.

4, 5. My manner of life from my youth, which was at the first among mine own nation at Jerusalem, know all the Jews; Which knew me from the beginning, if they would testify, that after the most straitest sect of our religion I lived a Pharisee.

Paul had been educated in Jerusalem with one of the most respected teachers (Acts 22:3). How long this took we do not know, but he was "brought up" there, perhaps from the early teens. And there in the center of Judaism he had proved himself one of the most intensely Jewish of the Jews.

6, 7. And now I stand and am judged for the hope of the promise made of God unto our fathers: Unto which promise our twelve tribes, instantly serving God day and night, hope to come. For which hope's sake, king Agrippa, I am accused of the Jews.

Paul was accused by the Jews, but he insisted that his activity was not anti-Jewish. On the contrary, he cherished the same hope that was treasured by all the twelve tribes of the Jews, a hope based on the ancient promise of God—the hope of redemption through the Messiah. His preaching was a declaration that the ancient promise was fulfilled in Jesus.

8. Why should it be thought a thing incredible with you, that God should raise the dead?

The statement that Jesus had been raised from the dead was rejected by many, and it still is. Why?

If anyone believes in the God who gave life in the beginning, why should he doubt God's power to give life to the dead?

9. I verily thought with myself, that I ought to do many things contrary to the name of Jesus of Nazareth.

So thoroughly had Paul been at one with the Jewish authorities that he had thought as they did that it was necessary to oppose *the name of Jesus,* that is, His cause and His way.

10. Which thing I also did in Jerusalem: and many of the saints did I shut up in prison, having received authority from the chief priests; and when they were put to death, I gave my voice against them.

Paul consistently did what he thought he ought to do. When he believed it right to oppose Jesus' way, he opposed it very strongly, working in complete harmony with *the chief priests* and by their *authority.* Some take the last part of this verse to mean that Paul had been a member of the Jews' supreme council or Sanhedrin and had voted for the death penalty for Christians. Other students think the expression may mean merely that Paul used his influence to secure a sentence of death.

11. And I punished them oft in every synagogue, and compelled them to blaspheme; and being exceedingly mad against them, I persecuted them even unto strange cities.

Blaspheme means primarily to speak against or to speak evil of. Paul punished Christians, trying to compel them to speak evil of Jesus, to say He was not the Christ but an imposter. Probably this effort succeeded in some cases. *Mad* here means furious, enraged. Paul was so violently aroused that he could not be content merely to persecute Christians in Jerusalem: he soon wanted to punish them in foreign places as well. *Strange* here means foreign rather than odd or peculiar.

12, 13. Whereupon as I went to Damascus with authority and commission from the chief priests, At midday, O king, I saw in the way a light from heaven, above the brightness of the sun, shining round about me and them which journeyed with me.

Paul's marvelous experience near Damascus has been considered in comments on chapters 9 and 22. These two verses are quite similar to corresponding parts of the chapters.

14. And when we were all fallen to the earth, I heard a voice speaking unto me, and saying in the Hebrew tongue, Saul, Saul, why persecutest thou me? it is hard for thee to kick against the pricks.

Since Paul had been emphasizing that he was as thoroughly Jewish as anyone could be, he now mentioned that the Lord spoke to him in the *Hebrew tongue,* the language of the Jews.

15, 16. And I said, Who art thou, Lord? And he said, I am Jesus whom thou persecutest. But rise, and stand upon thy feet: for I have appeared unto thee for this purpose, to make thee a minister and a witness both of these things which thou hast seen, and of those things in the which I will appear unto thee.

Only in this account are we told that Jesus thus explained His purpose in appearing, but Acts 22:14 records that Ananias gave the same explanation. Paul was not to be merely a Christian; he was to be an apostle. Therefore he, like Matthias (Acts 1:22) and the other apostles, must be a witness of the risen Lord. That he might be an eyewitness, Jesus appeared to him at this time and promised to appear to him at later times as well.

17. Delivering thee from the people, and from the Gentiles, unto whom now I send thee.

The people means the Jewish people. The Lord knew that His power and providence would be needed to *deliver* Paul from them, as well as from the *Gentiles.* Here the Lord announced that Paul's mission would be mainly to the Gentiles.

18. To open their eyes, and to turn them from darkness to light, and from the power of Satan unto God, that they may receive forgiveness of sins, and inheritance among them which are sanctified by faith that is in me.

Here is a magnificent statement of the purpose and result of Paul's preaching to the heathen Gentiles. His good news would *open their eyes* to the truth revealed in Jesus. It would *turn them* in repentance from the ways of *darkness* to the ways of *light,* truth, righteousness. Thus they would escape from *the power of Satan* and give themselves to *God.* Thus they would *receive forgiveness of sins,* and share the *inheritance* of eternal life and blessing that is given to all who are *sanctified,* or set apart, as God's people through their *faith* in God's Son, Jesus, the Christ.

19. Whereupon, O king Agrippa, I was not disobedient unto the heavenly vision.

A Sadducee would have scoffed at the story of Christ's appearance to Paul. Agrippa, a Pharisee in his sympathies, would respect it, as he would also respect Paul's emphasis on obedience. The vision, as Paul recalled it here (vv. 16-18), was principally a commission, demanding obedience.

20. But shewed first unto them of Damascus, and at Jerusalem, and throughout all the coasts of Judaea, and then to the Gentiles, that they should repent and turn to God, and do works meet for repentance.

Paul omitted details of his preparation (Galatians 1:16, 17), but emphasized the fact that his labors had been in obedience to divine commission. Acts 9:27 tells of his labor in Damascus. *And at Jerusalem* (see 9: 28, 29). We learn also of the difficulties attending that ministry. "And throughout all the country of Judaea" (American Standard Version). This may have taken place when Paul came to Jerusalem with gifts from the church at Antioch (11:30). *Then to the Gentiles.* To the nations. This was the greater part of his ministry. The mention of it was not offensive to Agrippa as to the Jewish leaders. "That they should reform, and turn to God, performing deeds worthy of reformation" (Living Oracles translation). The gospel of Christ is practical, more than theoretical. This the dissolute Agrippa needed to be told. "And live as men who have repented should" (Goodspeed translation).

21. For these causes the Jews caught me in the temple, and went about to kill me.

"For this cause the Jews seized me in the temple" (American Standard Version). For preaching to the Gentiles, and for requiring a new life in Christ rather than conformity to the law of Moses. "Attempted to have killed me with their own hands" (Living Oracles translation). This happened twice, once at the first onslaught (21:31), and again in the Sanhedrin (23:10).

22. Having therefore obtained help of God, I continue unto this day, witnessing both to small and great, saying none other things than those which the prophets and Moses did say should come.

God's help had been a feature in all of Paul's ministry, especially in bringing him through such dangers as he had experienced on his last visit to Jerusalem (chapters 21-23). Even in this present moment Paul was engaged in obeying Christ's commission to speak the word to one that was "high" in his position among men. "Saying nothing but what the prophets and Moses did say should come" (American Standard Version). Far from having flouted the law of Moses, as the Jews accused him of doing, Paul was proclaiming its perfect fulfillment.

23. That Christ should suffer, and that he should be the first that should rise from the dead, and should shew light unto the people, and to the Gentiles.

These were the principal points of Christian doctrine established by prophecy, and they were the very points to which the Jews objected most strenuously. *That Christ should suffer.* The preaching of the cross was a stumbling block to Jews, who expected a triumphant Messiah (1 Corinthians 1:23), but it was central in some of the clearest Old Testament prophecies, such as Psalm 22 and Isaiah 53. "That he first by the resurrection of the dead should proclaim light both to the people and to the Gentiles" (American Standard Version). To the Sanhedrin Paul had declared that the preaching of the resurrection was the central charge against him (23:6). Again in spite of the clear prophecy of Isaiah. (60:3), the Jews would not believe that the Messiah would come to save the Gentiles equally with the "people"—the children of Israel.

24. And as he thus spake for himself, Festus said with a loud voice, Paul, thou art beside thyself; much learning doth make thee mad.

Poor Festus found himself increasingly bewildered by what Paul was saying to Agrippa. With arrogance typical of ignorance he concluded that if it made no sense to him, it simply made no sense! *Said with a loud voice.* Completely absorbed as well as bewildered, he forgot the dignity of the occasion and expressed his frustration in the most natural manner.

25. But he said, I am not mad, most noble Festus; but speak forth the words of truth and soberness.

This patient, respectful declaration is the only word addressed to Festus. Paul was addressing himself to Agrippa, who had been asked to conduct the inquiry, who knew the facts involved in it (v. 3), and whom Paul fervently hoped he might bring to faith in Christ. "Most excellent Festus" (American Standard Version). The title of respect befitting his office.

26. For the king knoweth of these things, before whom also I speak freely: for I am persuaded that none of these things are hidden from him; for this thing was not done in a corner.

As a member of a Jewish family involved, even as persecutors, in the affairs of Christ and the apostles, Agrippa was familiar with the prophets and Moses, with the Messianic hopes of Israel, with the death of Christ, and with the spread of Christianity. *This thing was not done in a corner.* The Scriptures were widely known, read, and discussed. The ministry and crucifixion of Christ had taken place in the chief city of Palestine with thousands of witnesses, and gospel preaching had stirred the empire. How could any normally intelligent man be unaware of these things?

27. King Agrippa, believest thou the prophets? I know that thou believest.

As he explained the king's familiarity with the facts of the gospel, Paul had seen some response in Agrippa, which led him to this bold word in pressing for a commitment of faith. *Believest thou the prophets?* With Paul, to believe the prophets was to accept the One of whom they spoke. There was no logical alternative. *I know that thou believest.* Some look or gesture gave Paul this confidence, so that he pressed his advantage.

28. Then Agrippa said unto Paul, Almost thou persuadest me to be a Christian.

Herod chose to turn the appeal with an objection, not resentful and not quite flippant, but indicating an

uneasy response to a stirred conscience. "With but little persuasion
thou wouldest fain make me a Christian" (American Standard Version).
He thought it unreasonable that Paul
should expect to convert him with
one sermon. In that he was different
from the believers at Pentecost (Acts
2:37-41), the Ethiopian eunuch (8:
35-38), Lydia (16:14, 15), the Philippian jailer (16:30-33), and many
others. *A Christian.* The name first
used at Antioch had come to be
widely accepted. Agrippa was familiar with it.

**29. And Paul said, I would to God,
that not only thou, but also all that
hear me this day, were both almost,
and altogether such as I am, except
these bonds.**

In this last appeal the fervency
of Paul's yearning spent its force.
"Whether with little or with much"
is added in the American Standard
Version. This was a direct answer
to Agrippa's reference to "little persuasion." With one sermon or a hundred, Paul labored "that I might by
all means save some" (1 Corinthians
9:22). *Not only thou, but also all
that hear me this day.* Paul's discourse had been addressed to Agrippa
personally, but neither the gospel nor
his concern was so limited. "Might
become such as I am" (American
Standard Version). Paul was not
ashamed, either of the gospel, or of
his application of the gospel to his
life. *Except these bonds.* An after-
thought, probably accompanied with
a gesture of his manacled hands.
How could a man so completely self-
less and lacking in vindictiveness
be held as a criminal?

**30. And when he had thus spoken,
the king rose up, and the governor,
and Bernice, and they that sat with
them.**

With this gesture Agrippa closed
the interview. He had decided two
things: Paul was innocent, and that
he did not wish to face further appeals to his own responsibilities before God and Christ. Paul had
sought to vindicate the gospel rather
than himself. He had succeeded in
winning a verdict for himself, but
not for the gospel.

**31. And when they were gone
aside, they talked between themselves,
saying, This man doeth nothing worthy
of death or of bonds.**

The judges took counsel as to their
verdict. It was not difficult. Agrippa
had not heard the charges against
Paul, but knowing the temper of the
Jewish leaders and having heard
Festus' version of the charges that
had been brought (25:7, 18, 19), he
could make his own comparisons.
"This man has not done anything
to deserve death or imprisonment"
(Goodspeed translation). Festus was
now right back where he started in
his search for a plausible charge to
send to Caesar with the prisoner.

**32. Then said Agrippa unto Festus,
This man might have been set at lib-
erty, if he had not appealed unto
Caesar.**

The decision was too late. If Festus
had used intelligent courage in rejecting the Jews' demand that Paul
be returned to Jerusalem for trial
(25:9-12), the appeal to Caesar
would not have been made, and the
matter would have been closed.

CHAPTER 27

1. And when it was determined that we should sail into Italy, they delivered Paul and certain other prisoners unto one named Julius, a centurion of Augustus' band.

When it was determined. When all plans and arrangements for the voyage had been completed. *We should sail into Italy.* "We" includes Luke, who had probably been nearby during Paul's stay in Caesarea, very likely employed with writing the Gospel which bears his name. He was an eyewitness of the events that followed. *Paul and certain other prisoners.* Verse 2 tells that Aristarchus, of Thessalonica, was with them, and in Colossians 4:10 he is, referred to as Paul's fellow prisoner, perhaps, however, meaning only that he was Paul's voluntary companion to Rome. Others, unnamed, were also being delivered as Roman citizens to the imperial court. *One named Julius, a centurion.* Scriptural notices concerning centurions—officers over a hundred soldiers each—are uniformly favorable (Matthew 8:5; 27:54; Acts 10:1; 23:17). Julius was perhaps favorably impressed with Paul both from Festus' report of him and from his own observation of Paul's demeanor. *Augustus' band.* The band was also known as the "imperial regiment" (Moffatt).

2. And entering into a ship of Adramyttium, we launched, meaning to sail by the coasts of Asia; one Aristarchus, a Macedonian of Thessalonica, being with us.

The ship's home port was *Adramyttium* in northwest Asia; and probably the correct meaning is that the ship, not Paul and his companions, was about to sail for places in Asia. The passengers we are following were transferred to another ship before reaching Asia (Acts 27:5, 6). *Asia* was the province on the east side of the Aegean Sea.

3. And the next day we touched at Sidon. And Julius courteously entreated Paul, and gave him liberty to go unto his friends to refresh himself.

The first day's trip was northward along the coast to *Sidon.* In modern English we would say "treated" where our text has *entreated.* The centurion, *Julius,* who had the prisoners in his charge, allowed Paul to be a guest in the home of friends. Probably a soldier accompanied him.

4. And when we had launched from thence, we sailed under Cyprus, because the winds were contrary.

With a following wind, the ship might have sailed across the open sea in a straight line toward Asia, passing southwest of the island of Cyprus. But the wind probably was from the southwest, so the ship went east and north of Cyrus. *Under* means on the lee side.

5. And when we had sailed over the sea of Cilicia and Pamphylia, we came to Myra, a city of Lycia.

Cilicia and Pamphylia were provinces of the south coast of Asia Minor. *The sea* mentioned was that part of the Mediterranean that touched those provinces. Myra was a seaport in the province of *Lycia.*

6. And there the centurion found a ship of Alexandria sailing into Italy; and he put us therein.

Alexandria was a prominent port of Egypt; this ship was carrying Egyptian wheat (Acts 27:38) for the cities of *Italy*.

7. And when we had sailed slowly many days, and scarce were come over against Cnidus, the wind not suffering us, we sailed under Crete, over against Salmone.

Beating its way against the contrary wind, the ship *sailed slowly* till it *came over against Cnidus,* at the southwest point of Asia Minor. Apparently the wind was now from the northwest, and the ship was able to make its way to the island of *Crete* and find shelter in its lee.

8. And, hardly passing it, came unto a place which is called The fair havens; nigh whereunto was the city of Lasea.

Even in the lee south of the island, the ship could move westward only *hardly,* that is, with difficulty. However, it did manage to reach the port of Fair Havens, about midway of the length of the island.

9. Now when much time was spent, and when sailing was now dangerous, because the fast was now already past, Paul admonished them.

The voyage had been slow all the way from Sidon, and perhaps the mariners then waited some time at the Fair Havens. *The fast* probably was the Jewish Day of Atonement, which came in the fall, perhaps in October. After that time *sailing was now dangerous* because severe storms could be expected. Paul therefore ventured a word of advice.

10. And said unto them, Sirs, I perceive that this voyage will be with hurt and much damage, not only

of the lading and ship, but also of our lives.

We are not told whether Paul perceived this by divine revelation or merely by his own wisdom. Some point out that no lives actually were lost, and therefore they conclude that Paul here gave only his own uninspired predictions. It is possible, however, for God to announce a coming disaster and then modify it in response to prayer (Numbers 14:11-24), and Acts 27:22-24 indicates that God granted to Paul the lives of those on the ship.

11, 12. Nevertheless the centurion believed the master and the owner of the ship, more than those things which were spoken by Paul. And because the haven was not commodious to winter in, the more part advised to depart thence also, if by any means they might attain to Phenice, and there to winter; which is an haven of Crete, and lieth toward the south west and north west.

Obviously the point of Paul's advice in verse 10 was that it would be safer to winter where they were. Only a short distance to the west, however, was a harbor much better protected from the winter storms. The centurion conferred with the captain of the ship and the owner, and they agreed to go on to the better harbor as soon as there was a break in the weather. The closing part of verse 12, more literally translated, describes the desired harbor as "looking toward [or looking down] the southwest wind and the northwest wind." Since the harbor today opens toward the east, probably this description should be taken to mean that it looks in the direction toward which these winds blow, not the direction from whence they come.

13. And when the south wind blew softly, supposing that they had obtained their purpose, loosing thence, they sailed close by Crete.

The break in the weather came, and the mariners lost no time in starting to the better harbor at Phenice or Phoenix.

14. But not long after there arose against it a tempestuous wind, called Euroclydon.

Euroclydon, or Euraquilo, seems to have been the sailors' name for a terrific wind from the northeast. The word may be a curious combination of the Greek word for east wind and the Latin word for northeast wind, so the precise meaning may be a wind from east-northeast.

15. And when the ship was caught, and could not bear up into the wind, we let her drive.

The wind was so violent that the sailors could not maneuver the ship effectively; they could only let it be driven in the direction the wind was blowing.

16. And running under a certain island which is called Clauda, we had much work to come by the boat.

The sailors could not keep the ship from being driven away from Crete, but they did manage to bring it into the lee of a tiny island to the south. There the storm was not quite so violent. In the short time before being driven out of that area the sailors did what they could to prepare for their stormy ride. A small *boat* had been towed behind the ship; they now hoisted it to the deck and secured it.

17. Which when they had taken up, they used helps, undergirding the ship; and, fearing lest they should fall into the quicksands, strake sail, and so were driven.

After lifting the boat on board, the sailors did what they could for the ship. The *helps* were ropes or chains wrapped around the hull and pulled tight with winches. They helped to keep the ship from being broken to pieces in the violent sea. The *quicksands*, or Syrtis, were shallows on the coast of Africa to the south. Having no way of judging their direction, the sailors thought they might go aground there. To slow their movement as much as possible, they lowered whatever small sails they had used in working the ship into the lee of Clauda.

18. And we being exceedingly tossed with a tempest, the next day they lightened the ship.

Perhaps the deck cargo was thrown overboard. The wheat in the hold' would serve as ballast and help to stabilize the craft. There is no record of what freight was carried in addition to wheat.

19. And the third day we cast out with our own hands the tackling of the ship.

Some good manuscripts have "they cast out" instead of *we cast out*. It seems more likely that the seamen, not Luke and the other passengers, would do this. They cleared the deck, throwing over the side some of the sails, ropes, booms, and other equipment. Enough gear was kept for emergency navigation (Acts 27:40).

20. And when neither sun nor stars in many days appeared, and no small tempest lay on us, all hope that we should be saved was then taken away.

The violent storm raged day after day. Tired and battered, seamen and passengers alike lost heart. Seeing *neither sun nor stars,* they could not tell which way they were drifting. They might run aground any day, they thought, and if they escaped that fate, the ship must finally break up in that terrible sea.

21. But after long abstinence Paul stood forth in the midst of them, and said, Sirs, ye should have hearkened unto me, and not have loosed from Crete, and to have gained this harm and loss.

"When they had been long without food" (American Standard Version). The storm had deprived them of the means, the time, and the inclination to prepare or to eat any regular meals. *Paul stood forth in the midst of them.* He had an important announcement to make. *Sirs, ye should have hearkened unto me.* He addressed especially the centurion, who was in ultimate command, having taken the vessel over in the service of the emperor. Paul had advised against leaving Fair Havens, warning that great loss and danger would result (vv. 10, 11). His present comment was more than "I told you so." He had something else to say, and it had even more authority in it than his former advice, sound as that had proved to be.

22. And now I exhort you to be of good cheer: for there shall be no loss of any man's life among you, but of the ship.

"Be of good courage" (Living Oracles translation). The morale of the entire company was at a dangerously low level. Paul had news designed to lift it. *No loss of any man's life.*

Paul's former warning had indicated fear for the lives of those on the ship (v. 10), but for the present assurance he had more than natural support. Later, when the sailors would have escaped alone from the foundering vessel (v. 31), Paul warned that lives would be lost if they were not kept on board. He recognized that God's promises include the expectation of human co-operation. *But of the ship.* The prophecy was specific and not completely optimistic. The ship would be lost.

23. For there stood by me this night the angel of God, whose I am, and whom I serve.

Paul gave the authority for his prediction. The presence was not the same as that of Christ on other occasions (18:9; 22:17, 18; 23:11), but brought a similar message. *God, whose I am, and whom I serve.* Before Paul were worshipers of many gods. He identified the source of his revelation as Jehovah, the one Creator worshiped by the Jews. His life of devotion and service would explain why God gave a revelation to him and not to others.

24. Saying, Fear not, Paul; thou must be brought before Caesar: and, lo, God hath given thee all them that sail with thee.

"Fear not, Paul; thou must stand before Caesar" (American Standard Version). The angel repeated the exhortation and promise formerly given by the Lord (23:11). "God hath granted thee all them that sail with thee" (American Standard Version). For ten righteous men Sodom would have been spared (Genesis 18:23-32). Now for the sake of an apostle needed to bear his testimony before

Caesar, 276 soldiers, sailors, and passengers were to be spared. Paul had evidently been praying for the whole company.

25. Wherefore, sirs, be of good cheer: for I believe God, that it shall be even as it was told me.

"Wherefore, take courage, men" (Living Oracles translation). The assurance gave them all reason to hope. "For I trust in God that it shall be so" (Living Oracles translation). Paul had complete confidence in the identity of his heavenly visitor, that he spoke for God. He would never question the will or the power of God to fulfill His promises. To the degree that the others shared Paul's faith, they would share also his confidence in ultimate safety.

26. Howbeit we must be cast upon a certain island.

"However, we are to be stranded on an island" (Moffatt). No light or easy escape was promised. Paul's prediction was confident and detailed. indicating a supernatural source of information. At the time the ship was apparently headed toward the mainland of Africa.

27. But when the fourteenth night was come, as we were driven up and down in Adria, about midnight the shipmen deemed that they drew near to some country.

Perhaps the practiced ears of the sailors could detect a new note in the roar of the storm—the sound of seas breaking on a beach. Probably they feared that they were at last about to be smashed on the shoals of Africa. After two weeks of blind drifting, of course they did not know where they were; but before writing the account, Luke deemed that they were in Adria,

the Adriatic Sea between Greece and Italy. The wind had shifted and carried them west instead of south.

28. And sounded, and found it twenty fathoms: and when they had gone a little further, they sounded again, and found it fifteen fathoms.

The water was shallower as they drifted on. This confirmed the guess that they were approaching land.

29. Then fearing lest we should have fallen upon rocks, they cast four anchors out of the stern, and wished for the day..

It would be almost certain death for all aboard if the ship were dashed to pieces on a reef in the middle of the night. The *four anchors,* it was hoped, would hold the craft offshore till daylight.

30. And as the shipmen were about to flee out of the ship, when they had let down the boat into the sea, under colour as though they would have cast anchors out of the foreship.

The seamen judged that it would be less risky to try to go ashore in the small boat, leaving ship and passengers to their fate. They pretended to be casting out more anchors, but really they lowered the boat.

31. Paul said to the centurion and to the soldiers, Except these abide in the ship, ye cannot be saved.

Apparently Paul was the only one who realized what the sailors were doing in the darkness. He promptly reported to the soldiers, for the experienced seamen would be needed to bring the ship to land in the morning. Without their help, all the passengers might well be lost.

32. Then the soldiers cut off the ropes of the boat, and let her fall off.

Perhaps with their swords, the soldiers cut the ropes with which the boat was being lowered. The boat was lost in the sea, but the seamen were kept aboard the ship.

33. And while the day was coming on, Paul besought them all to take meat, saying, This day is the fourteenth day that ye have tarried and continued fasting, having taken nothing.

To accept Paul's statement as true is not necessarily to insist that absolutely nothing had been eaten by anyone on board. Some or all may have found ability and opportunity to snatch a few bites now and then, but any eating that had been done was inconsequential—they had eaten practically nothing. They would need strength for the coming day, and Paul urged them to eat.

34. Wherefore I pray you to take some meat: for this is for your health: for there shall not an hair fall from the head of any of you.

Anxiety robbed them of appetite, so Paul assured them again that all of them would be safe.

35. And when he had thus spoken, he took bread, and gave thanks to God in presence of them all: and when he had broken it, he began to eat.

To his urgency Paul added his own example of confidence, gratitude, and trust toward God, and eating to prepare for the needs of the coming day.

36. Then were they all of good cheer, and they also took some meat.

Paul's words were effective, and his example was followed. *Meat* of course is used in its older sense, meaning food of any kind. It applies to bread (v. 35) as well as to the flesh of animals.

37. And we were in all in the ship two hundred threescore and sixteen souls.

The number of passengers and crew helps us realize that this was a large and important ship.

38. And when they had eaten enough, they lightened the ship, and cast out the wheat into the sea.

The remainder of the cargo now was thrown out so that the ship would float higher in the water and could come closer to the beach before running aground.

39. And when it was day, they knew not the land: but they discovered a certain creek with a shore, into which they were minded, if it were possible, to thrust in the ship.

The land before them was unknown to the sailors, but with the coming of day they could see the nature of it and make their plans. They saw a narrow inlet such as our English-speaking ancestors used to call a *creek*. They decided to drive the ship into this inlet, if possible, so that they could disembark with the least possible danger and inconvenience.

40. And when they had taken up the anchors, they committed themselves unto the sea, and loosed the rudder bands, and hoised up the mainsail to the wind, and made toward shore.

Translators of the American Standard Version render the first part of this verse differently, indicating that the anchors were not *taken up*, but simply cut loose and left in the sea. The *rudder bands* had secured the rudder so it would not be beaten about by the waves during the night. Now they were loosed so the rudder could be used in steering. *Hoised*

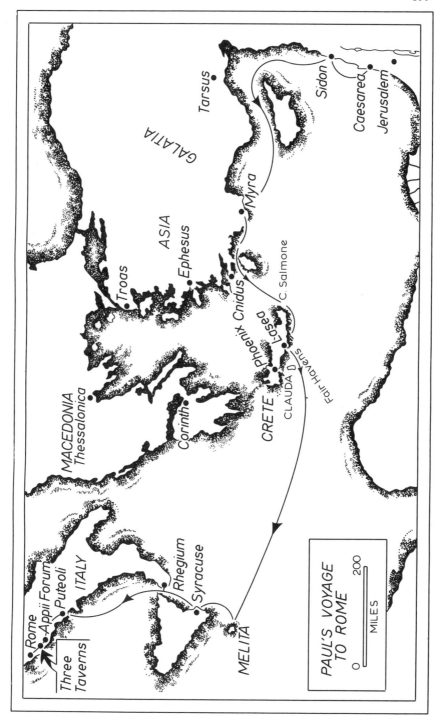

PAUL'S VOYAGE
TO ROME

0   200
|—————————|
MILES

means hoisted, raised. Instead of *mainsail* the American Standard Version has "foresail." It seems more likely that the foresail would be used in the circumstances, both because the wind was strong and because the foresail could be set to lift the bow of the ship and carry it farther into the inlet before grounding it.

41. And falling into a place where two seas met, they ran the ship aground; and the forepart stuck fast, and remained unmoveable, but the hinder part was broken with the violence of the waves.

The *two seas* or currents meeting evidently had built up a sandbar, leaving the water shallower than the sailors had thought it to be. The bow of the ship stuck fast in the sand, but the stern, lifted and dropped by the great waves, began to be pounded to pieces.

42. And the soldiers' counsel was to kill the prisoners, lest any of them should swim out, and escape.

Roman law was severe: a guard who let a prisoner escape might have to pay with his own life. The soldiers would rather kill all the prisoners than take a chance of losing any.

43. But the centurion, willing to save Paul, kept them from their purpose; and commanded that they which could swim should cast themselves first into the sea, and get to land:

Paul was no ordinary prisoner. Festus doubtless had made this clear to the centurion, and it had become increasingly clear during the voyage. Luke gives but few details; it may be that the officer sent some of the soldiers ashore first to receive the prisoners when they came. But he was willing to take the necessary chances to save Paul alive.

44. And the rest, some on boards, and some on broken pieces of the ship. And so it came to pass, that they escaped all safe to land.

Anything that would float and support a man could be used to help the people to land.

CHAPTER 28

1. And when they were escaped, then they knew that the island was called Melita.

As Paul said, the total company came ashore. "And being got safe to land" (Living Oracles translation), some swimming and some drifting on floating objects from the ship. "Then we knew that the island was called Melita" (American Standard Version). Having drifted for two weeks without compass or sight of sun, stars, or land, the company had no idea where they were. They learned, either from the people on shore, or from the known contours of the is-

land. Melita is now known as Malta.

2. And the barbarous people shewed us no little kindness: for they kindled a fire, and received us every one, because of the present rain, and because of the cold.

"The barbarians treated us with uncommon humanity" (Living Oracles translation). The word "barbarian" indicates only that the citizens of Melita were neither Greek nor Roman, being African or Asiatic in descent and speaking a mixed language. "Having kindled a fire, they brought us all to it" (Living

(Oracles). These island people must have come some distance from their homes on learning of the foundering ship approaching their shore. To find immediate lodging for so many would be impossible. They did the best they could to make the shivering refugees comfortable. "For it had begun to rain and was cold" (Revised Standard Version). It was early winter, and Malta is about as far north as Los Angeles.

3. And when Paul had gathered a bundle of sticks, and laid them on the fire, there came a viper out of the heat, and fastened on his hand.

Paul promptly joined in the work of gathering wood for the fire. He may have picked up a little heap of driftwood in which a *viper* was hidden, or perhaps the snake was in the wood someone else laid on the fire just before Paul brought his load. The poisonous snake emerged just as Paul's hand was in reach, and Paul was bitten.

4. And when the barbarians saw the venomous beast hang on his hand, they said among themselves, No doubt this man is a murderer, whom, though he hath escaped the sea, yet vengeance suffereth not to live.

The heathen on the island did not know the true God, but they firmly believed their imaginary gods were active in human affairs. They supposed some god or gods wished to punish Paul for his crimes. Failing to kill him by the storm, the deity or deities had caused a poisonous snake to bite him.

5. And he shook off the beast into the fire, and felt no harm.

This calls to mind the promise of Jesus in Mark 16:18: "They shall take up serpents; and if they drink any deadly thing, it shall not hurt them; they shall lay hands on the sick, and they shall recover." The last part of that promise also was fulfilled in the days that followed (vv. 8, 9).

6. Howbeit they looked when he should have swollen, or fallen down dead suddenly: but after they had looked a great while, and saw no harm come to him, they changed their minds, and said that he was a god.

The first part of this verse may be paraphrased simply, "They expected him to swell or fall down dead." A viper's bite is not always fatal, but at the very least it could be expected to result in painful swelling. When Paul suffered no harm at all, the islanders decided he must be a god.

7. In the same quarters were possessions of the chief man of the island, whose name was Publius; who received us, and lodged us three days courteously.

The island chief joined his people in caring for the shipwrecked travelers. Whether he had a palatial estate where all the 276 people could be lodged, or whether he lodged only a few of the more notable ones, Luke does not make clear. Neither does he tell what happened after the three days of lodging with Publius. Probably many of the islanders cooperated in providing food and lodging.

8. And it came to pass, that the father of Publius lay sick of a fever and of a bloody flux: to whom Paul entered in, and prayed, and laid his hands on him, and healed him.

The bloody flux probably was what we call dysentery. In fact, the English word "dysentery" is derived from the Greek term used here.

9. So when this was done, others also, which had diseases in the island, came, and were healed.

Although Luke does not mention it, we can hardly doubt that Paul's ministry of healing was accompanied by the preaching of the gospel.

10. Who also honoured us with many honours; and when we departed, they laded us with such things as were necessary.

Thus the islanders showed their appreciation of Paul's helpfulness.

11. And after three months we departed in a ship of Alexandria, which had wintered in the isle, whose sign was Castor and Pollux.

After three months, probably from late November to late February. Shipping in the Mediterranean was usually suspended for almost four months each winter. "We set sail in a ship of Alexandria which had wintered in the island whose sign was The Twin Brothers" (American Standard Version). The figurehead of the sailing vessel bore the insignia indicating its name. The *Dioscuri* were supposed to be twin sons of the god Jupiter and were regarded by Greeks and Romans as the patron gods of seamen.

12. And landing at Syracuse, we tarried there three days.

Syracuse, a chief city of Sicily, was most favorably located on an excellent harbor less than a hundred miles north of Malta and across the straits from the southern tip of Italy. The *three days* may have been spent in transacting ship's business, or in waiting for favorable winds to continue the journey.

13. And from thence we fetched a compass, and came to Rhegium: and after one day the south wind blew, and we came the next day to Puteoli.

"From thence we made a circuit" (American Standard Version). A roundabout, tacking course was necessary because of adverse winds. "And came over against Rhegium" (Living Oracles translation). The modern city of Reggio, at the toe of the Italian boot, lies opposite Sicily. *After one day the south wind blew.* This was worth waiting for. Their course lay northward along the west coast of Italy to Puteoli. *We came the next day to Puteoli,* making 180 miles in little more than a day. Earlier in the voyage it had taken "many days" to cover 150 miles from Myra to Cnidus (27:6, 7). Puteoli, modern Pozzuoli, is located on the northern shore of the Bay of Naples.

14. Where we found brethren, and were desired to tarry with them seven days: and so we went toward Rome.

We found brethren. The gospel had been preached for some time in Italy, and the church established in many of the towns about Rome. (Compare the greetings of Romans 16 written three years before this event.) "And were entreated to tarry with them seven days" (American Standard Version). Thus Paul and his party would be with the Christians at the Lord's table on the Lord's Day, as they had been at Troas (20:6, 7) and at Tyre (21:4). That the centurion Julius consented to so long a delay indicates a high degree of sympathy with Paul. Perhaps by this time he also had become a Christian. "And so we came to Rome" (American Standard Version). This was approximately a hundred fifty miles by the Appian highway from Puteoli.

15. And from thence, when the brethren heard of us, they came to meet us as far as Appiforum, and The three taverns: whom when Paul saw, he thanked God, and took courage.

News of Paul's arrival had gone before him to Rome, and other Christians met the party at the Appii Forum and the "three taverns," fifty and forty miles from Rome, respectively.

16. And when we came to Rome, the centurion delivered the prisoners to the captain of the guard: but Paul was suffered to dwell by himself with a soldier that kept him.

"When we entered into Rome" (American Standard Version). The company included Luke and Aristarchus, who had come with Paul from Caesarea (27:2) and remained as his companions (Colossians 4:10, 14). Hence what Luke wrote in the book of Acts was the testimony of a firsthand witness. *The centurion delivered the prisoners to the captain of the guard.* Julius had completed his duty. This line does not appear in the most ancient manuscripts of Acts, and so is omitted from the American Standard Version and other late translations. "Paul was given permission to live by himself, with a soldier to guard him" (Goodspeed translation). That Paul was not confined in the common prison was probably due to the report of him conveyed by Julius from Festus, together with Julius's account of Paul's demeanor during the voyage.

17. And it came to pass, that after three days Paul called the chief of the Jews together: and when they were come together, he said unto them, Men

and brethren, though I have committed nothing against the people, or customs of our fathers, yet was I delivered prisoner from Jerusalem into the hands of the Romans.

After three days. Paul was wasting no time. He had come to Rome to speak for Christ, and he would be about his Master's business. The first days were probably spent with the brethren. "He called together those that were the chief of the Jews" (American Standard Version), the rulers of the synagogues, the scribes, and heads of the leading Jewish families. This was in harmony with Paul's declared purpose to preach "to the Jew first" (Romans 1:16). *Men and brethren.* The familiar address of one among his own people. *I have committed nothing against the people.* As a prisoner Paul might naturally be supposed guilty of crime. He here declared his innocence of wrong against the Jewish nation—"the people" as opposed to "the nations," or Gentiles. *Or customs of our fathers.* The Asiatic Jews had charged him with teaching against the people, the law, and the temple (21:28). He pleaded innocent to the charge. *I was delivered prisoner from Jerusalem into the hands of the Romans.* Paul prudently omitted details of the attack made against him in the temple, although he probably made a much more lengthy explanation than is given in these brief verses.

18. Who, when they had examined me, would have let me go, because there was no cause of death in me.

The inquiries conducted by Lysias, Felix, and Festus are compressed into this brief report. "Desired to set me at liberty" (American Standard Version). Both Felix and Festus kept Paul in bonds only because they were willing to favor the Jews (24: 27; 25:9). "There was no reason for the death penalty in my case" (Revised Standard Version). Actually he had committed no crime at all, but the death penalty had been demanded by the Jews (22:22).

19. But when the Jews spoke against it, I was constrained to appeal unto Caesar; not that I had ought to accuse my nation of.

"But the Jews objected" (Goodspeed). This is Paul's first use of the word "Jews" to identify his persecutors. Their objection to Paul's release was made most insistently before Festus, who did not know of their plots to seize and kill Paul. This was the occasion of Paul's *appeal unto Caesar*, to avoid being returned to Jerusalem and certain assassination (25: 1-12). *Not that I had ought to accuse my nation of.* The appeal to Caesar might naturally imply a desire to bring charges against his persecutors. Paul had no such intention.

20. For this cause therefore have I called for you, to see you, and to speak with you: because that for the hope of Israel I am bound with this chain.

"For this cause therefore did I entreat you to see and to speak with me" (American Standard Version). He wished to explain his presence in Rome so as to avoid misunderstanding and further bitterness between the Christians and the Jews. He also had a strong evangelistic motive. "I am wearing this chain because I share Israel's hope" (Moffatt). Paul indicated the chain that bound him to his soldier guard. He was a pris-

oner because he preached the fulfillment of the national hope for the coming of the Messiah. That hope, as he had asserted before (23:6; 26: 6, 7), should have identified him with the Jews rather than set him apart as an enemy.

21. And they said unto him, We neither received letters out of Judaea concerning thee, neither any of the brethren that came shewed or spake any harm of thee.

No official charge or complaint against Paul had come to the synagogues at Rome. It is hard to believe that they had no information at all. They knew enough about him to be interested in what he had to say. "Nor did any of the brethren come hither and report or speak any harm of thee" (American Standard Version). This was a new experience for Paul, who was accustomed to having the Jews pursue him from place to place with accusations.

22. But we desire to hear of thee what thou thinkest: for as concerning this sect, we know that every where it is spoken against.

"We think it only right to let you tell your own story" (Moffatt). They were willing to hear about Christianity from its greatest advocate. "As far as this sect is concerned" (Goodspeed). The Jewish leaders obviously had a low regard for what they regarded as a heretical splinter faction of Judaism. "We understand that everywhere it is denounced" (Goodspeed). They were dependent on hearsay for their information. They had probably refused to listen to Christian teaching, if they had previously had the opportunity. The unbelieving Jews uniformly contemned the "sect of the Nazarenes" (24:5), and the Roman Tacitus dismissed Christianity as "a detestable superstition."

23. And when they had appointed him a day, there came many to him into his lodging; to whom he expounded and testified the kingdom of God, persuading them concerning Jesus, both out of the law of Moses, and out of the prophets, from morning till evening.

The Jewish leaders made an appointment and told the members of the synagogues what was planned. "They came to him into his lodging in great number" (American Standard Version). The fact that the Jews took the initiative in coming to hear gave Paul a great advantage. The house must have been packed. "To whom he expounded the matter" (American Standard Version). The evidences for Christianity were studied and discussed. "He explained the Reign of God to them from personal testimony" (Moffatt). As one who had seen Jesus, and had served Him for many years, Paul knew the authority of the King in His realm, the church. "Trying to convince them about Jesus from the Law of Moses and the Prophets" (Goodspeed). The Lord himself had used this method of teaching about himself (Luke 24:27, 44) and Paul had insisted that his gospel did not go beyond what was written and foreshadowed in the Old Testament (26:22). The present discussion would explain the ordinances, sacrifices, priesthood, and prophecies of the Mosaic dispensation in their significance as preparation for the coming of Christ. *From morning till evening.* There may have been some coming and going among the audience dur-

ing that time, but these people were less bound to timepieces than are modern Americans, and they had a vital interest in the subject.

24. And some believed the things which were spoken, and some believed not.

"Some of them were convinced by what he said, but others would not believe" (Goodspeed). The gospel made its customary division between believers and unbelievers. Those who had open minds and searched honestly for the truth found it, as they had at Berea (17:11, 12). Those who did not wish to accept the responsibilities laid on them by the gospel could find reasons to reject it.

25. And when they agreed not among themselves, they departed, after that Paul had spoken one word, Well spake the Holy Ghost by Esaias the prophet unto our fathers.

The Jews who "believed" and those who "believed not" probably argued among themselves more and more hotly as the day passed. When they were about to leave in the evening, Paul had a final word for them. He made it very plain that it was not his own word, but God's—a message the Holy Spirit had given to Isaiah to be recorded in the sacred Scriptures.

26. Saying, Go ye unto this people, and say, Hearing ye shall hear, and shall not understand; and seeing ye shall see, and not perceive.

Referring to Isaiah 6:9, 10, Paul reminded the Jews that it was quite the customary thing for their people to hear God's inspired message and fail or refuse to understand and accept it. Some of those in Rome were rejecting the gospel just as their forefathers had rejected God's message given through Isaiah.

27. For the heart of this people is waxed gross, and their ears are dull of hearing, and their eyes have they closed; lest they should see with their eyes, and hear with their ears, and understand with their heart, and should be converted, and I should heal them.

With devastating impact God told why His message was unacceptable to the Jerusalem Jews of Israel's time and the Roman Jews of Paul's time— also to multiplied thousands of Jews and Gentiles in every century since that time. God's message is a demanding message. It calls people to repent, to give up greed and selfishness and pride, to sacrifice for truth and righteousness and love. Many people therefore stop their ears and close their eyes and harden their hearts against such a message, and in rejecting the message they reject also God's healing: they reject forgiveness, redemption, eternal life.

28. Be it known therefore unto you, that the salvation of God is sent unto the Gentiles, and that they will hear it.

How wonderful it would be if the Jews would all unite in accepting their Messiah and then would work together in presenting Him to the Gentiles! But here as elsewhere the Jews fell to arguing among themselves, and here as elsewhere Paul told them plainly that he would take the gospel to the Gentiles, and he knew from experience that many Gentiles would accept it. Note in Acts 13:46, 47, a comparable announcement during Paul's earliest missionary tour.

29. And when he had said these words, the Jews departed, and had great reasoning among themselves.

The Jews went on with their debating, no one knows how long, while Paul went on with his ministry to others as described in the two verses that follow.

30. And Paul dwelt two whole years in his own hired house, and received all that came in unto him.

Two whole years. The book of Acts was evidently completed at the end of those two years, before the tangle of Paul's legal status had been resolved. During that time he wrote (according to most Bible students) the epistles to the Ephesians, the Colossians, Philemon, and the Philippians. The Christians at Rome seem to have borne the cost of his ministry. The pinch of need was felt occasionally, and then such gifts as *unto him.* From letters written during this time we learn that Paul had a number of faithful companions and helpers, who carried his message to the city and brought many to receive preaching and instruction from him. Among these helpers were Luke, the beloved physician and writer of Acts; Timothy of Lystra, Paul's son in the faith; John Mark, who had returned to faithfulness and favor after turning back from the first missionary journey; Epaphras of Colosse; Tychicus who became Paul's messenger to Colosse; and Demas, who finally forsook Paul, "having loved this present world" (2 Timothy 4:10). Besides these, Onesimus, Philemon's runaway slave, was for a time with him as a helper (Philemon 13). that which the Philippians sent were most gratefully received (Philippians 4:10-18). *Received all that came in*

31. Preaching the kingdom of God, and teaching those things which concern the Lord Jesus Christ, with all

confidence, no man forbidding him.

"Announcing the kingdom of God" (Living Oracles translation), especially to unbelievers. "And taught about the Lord Jesus Christ" (Moffatt), especially to those who were already Christian. Even in prison, Paul fulfilled the preaching and teaching functions commanded in the great commission (Matthew 28:18-20). "With all freedom of speech, and without any restraint" (Living Oracles translation), or "quite openly and unmolested" (Moffatt). Thus the ministry that seemed to have been brought to an end with Paul's arrest was actually continued under Roman protection, and Paul was saved the hardships, persecutions, and afflictions that had attended his preaching in the cities of Greece and Asia Minor.